W9-BCF-862

CHOOSE RETIREMENT SERIES

Retirement on a Shoestring

FIFTH EDITION

John Howells

The Globe Pequot Press

GUILFORD, CONNECTICUT

Text design by Joanna Beyer

ISSN 1537-0518
ISBN 0-7627-2849-3

Manufactured in the United States of America
Fifth Edition/First Printing

Help Us Keep This Guide Up to Date

Every effort has been made by the author and editors to make this guide as accurate and useful as possible. However, many things can change after a guide is published—establishments close, phone numbers change, facilities come under new management, etc.

We would love to hear from you concerning your experiences with this guide and how you feel it could be improved and kept up to date. While we may not be able to respond to all comments and suggestions, we'll take them to heart, and we'll also make certain to share them with the author. Please send your comments and suggestions to the following address:

The Globe Pequot Press
Reader Response/Editorial Department
P.O. Box 480
Guilford, CT 06437

Or you may e-mail us at:

editorial@GlobePequot.com

Thanks for your input, and happy travels!

Contents

Chapter One
Golden Retirement Years

When people speak of retirement, the words *golden years* commonly come to mind. Golden, because these years are considered to be a reward—a substantial reward for a lifetime of productive work and loyalty to the workplace. Most workers eagerly look forward to these happy years as the time when they can enjoy the fruits of their labor and bask in the sunshine of leisure. A company pension, stock dividends, annuities, interest on savings, and Social Security provide the income to enjoy this new, carefree career as a retiree.

For the majority of those entering the retirement phase of their careers, this rosy scenario will play out. However, many others find themselves facing some tough choices that could make their "golden years" look somewhat tarnished. This is particularly true at the time of revising this fifth edition of *Retirement on a Shoestring*. The U.S. economy is going through an unsettling period, with the stock market wallowing in the worst bear market in more than seventy years. The economy is sliding downhill, with no clear end in sight. Today's economic crisis shows interesting similarities to the stock market crash of 1929 and the beginning of the Great Depression. The flash point at that time was the discovery of widespread corporate fraud and manipulation of stock values, followed by a rash of bankruptcies of supposedly solid companies. The beginning of the end was preceded by wildly fluctuating stock prices, the disappearance of hundreds of thousands of well-paying jobs, and spreading unemployment throughout the land. As during the Great Depression of

1929–1939, our falling economy threatens to drag the world economy with it. The chances of a free fall into a real depression are small, due to many reforms and safeguards put in place during the 1930s. With luck, this dangerous situation will soon reverse itself, but there are no guarantees when it comes to predicting the economy. The recession could drag on for some time.

Adding to the problem: Countless retirees are finding that company pensions have evaporated along with the value of their stock investments. Savings account interest has fallen to the 1 or 2 percent level. Dividends from major corporations that traditionally paid well, never missing a beat even through the last depression, are now history. Many workers who lost well-paying jobs when their companies disappeared are considering retirement as an alternative to working at minimum-wage jobs when unemployment benefits expire. Many are too young to qualify for Social Security. There's a new economic reality out there today.

Traditionally, retirees depended on Social Security benefits as a welcome part of their retirement income. But today, vanished company pensions and devalued investments cause many to count on Social Security as a *major* source of income. When Social Security checks do arrive, they're often dismally inadequate. To be fair, we should recognize that Social Security was never designed as a retirement fund, but rather as *a supplement* to retirement. But in real life, untold thousands of retirees depend on Social Security as their *only* source of income.

A large percentage of those couples approaching retirement today own their own homes. Some bought them twenty or thirty years ago. Today that $25,000 house might be worth $100,000 or even $250,000, and the older the couple, the more likely the home will be paid for. When this equity is the major part of a couple's assets, strategies are needed to take advantage of this untapped money. Of course, many *didn't* have the foresight, opportunity, or wherewithal to purchase one of those

$25,000 homes thirty years ago. Many others worked hard all their lives yet never earned enough money to do much more than survive, much less put aside money for retirement. Now more than ever, a book like this one is needed. Perhaps it should be renamed: *Strategies for Retirement in a Downsized Economy.*

Another group with much to worry about are single women. They make up almost three-quarters of the older Americans who must exist on poverty-level incomes! Because retirement income is tied to earnings and time spent on the job, women are deprived in two ways. First of all, they're traditionally paid less than men. Secondly, women who are covered by pension plans are more likely than men to lose their jobs before becoming vested in the plans. Low wages mean that women can't put aside enough money for a comfortable retirement. Women's traditional role as family caregivers means that they are also more likely to work part-time or have gaps in their work histories, which means reduced Social Security and pension benefits. The result? Women make only 71 percent of what men earn, and the wage gap widens with age.

It isn't just those on Social Security who need to plan on getting by on a shoestring. Workers forced into early retirement because of corporate mergers or industrial doldrums, say at age fifty-five, won't qualify for Social Security until they reach the age of sixty-two. Jobs aren't plentiful for those displaced over-fifty employees, because employers prefer to hire younger workers who aren't used to high wages and good benefits. Workers whose skills or crafts have been made obsolete by modern technology often have slim hopes of finding new jobs. These folks are forced to live on savings or on income from part-time jobs.

This book provides strategies for maximizing the use of scarce retirement dollars for *everybody*, no matter what their level of income or how high their current net worth.

Retirement on a Shoestring

For the past fifteen years, my wife and I have been doing research on retirement lifestyles. Most of our books deal with *where* to retire, rather than *how* to retire. Our method is to visit each potential location and investigate the town or city in person. We've traveled many thousands of miles by car, motor home, travel trailer, and airline, crisscrossing the country many times. As we visit cities, towns, and hamlets, we try to imagine ourselves actually living in each place. We routinely look at rentals and property for sale, and we check prices in stores and restaurants. We examine newspaper classified sections for prevailing wages, a big help in calculating the cost of living. In each location, we estimate how much income we would need if we were to retire in the town. We try to visualize the lifestyle we could have in each place, whether on a high, medium, or low income.

Early on, we discovered that the cost of living varies markedly from region to region and from town to town. The biggest differences are generally in housing costs and utilities. Restaurant meals and grocery store prices also vary, as does the cost of labor involved in services like auto repair, home repair, and gardening. The number and quality of senior services also fluctuate widely from locality to locality, particularly in services geared toward low-income families.

The idea for this book came one day as we were having lunch in a small city on the coast of Washington. Housing prices and rentals seemed exceptionally low, the cost of living quite afford-able. We began wondering how a retired couple could make out on an absolutely *minimum* budget in this town. After all, millions of American retirees do live below the poverty level. What if our worst fears were realized and our only income came from a Social Security check? What kind of a lifestyle could we create for ourselves in this low-cost town? We realized that there is a need for a book not only on where to retire, but also on *how to retire on a shoestring*. The fact is that many folks must get by on a Social Security check. If they were to retire *here*, in this little coastal community, could they survive? And at what standard of living?

The first thing we did was to check a real estate office for their least expensive listings. We found an older, two-bedroom frame

At age sixty-two, a single person who earned an average salary during his or her working career, and retiring in 2003, can expect a monthly Social Security benefit of $927 per month (depending on the worker's earnings record, the figure could be more or less). For married couples who both qualify for Social Security (both at age sixty-two), the payment will be around $1,400 a month. Although an income of this magnitude would barely cover rent in many towns we've researched, we've found numerous pleasant retirement locations where a retired couple would do just fine on $1,400. For $927, you'll have to be creative, but it can be done. In fact, about 4.5 million retirees have to get by on Social Security; that's all the income they have! Another 7.5 million households count on Social Security checks for 90 percent of their income. For those who do not care to move away during retirement (and most folks don't), we'll take a later look at strategies to live within your income without moving away from home.

SOCIAL SECURITY
MONTHLY RETIREMENT BENEFITS AT AGE SIXTY-TWO ($)

	WAGE EARNER ONLY	WAGE EARNER AND SPOUSE
Low	636	954
Average	927	1,390
High	1,161	1,741

house in town selling for $35,000. There was another house, a brick ranch-style home, located outside of town and priced at $59,000. (These figures have been adjusted to reflect inflation and current real estate prices.)

Don't misunderstand: We're not suggesting that you can go just anywhere and pick up a house for $35,000! These houses were priced exceptionally low because the town's two major industries had closed, jobs had disappeared, and small businesses were struggling to survive. Houses were difficult to peddle because everybody wanted to sell and nobody wanted to buy. Empty houses weren't renting because tenants were moving away to seek work elsewhere. For many retirees, however, employment opportunities don't matter nearly as much as affordable housing costs.

We located the first house—a slightly run-down place not far from a supermarket and shopping center. As you can imagine, it needed paint, cleaning, and repairs. Yet the house looked like a bargain at $35,000. Yes, we could easily imagine ourselves living here, and the price was affordable even with the needed repairs. But suppose we couldn't afford to buy a house and needed to rent? The local newspaper listed several rentals, some furnished, for as little as $250 a month.

We figured out two "bare-bones" budgets for living modestly but comfortably in this town. The itemized budgets, given in the tables below, call for monthly expenses ranging from $954 to $1,576. These match the average monthly income from Social Security checks for a couple with one wage earner and two wage earners, respectively. Automobile expenses accounted for about $100 in both budgets. While car expenses might seem like a big chunk out of the budget, living here without a car would be difficult—and this is true of most small towns without local or intercity bus service. Of course, these bare-bones budgets don't allow for items like automobile depreciation, life-insurance premiums, club dues, loan payments, or other expenses that vary with individual circumstances. Also, because the town's ocean-tempered climate is cool year-round, there is no need for air conditioning, and the heating demands are minimal. Assuming that we could qualify for Medicare, we added $75 for supplementary medical insurance. We had sold our car, we had cashed in our life insurance policies after the children were grown, and we have no outstanding loans. Our conclusion: Yes, living here, we could make all of our basic expenses on Social Security! No, it would not be easy, but a Social Security check that size wouldn't even cover rent in some towns we've visited!

Please note that throughout this book, *cost of living* refers only to basic expenses, those items most people simply cannot avoid. Obviously, individual circumstances differ. To our sample budgets, you'll need to add your own extras. When you retire, if you still have big car payments, mortgage payments, huge insurance premiums, back taxes, alimony, or gambling debts, you don't need a book on how to retire on a minimum income, you need a book on how to win the lottery. If you don't qualify for Medicare

BARE-BONES BUDGET FOR A COUPLE, ONE PERSON DRAWING SOCIAL SECURITY, (2003 DOLLARS)

Cable TV (minimum service)	20
Clothing, laundry, grooming	70
Groceries	230
Bus, taxi, and other transportation	50
Medicare supplement B	75
Miscellaneous	54
Rent, two-bedroom apartment	400
Utilities (gas and electric)	65
Total	954

BARE-BONES BUDGET FOR A COUPLE, BOTH DRAWING SOCIAL SECURITY, (2003 DOLLARS)	
Cable TV (with extra channels)	35
Clothing, laundry, grooming	100
Groceries	300
Automobile insurance (liability and property damage)	32
Gasoline and maintenance	95
Medicare supplement B	75
Miscellaneous	79
Rent, three-bedroom home (small)	650
Utilities (gas and electric)	95
Total	1,576

or Medicaid and you have no other medical coverage, you don't need someone telling you that you are in trouble. Until our system catches up with the rest of the world in assuring medical care for all its citizens, millions of Americans will be without protection. Let's hope that you're among the lucky Americans who can afford the care you need. If not, be assured that you have plenty of company.

But let's say that you do have medical coverage and don't have any extraordinary expenses. You really could retire to this Washington coastal town in reasonable comfort. That's wonderful, you might say, but suppose we don't want to move? What if we want to stay right here, where we've lived almost all our lives? We'll discuss this later on, and as we shall see, no matter where you live you can control your budget. The secret is taking command of the two factors that drive expenses up: housing and utility costs. For the moment, let's look at an extreme example.

Home Base

At first glance, our small coastal town looks like great place to retire. With wooded hills, a lazy river, and lovely seascapes, summers here are delightful. Temperatures rarely rise above 75°F, and sunny days invite residents outside to enjoy the season. However, although winters rarely bring even a hint of snow, some residents complain about damp and overcast days with shortened daylight hours. Some folks love cool weather like this, but our personal tastes lean toward hot summers, when we can wear swimsuits instead of sweaters.

Another problem is the lack of community services for senior citizens. Towns where population and tax money are dwindling sometimes have few funds left over for retirement centers and other amenities for retirees. This can be an all-important consideration for retirement on a shoestring, as we shall see later in this book.

Even though we recognized that this town was not the perfect retirement setting for us, we became interested in the possibility of using it as a home base. The home's wide lot would make a great place to store our small motor home while we enjoyed an inexpensive summer and fall living in a peaceful ocean setting. When winter rain and gloom threatened, we could store our things, winter-proof the house, and drive our motor home to Arizona, Florida, or Mexico for inexpensive RV living. Small-town safety and neighbors would protect our valuables while we were on the road. Part-time retirement is a concept that is swiftly growing in popularity.

The more we thought about having a home base for summer, the closer we came to actually buying the house! This often happens when we are researching a place; we become so enthusiastic that we begin scheming a way to live there part-time. We came very close to buying a condo in Hawaii once, not considering how difficult it would be to commute to our work in California. We actually did buy a home on the Rogue River in Oregon, simply because we were so delighted with the setting. We also bought a home in Costa Rica while researching retirement there.

Granted, places like this Washington town aren't representative of the normal, everyday real estate market. But dedicated bargain hunters can find similar conditions in many parts of the country. A factory goes bankrupt and workers follow jobs elsewhere. Logging and fishing industries fall into the doldrums. A military base closes its gates and the local economy collapses. Any number of business-related disasters can turn a wonderful residential community into a nightmare for people who must work. Yet this same disaster can be a windfall for those who don't *have* to work. Later in the book, we'll talk about ways to locate these bargains.

Mind you, finding depressed towns is just one solution for low-cost retirement. If we all crowded into these places, costs would soon begin to rise until they were no longer bargains. Furthermore, too many depressed towns are depressed simply because they are boring places to live! Being able to buy a house for $35,000 does not guarantee you'll enjoy living there. If the most exciting thing to do is sit on your front porch rocker swatting flies, you might as well enter a rest home.

Senior Boomers and Social Security

Many of you who are considering retirement this year are members of the baby boomer generation, that titanic wave of children born after the end of World War II and during the following decade. This boom triggered a tremendous expansion of home building and school construction. An enormous number of tax dollars went to educate baby boomers, making this the best-educated generation in our history, the innovators of Internet and other high-tech industries. You were the ones who used to say, "Don't trust anyone over thirty!" Remember? Well that was thirty-five years ago. Today, baby boomers are middle-aged and heading for retirement, with graying hair and sagging bellies. Welcome to old age, kids. Don't trust anyone over thirty, indeed!

For years, retirement experts took it for granted that baby boomers, when they entered retirement, would step right into the affluent lifestyle enjoyed by their parents. Not necessarily so. For one thing, this younger generation was famous for "instant gratification," not for thrift. Whereas their parents remembered the Great Depression and were careful not to waste money, always putting something aside for the future, many baby boomers spent their money on luxury cars, fast lifestyles, and unaffordable homes. Many purchased homes when real estate was at its peak, so they'll never see the tremendous appreciation of home equity that their parents enjoyed. Furthermore, this is the group most affected by the disappearance of "dot-com" and high-tech jobs. Some cashed in before the bubble popped, but others will truly need economical retirement strategies.

An ironic twist is that baby boomers are now being subjected to age discrimination, as employers choose to replace them with younger workers who are so eager for work they will accept much lower salaries in this era of sluggish economy. Age bias complaints by those between the ages of forty and fifty increased by 41 percent from 2000 to 2003.

Curiously, the baby boomer generation opted not to have as many children as their parents did. The birth rate declined—to one of the lowest points in our history. The result is that the number of children has been shrinking while the number of elderly is on the rise. This will have consequences later on, when fewer children will pay higher Social Security taxes to fund their parents' retirement.

The overall number of retirees is also growing because we are living longer. In 1900, the average length of a woman's life was forty-eight years; today it's almost eighty-two years. Men usually die younger; their average life span is closer to seventy-five years. Of course, when we talk about life span, we include in our averages all those who die in childhood, adolescence, and middle age. It certainly doesn't mean that all men will die at age seventy-five! If you arrive at age seventy-five in good health, you could easily expect another ten to fifteen good years. In fact, the fastest-growing segment of the population are folks over eighty-five!

Because we are living longer than ever before, and the baby boomers are nearing retirement age, this country will soon experience a "senior boomer" generation! Demographers estimate that at some point, those over sixty-five years of age will outnumber teenagers by a two-to-one margin.

A problem arises with this overbalance of retirees. Bear in mind that taxes and Social Security payments supported our retired parents and grandparents when we were working. What's going to happen when there are fewer workers and taxpayers in the younger generation to support *us?* As more and more baby boomers join today's seniors in the golden years of retirement, the grandkids are going to have a heck of a time supporting Social Security, Medicare, and other senior-citizen programs! At that point, maybe the younger generation will be saying, "Don't trust anyone *over* sixty-five!" We'll discuss Social Security's future in Chapter 4.

Poverty and the Cost of Living

Again, as we studied retirement lifestyles and economic conditions in various sections of the country, we were impressed by wide differences in the cost of living. Some couples reported they couldn't make it on less than $22,000 a year, while others do okay on incomes of $12,000 a year. Of course, millions of folks in the United States would consider a $12,000 income a blessing. Those who work at minimum-wage jobs find it even tougher, with before-tax incomes of $10,712 a year, about $200 a week.

Do you earn more than $8,980 a year as a single person, including Social Security benefits? Then congratulations. According to the U.S. government, you are *not* poor! If you're married, your annual income must be less than $12,120 for you to be considered poor. That's $173 a week for a single person and $234 for a couple (less income tax and Social Security deductions, of course). If you earn more than that, your representative in Congress is likely to tell you that you're too affluent to be entitled to many federal programs aimed at helping the country's poor. How the government arrives at this figure is difficult to understand, yet $8,980 a year is what the fat cats figure is an adequate income for an ordinary citizen to live on. That's only $4.32 an hour or $172 a week, compared with $206 a week for a minimum-wage job! I'd be willing to bet that the average congressman spends more than that each month for lease payments on his Mercedes-Benz or Jaguar.

Even worse, some politicos complain that today's retirement generation is *too affluent!* They feel that too much is being spent on the elderly, at the expense of the country's youth. They want to cut Medicare benefits and slash Social Security payments at the same time they increase their own salaries and medical benefits. By the government's own statistics, more than three million senior citizens are living below the poverty line.

Women over sixty-five have double the poverty rate of men of the same age; more than 15 percent fall into this category. Because women's wages historically have been less than men's, women's Social Security payments are also low—disgracefully low. Poverty among the elderly is highest among single black women over seventy-five (40 percent of them are poor), compared with 32 percent of Hispanic women and 18 percent of white women over seventy-five.

An Ace in the Hole

This book isn't just for those who need to survive on minimal budgets. Many readers will probably enjoy perfectly adequate incomes, but they'd rather not spend everything they have on basic living expenses. Cutting back on one area of the budget will release funds for travel, recreation, and luxuries. Keeping money aside for emergencies is prudent and reassuring. Besides, just knowing that it's possible to live on a lower income is a reassuring thought—you'll always have that "ace in the hole."

Other readers, while they may own property worth a small fortune, don't feel particularly rich. Owning a home doesn't do a thing toward boosting income. Home ownership usually *absorbs*

2003 FEDERAL POVERTY GUIDELINES

Incomes at or above figures are above poverty levels

	Yearly Income	Monthly Income	Weekly Income	Hourly Income
Single person	$8,980	$748	$173	$4.32
Married couple	12,120	1,010	233	5.83
One dependent	15,260	1,272	294	7.34
Two dependents	18,400	1,533	354	8.85
Three dependents	21,540	1,795	415	10.36

Programs using the federal poverty guidelines to determine eligibility include the Food Stamp Program and the Low Income Home Energy Assistance Program. Note that in general, public assistance programs such as Aid to Families with Dependent Children, Supplemental Security Income, and the Earned Income Tax Credit Program do not use the poverty guidelines in determining eligibility.

money from the home owner's monthly income. After paying taxes, maintenance, and miscellaneous costs of home ownership, some folks are lucky to have enough left over to buy groceries—even though their home is worth hundreds of thousands of dollars.

For those who aren't lucky enough to be comfortably affluent, things are not likely to change for the better. In fact, we must face the fact that the trend will continue—at least through the next decade. That is what this book is all about: facing facts and planning how to live with them.

Chapter Two
Retirement Strategies

How do folks manage to retire on Social Security or its equivalent? Unless you're already accustomed to living on a limited income, it's going to take some adjusting. Not only adjusting financially, but mentally as well. The old notion of "keeping up with the Joneses" has to be set aside. Instead of feeling depressed because your neighbors buy a new Buick every other year, you need to feel proud that you don't waste money on frills and that your old Plymouth takes you just as many places, perhaps more, because you can afford to keep gasoline in the tank.

Most folks who plan on retiring on a shoestring budget are familiar with ordinary tricks for saving money and economizing. Buying on sale, clipping coupons, finding bargains—you already know all the standard maneuvers. Chances are you could write your own book about keeping costs down.

But there's only so much you can save on many common expenses—items like clothing, automobiles, and so forth—because prices don't vary significantly between one store and another. Prices do vary among different cities, towns, and states, but many commodities are sold through national chain stores, so retail prices of many items tend to be similar anywhere you go. Grocery costs can be lower in some communities, depending upon competition from chain stores and the availability of local produce. They can vary as much as 10 percent from place to place. Gasoline prices, however, can vary wildly, depending on state and local taxes, state regulations, and pricing strategies by local dealers. For example, during our last trip through Georgia, the price of a gallon of gasoline was about 50 cents higher than we pay in our California hometown. And there were places in California where gasoline was 25 cents less than where we live. If you need to drive, the difference in price will make a big difference in your budget.

Nevertheless, some monthly expenses can be cut dramatically and can help control your budget. The most important strategy for low-cost retirement is to take control of the two most expensive budget variables: housing and utilities. First, let's look at the price of housing.

Cutting Housing Costs

Your largest savings potential lies in finding creative ways of keeping a roof over your head. This is typically the largest single outlay in any budget. You have a number of cost-cutting options available to you that don't involve moving away from your home town. Low-cost rentals, government subsidies, and alternative housing strategies can reduce your outlays dramatically. We'll discuss these strategies later on in this chapter.

If you're willing to relocate to a low-cost area in your state, or to another state, your house payments or rents can be slashed spectacularly. Home prices vary widely for two reasons: Construction wages fluctuate, and real estate and rental prices are based on supply and demand. When local wages are low, you can be sure that housing costs will be moderate; otherwise residents couldn't afford to buy. A house that sells for $625,000 in one part of California can be duplicated in another part of the state for $125,000, or in Georgia for $65,000. A house that rents for $900 a month in one city can have counterparts in equally nice neighborhoods in smaller towns for $350, a potential savings of $550 a month. That extra

$550 will buy groceries for the month, with enough left over to buy a set of tires for the car!

Of course, moving to a low-cost community in some distant part of your state in order to find reasonable housing may not appeal to you. Relocating to another part of the country, in a far-away state, could be an even worse idea! After all, you may love your hometown. Your grandchildren live nearby, and your life-time friends and beloved neighbors live here. Why move if it isn't necessary?

One option for staying where you are, yet cutting your housing expense to zero, is property management. It's entirely possible to enjoy free rent plus a small salary in exchange for your services as property managers. Example: An apartment complex in our hometown is currently advertising for a married couple to take over management in return for a small salary ($1,000 a month) plus a two-bedroom, two-bath apartment and expenses. The smaller the property, the less will be your obligations and responsibilities, and (of course) the less the pay. Often you can find an absentee owner of a six- or eight-unit apartment complex who is delighted to offer a nice reduction in rent for someone to watch over things, to call the plumber when necessary, to collect rent checks and deposit them, and generally solve problems.

Another situation offered in our local newspaper's classified section was management of a mobile home park in return for free housing (presumably in a mobile home), medical benefits, a modest monthly salary, plus two weeks vacation. The downside to this job is the obligation to keep the office open on a forty-hour-a-week basis. Not exactly retirement, but the housing expense is affordable!

Trimming Utility Bills

Utilities, the second big category of potential savings, also differ from place to place. Moving to a warmer climate where real estate sells for a fraction of what you're used to and where cold-weather heating costs don't gobble up your spare cash will give your budget a real boost.

Electricity and natural gas can cost 20 percent less in some communities. When you live in a particularly high-cost, cold-weather environment, moving to a warmer climate will cut your budget in a meaningful way.

The biggest energy hog—heating—varies with the climate. Your electric and heating-fuel expenditures can dwarf your grocery bills when you stave off cold weather with an energy-gobbling furnace half the year, and then fight stifling temperatures with an air conditioner during the other half. Bills of $250 a month for heating and $175 a month for air conditioning are common in many locations. We've visited places in Wyoming and Montana where monthly heating bills of $350 to $400 are normal in winter. Ironically, people living in sunny California were receiving similar utility bills until the state deregulated the industry a couple of years ago.

You can cut utility bills by a third by moving to a section of the country where you can live without air conditioning. And if you go someplace where you need neither furnace nor air conditioner, you'll save at least another third. We've interviewed folks who cut their average utility bills from $250 a month to $40 simply by moving to a mild climate. That means $210 a month left for luxuries—or other necessities.

Adding your $210 savings in utility bills to potential housing savings of $550 (a total of $760), you've saved more than the total Social Security check for millions of retirees. When you cut expenses this drastically, you are well on your way to living on a shoestring.

Everybody can't move to a mild climate to avoid high heating bills in the winter. In fact, most people don't want to move away. If you choose to stay put in your hometown—as the majority of retirees do—there are ways of cutting utilities without pulling up stakes and leaving the kids and grandchildren. Fortunately, several assistance programs are out there to help low-income home owners and renters cut energy costs. A federal effort you should know about is the Home Energy Assistance Program (HEAP), which comes to the rescue of low-income people who face unaffordable energy bills.

In December 2002, the Bush administration announced that it planned to cut nearly $300 million from the program. Throughout the nation, desperate communities put pressure on Congress to restore the cuts, partly by releasing $100 million in emergency contingency funds. The budget for 2003–2004 is now slightly higher than before.

Although in some states HEAP assistance is limited to heating expenses, in other states HEAP also helps with lighting and cooking costs. As a renter, even if heating is included in the rent payments, you may be still be eligible for reimbursement. The more liberal states allow HEAP funds to pay for maintenance and repair of heating equipment. Sometimes HEAP assistance will even pay for weatherizing your home or apartment. In many areas, your local utility company gets into the act, helping you maximize your energy efficiency through weather stripping and insulating water heaters as a free service.

To qualify for HEAP, you must file an application with your local department of social services or public welfare. Regulations for qualifying vary from state to state. Wisconsin, for example, requires that you meet the following criteria: a household of one person, a three-month income of no more than $3,322; a couple, less than $4,477; three persons, less than $5,632.50; and no more than $6,787 for a household of four. Remember, you should be prepared to prove that you are truly needy. This will be no problem if you already qualify for food stamps or receive welfare or Supplemental Security Income (SSI). In any event, remember to apply for assistance as early in the year as permitted, because the federal funds for HEAP are limited; once they've been allocated, no more help is available. For information about HEAP, contact your local office of public welfare or social services department.

While you're at it, inquire about energy- and utility-company discounts for low-income families; it's worthwhile to check this out. Put your bid in early in the year; there's often a limit on the amount of relief available. If you use oil for heating, ask whether there's an oil buyer's cooperative in your area. Sometimes residents band together to cut fuel costs through group purchasing power.

Recognizing that cold weather hits the low-income family hardest, many utility companies join with state and local governments to conduct energy audits and weatherization assistance. Experts will survey your home at no charge and show you how to save money on heating bills. Low-interest or interest-free loans are then available for you to follow through with recommendations—things like adding insulation to critical parts of the house and weatherizing doors and windows.

Eligibility rules and the scope of help vary from locality to locality, but generally preference is given to home owners or renters with homes built before a certain year. Eligibility for these audit and weatherization programs usually doesn't depend on income. To find out about programs in your area, call your state public service commission or contact the Department of Energy, Division of Weatherization Assistance, 1000 Independence Avenue SW, Washington, DC 20585; (202) 586–2207.

Another way of cutting heating costs is to live in an apartment or condominium complex instead of individual housing. Because the living quarters have less exposed outside wall surface and because costs are shared between living units, you'll usually find lower heating and cooling bills. Utilities are often included in the rent. Although you pay indirectly through rent, the landlord assumes the problem of insulation and getting the best rates in order to keep his rents competitive.

Real Estate Tax Squeeze

A third item, real estate taxes, can have a huge impact on those who insist on home ownership yet want to live on a tight budget. There are only two ways to reduce your real estate taxes: Either move to a less expensive home or move to a low-tax area. Moving doesn't necessarily mean moving out of the state or even out of the area where you live. In most states you'll find dramatic differences in property tax rates in neighboring communities, sometimes in the same county. Each state has its own unique tax structure and each county, township, and city adds its own assessments to create a bewildering patchwork of rates throughout the nation.

Choosing the right tax niche is where you could save enough to cover your monthly grocery bills and then some. I recently interviewed friends, who live in a San Francisco suburb and were ecstatic about the future retirement home they purchased in Fairhope, Alabama (a popular retirement community near Mobile and just a few miles from the Gulf Coast beaches). They fell in love with the town while vacationing in the area and visiting friends. Almost on impulse, they came up with a small down payment and became owners of a beautiful $89,000 home just a little larger than their $350,000 California home. (Of course, $350k doesn't buy much near San Francisco!) Since the Fairhope home was rented and the rent almost covered the mortgage payments, the transaction was painless. They will be building equity until retirement. The interesting part of the story is that taxes on their California home were a little over $4,000 ($333 a month), but their taxes on their future retirement home will be about $450 a year (that's only $37 *a month!*). This $300 extra each month can cover the grocery bills, a vacation in Costa Rica, or a Caribbean cruise every year.

Below is a list of some of the more popular retirement states, with an approximate ranking from lowest to highest property tax rates per capita:

1. Alabama	6. Kentucky
2. New Mexico	7. West Virginia
3. Arkansas	8. Delaware
4. Louisiana	9. Tennessee
5. Oklahoma	10. Mississippi

11. Missouri
12. North Carolina
13. Utah
14. Idaho
15. South Carolina

16. Nevada
17. Georgia
18. Indiana
19. Pennsylvania
20. Virginia

I must caution you not to take these rankings as absolute. Property taxes are so variable, depending on so many individual conditions and changing so much between communities even in the same county, that it's impossible to quote taxes state by state with any precision. Your assessments also will vary depending on the following:

1. Are you a veteran?
2. Do you have a low income?
3. Are you over sixty-five or disabled?
4. Is your house undervalued or overvalued?
5. Does your community have unusual bond debts?

Income Taxes

Don't get the idea that finding a no-income-tax location equals finding a low-tax situation. After all, state and local governments have to get money somehow. Texas, Nevada, Florida, Washington, South Dakota, Wyoming, and Alaska collect no state income tax, and Tennessee and New Hampshire tax interest and dividends only. But if you are retiring with a modest or tax-exempt income, what difference does this make? States that have no income tax use other methods to make up the shortfall. Property taxes, sales taxes, high automobile license fees, and other fees will always find their way into the state treasury. Some states collect no sales taxes and boost property taxes to make up the differences. Unless you have a substantial taxable income, state income taxes should be among the least of your concerns.

Medical Costs

Another significant cost item that varies from one part of the country to another is medical care. Of course, doctors and hospitals are expensive everywhere, but in some areas—notably larger cities—medical costs are out of control. In many localities, an inexpensive hospital charges $1,000 per day just for the room. Aspirins can cost several dollars each. And this is an *economy* hospital! The more expensive ones charge $2,000 per day. How many days can you afford at these rates? Therefore, local medical expenses are something to consider before you decide to relocate.

Don't feel smug because you are old enough to be covered by Medicare. The system is under attack by its enemies and is being underfunded on one hand and bashed by soaring health premiums on the other. The government, along with private insurance companies, is trying to force people into HMOs, where doctors work on a piecework basis, with an emphasis on saving money rather than quality health care. The worst part about HMOs is that they hustle to recruit patients, but when they find a coverage area not profitable enough, the insurance company simply cancels the program, forcing patients to scramble in search of an insurance provider willing to accept them for supplemental coverage. Those with existing problems or with expensive medical histories: good luck! Not only that, many private doctors find Medicare patients a bother and limit the number of patients they will accept, or refuse to deal with Medicare at all. See Chapter 5 for hints on how to protect yourself.

Sacred Home Ownership

Let's examine some common beliefs about home ownership and see if they're still valid on your retirement agenda. Most readers who will be retiring in the new millennium entered adulthood during an era of cheap and abundant real estate. Buying a house was easy. In the years after World War II—up until the 1970s, when inflation began pushing real estate prices past the clouds—anyone with a few hundred dollars in savings could buy a home. Monthly payments were often less than rent. For the first time in history, home ownership became so common that it was taken for granted. Our generation grew up with the conviction that it didn't make sense *not* to own your own home. Those retiring in 2003 probably paid less than $20,000 for their first home, with monthly payments around $160 or less. Renting a similar house would have been more expensive. Not everyone has this kind of equity, of course. Many sold their homes and kept "moving up" and could have more or less equity than those who held onto that original abode. Others had neither the foresight nor the wherewithal to buy a house in the first place. They really need this book.

The deal was irresistible. Home ownership was doubly important during our working years because interest and property taxes were deductible, thus reducing our income taxes. However, if you are retired and have a low income, you'll be paying little or no income tax, so deducting property taxes and interest probably won't affect your income tax liability.

When we were kids, one man's salary could support a family, send the kids to college, and maintain a comfortable, suburban, two-car lifestyle. Most wives didn't have to work; they stayed home to take care of the house and kids. A visit to the doctor was $20, and adequate health insurance cost $30 a month. The United States made the best cars, television sets, and sewing machines money could buy, and we enjoyed the highest living standard in the world. Those were the "good old days" everyone talks about.

You don't need to be reminded that times have changed. Today, we buy our autos, sewing machines, and TVs from foreign countries. College tuition is so high that children and their parents must borrow heavily to pay for a top-quality education. Today, young married couples take it for granted that both will work until retirement. Whatever happened to the "Ozzie and Harriet" scenario, with the wife as homemaker and the husband the breadwinner? Today, unless their parents can dredge up the down payment, many young adults will be renting for the rest of their lives. Even if they manage the down payment, they both will have to work full-time in order to make the monthly payments, which today are usually far *higher* than rent on a similar place. Yes, things have changed.

Many of us of who bought homes thirty years ago take it for granted that property appreciation will continue on indefinitely. Maybe it will. At least we can be confident that prices will increase in tandem with inflation, which would maintain your home equity. Yet we must recognize that, at the time of writing, our economy appears somewhat uncertain. Increasing long-term unemployment means some people cannot manage high mortgage payments, which could lead to distress sales and the probability that real estate will have reached a long-term plateau, perhaps even a decline in prices. Should this happen, prospects for property appreciation are dim.

In any event, many retirement-age people cling to the conviction that owning a home is essential for stability and safety. They would rather cut back drastically on their budgets than lose the feeling of permanence and security that home ownership provides. This is fine for those who can afford to live where they are upon retirement, those who have enough income that their lifestyles won't change appreciably when they no longer have weekly paychecks. Still others, even though they may be financially strapped, feel that staying in their homes is worth it. After all, the grandkids live nearby, many of their neighbors are close friends, and they simply enjoy living where they are.

However, you may find it worthwhile to examine your attitudes toward home ownership and see if alternatives might be worth exploring. Each case is different.

Costs of Home Ownership

An impressive number of couples approaching retirement today own their homes outright. That's not surprising, given the fact that the original purchase price was in the $30,000 to $40,000 range, with monthly payments about $130 a month. For many, the mortgage went up in smoke long ago. But the value of the homes also went up. Depending upon the part of the country where you live, your $30,000 home could be worth from $150,000 to more than $300,000. That's a lot of money and very tempting for someone who may have to retire on a shoestring. But many would never consider selling and using the money to finance a new, downsized budget and a comfortable lifestyle at the same time.

"After all, my house is paid for now, and I'll live rent-free," you might insist. "I may have to pinch pennies from time to time, that's true, but at least I'll always have a roof over my head."

While it is comforting to own your home outright, you cannot realistically figure that you'll be living there "rent-free." Look at it this way: A business considers its store, office, or factory to be a capital investment; your home is exactly the same type of investment. Let's suppose your home is worth $275,000. That's your capital investment. If that $275,000 equity were placed in a safe, interest-producing investment (say earning 5 percent interest), your income would be $13,750 a year. When you figure it that way, the actual cost of living in your own home is $1,145 a month plus taxes, insurance, and upkeep, which could add another $2,500 a year. (Depending upon the state and locality where you live, you may have to double that figure.) This brings the cost of a "rent–free" home to $1,400 a month, or $16,800 a year. Depending upon financial market conditions, your income could be much higher. At the time of writing, stocks, bonds, and other investments are fluctuating. Should you decide to sell, you'll not only have to do your homework but also be willing to spend the time to keep abreast of developments.

However, suppose you were to sell your home, invest the proceeds, then lease your neighbor's place for $1,000 a month and allow the landlord to pay taxes, insurance, and repairs. Your rent would come to $12,000 a year. You would be ahead more than $4,800 a year. Instead of paying for real estate taxes, insurance, and upkeep, you could use that money for travel or upgrading your automobile. Finally, you would have an additional $275,000 in tangible wealth, quickly available in cash should you need it.

There's another side to the coin, so you need to do a lot of math before sticking a FOR SALE sign in your front lawn. During periods of inflation, your equity (capital investment) will be increasing. This can be significant in regions where real estate is appreciating rapidly, like parts of California, Connecticut, and other states with unusual economic growth. We've looked at regions where the price of a $275,000 home can each year easily increase by the $20,000 that you could save by selling your home and investing in high-grade securities. The question is, will this increase in real estate prices continue? (Don't ask me. I've been predicting the collapse of the California real estate market for the last thirty years. Some day, I may be right.) So ten years down the line, your home might increase in value by $100,000. So then the question might be: Do you need the extra money now, or should you wait until some future time when you do need it and let your equity build up in the meantime?

I'll admit that this case is a bit extreme—few readers of this book have $275,000 homes, and most parts of the country haven't experienced runaway real estate prices. In order for this strategy to work, there should be a wide difference between local market values and national values. Making a decision to pull down equity is not easy, and it shouldn't be made until all factors are considered and you have consulted a reputable financial adviser.

I'm certainly not urging everyone to put his or her home up for sale upon retirement. In fact, for many people selling would be a terrible mistake. There are several advantages that come with owning property. For one thing, property ownership is a

hedge against inflation. Should the economy go into an inflationary spiral, property values will follow. Another benefit is that
you can often "homestead" your residence in the event of a law-
suit or personal bankruptcy.

An alternative to selling your house or sitting on your equity is
to consider a "reverse mortgage." We'll discuss reverse mortgages
later on.

Why Not Rent?

If, after analyzing your situation, you find you would be better
off using your home equity as a cash investment, you might
consider renting as an alternative to home ownership. One
benefit of renting is that the landlord—not you or your
spouse—is responsible for fixing that leaky roof or repairing tor-
nado damage.

Another happy thought is the knowledge that you don't *have*
to live there. When your lease is up, you are perfectly free to look
for a better place. Since you aren't tied to a particular locality,
you can move someplace where rents are cheaper. For example,
an apartment that rents for $425 a month in Daytona Beach or
Austin couldn't be duplicated in a similar Chicago neighborhood for less than $950 a month.

Another argument against renting I often hear is, "Paying
rent is like pouring money down a rat hole—no tax breaks."
Maybe there was a time in your life when that was true, when
you were earning good wages and when those high property
taxes and interest payments brought you a tidy income tax
refund at the end of the year. During those days when housing
was appreciating at a high yearly rate, and when capital gains
ate up 20 percent or more of the profit, holding onto property
was quite prudent. Things are different today. With a couple's
$500,000 deduction for profits on a home sale, capital gain
taxes have been eliminated on all but the most expensive
homes. If your retirement income is low, your Social Security

will be nontaxable, so you'll have little income to shelter with the tax breaks that come with home ownership.

Home ownership, even though monthly payments are high, clearly makes sense for a young couple whose earning power will probably grow over the years. As time goes by, they pay off the loan with larger paychecks, with dollars that will probably shrink from inflation. They are building for the future, just as you did at their age. But before you enter an expensive, long-term commitment to build for the future, you might want to consider whether it wouldn't be better to invest your money in your *retirement* rather than in some nebulous future thirty years down the line. Will you be able to enjoy your money as much thirty years from now as you can today? How old will you be then? In short, don't automatically fall for the "money down a rat hole" line. Figure out the financial advantages for yourself realistically, with an eye on today, not thirty years in the future.

What are the disadvantages of renting? For someone who's always owned a home, there's a vague feeling of insecurity. If you're renting a house, you never know if the owner is going to put it on the market, and you'll have to move. When you were younger, moving was no big deal, but as you grow older, the chore looms larger and more distasteful. The bottom line is undeniable: You lose the sense of security that comes with home ownership.

Reasonable Rents

When working on the original edition of *Retirement on a Shoestring*, we mailed questionnaires to retirees in all parts of the country, inquiring about housing and other living costs in their areas. When we examined several hundred responses, our figures differed significantly from the widely published cost-of-living charts. This is because the usual surveys average in people of all incomes and expenditures, including families with exceptionally high monthly incomes. Our questionnaires, however, targeted lower-income, retired folks, people who know how to economize and get along on very little. Their comments were very enlightening.

For example, some reported that two-bedroom apartments in their small towns rented for $100 to $150 a month more than a three-bedroom home. These figures ran counter to our expectations: Houses should rent for more than apartments. We solved this puzzle when we found that in many towns, the major building emphasis in recent years has been on luxury apartments. Landlords can ask top rent for a place with a swimming pool. Older homes are less in demand, and rents drop accordingly. The second factor is that our questionnaires were filled out by people on tight budgets who wouldn't be interested in yuppie-type houses or apartments. Therefore, they reported lower grocery budgets and tax bills, as well as lower housing and utility costs.

Rental Assistance

For those who absolutely cannot afford conventional rents where they live, some special federal government programs can sometimes come to the rescue. One program is called the Housing Choice (Section 8) Voucher Program, designed to provide rental assistance for very low-income families, the elderly, and the disabled. The idea is to subsidize rents for decent, safe, and sanitary housing in the private market. Because the rental assistance is provided on behalf of the family or individual, you are free to find and lease privately owned housing: single-family homes, town houses, or apartments. This means you're not limited to units located in housing projects, which can sometimes be dreary.

Of course, once you qualify, you have to find a landlord who is willing to participate in the Section 8 Program, and the rent must fall within the limits set by the federal government. The landlord gets assurance that HUD will take care of unusual wear and tear of the property and guarantee the rent should the renter skip out. Renters get the security of never having to pay more than 30 percent of their income for rent. Sometimes another rental assistance approach is taken when the qualifying applicant is given a coupon or voucher that's worth the difference between 30 percent of the tenant's income and the market rental value of the apartment. The landlord doesn't have to agree to the Section 8 Housing Program to participate in the Housing Voucher Program. This plan is also administered by your local housing authority.

The program is funded by the U.S. Department of Housing and Urban Development (HUD), but it is administered locally, usually by a county or city housing agency. When you qualify and are issued a rental voucher, you are responsible for finding and selecting a suitable rental unit of your choice. This could be your present rental residence. Rental units must meet minimum standards of health and safety, and they could be inspected by the housing authority before being approved. A rental subsidy is paid directly to the landlord by the housing authority. You then pay the difference between the actual rent charged by the landlord and the amount subsidized by the program.

Eligibility for rental assistance is determined by the housing authority based on the total annual gross income and family size and is limited to U.S. citizens and specified categories of noncitizens who have eligible immigration status. In general, the family's income may not exceed 30 to 50 percent of the median income for the county or metropolitan area in which the family chooses to live. This figure can vary widely, depending on the part of the country where you live. For example some localities in Florida allow a maximum income of $7,800 for a couple, whereas Connecticut sets the limit at $21,000.

Once the housing authority determines that you are eligible, your name usually goes on a waiting list, but you may get immediate assistance. When your name reaches the top of the waiting list, the housing authority contacts you and issues a rental voucher.

When selecting a family from the waiting list, preferences are given to those who are (1) homeless or living in substandard housing, (2) paying more than 50 percent of the family's income for rent, or (3) involuntarily displaced. Those who qualify for these preferences will move ahead of other families on the list who do not qualify. Each local housing authority has the discretion to establish additional preferences to reflect other needs of its particular community. Once enrolled in the program, under certain circumstances, it is possible to move to another part of the United States and lease another subsidized rental.

Depending on the locality, the waiting list could be long, with the demand for housing assistance exceeding the limited resources available. When this is the case, it pays to look around at other nearby areas and check to see how long other waiting lists are. Sometimes there are plenty of funds in one district and none in another. We personally know of a woman whose only income was minimum Social Security benefits, who applied for rental assistance and found that the waiting list in her city was so long that it would take years to get a place. She checked around and found a small town about seventy-five miles away where she could be accepted immediately. She moved into a lovely two-bedroom apartment for about $50 a month.

Conventional public housing is somewhat easier to obtain, but you have fewer choices as to where you live. The U.S. Department of Housing and Urban Development also administers public housing programs and also through local housing agencies. Qualifying standards are the same as for the voucher program.

Public housing is a valuable source of living accommodations for many elderly and disabled populations in our society. Contrary to stereotype, tenants aren't restricted to welfare recipients and single mothers with kids. Retired and disabled households without children account for 43 percent of all public housing residents. (This percentage does not include elderly and disabled folks who also have dependent children.) And, contrary to popular belief, the primary source of income for more than two-thirds of public housing residents comes from wages, Social Security, and pensions, not welfare.

Inexpensive Home Ownership

Some people absolutely cannot bear the thought of retiring without owning their own home. A castle that belongs to them alone, even if a small castle, is more than a luxury; it's a necessity. Having to sell the home they've lived in for years would be too much of a hardship unless they could replace the home with a less expensive place of similar quality. In many cases, this requires a move to another area or even to another part of the country—a place where prices haven't kept pace with the galloping inflation of the 1970s and 1980s. But there's no law that says you can't trade your expensive home for a less costly one. You might find a bargain not very far from your old neighborhood. A good place to begin your search is with HUD.

HUD will help you purchase a home, assist you with federal mortgage programs, and even sell homes to low-income families. If HUD can't help you with a home purchase, it might be able to help you find low-cost public housing or privately owned subsidized housing. The department wears many hats.

When someone with a HUD-insured mortgage can't meet the payments, the bank forecloses on the home. HUD then pays off the mortgage and takes ownership of the home. The home is then offered for sale as quickly as possible. Prices are often at the low end of market value so that the property will sell quickly. You should make a bid (well below the asking price) during the "offer period." At the end of the offer period, the offers are opened and the highest bid is accepted. If the home isn't sold in the offer period, you can submit a bid on any business day.

These homes are sold by HUD "as is," without warranty. The agency cannot pay to correct any problems or to spiff up the place. This means that HUD's asking price takes into account that the buyer will probably have to invest work and maybe some money to bring the house up to standard. In some cases, HUD will offer special incentives to make a sale. It will make adjustments in the asking price to upgrade the property, or may offer an allowance for moving expenses or a bonus for closing the sale early. You can often find true bargains in these sales. Furthermore, the buyer can usually get HUD to pay all or a portion of the financing and closing costs.

HUD makes it easy to find out what is available and how to go about buying a HUD home through its Housing Counseling Clearinghouse (HCC), which operates a toll-free, twenty-four-hour automated voice response system that provides home owners and home buyers with referrals to local housing counseling agencies. The number is (800) 569–4287.

When an economic downturn hits an area, you will find many homes on the verge of foreclosure. The possibility here is finding a home about to be foreclosed, with an assumable loan. Often the owners owe more on the home than they could get on the market. In this case, they are happy to get someone to take the home off their hands to protect their credit.

When homes aren't selling, lenders and government agencies will sometimes let you take over a foreclosure with no down payment if your credit is good. They're often anxious to have the home occupied, especially if you have skills, such as carpentry, painting, or landscaping, that you can use to maintain or increase the property's value.

Credit Reports

Don't know if your credit is good? Before making an offer on a HUD property, it's a good idea to check your credit status by ordering copies of your credit report from one of the three largest national credit bureaus. These are: Experian (formerly TRW), (800) 392–1122; Equifax, (800) 685–1111; and Trans Union, (800) 888–4213. A report costs about $8.00. A combined report from all three companies can be ordered from First American Credco for about $30. Call (800) 637–2422.

If your credit is questionable, you can improve your chances of getting a loan if you take the following actions. It may take several months for your new status to be reflected in the report.

1. Pay off as much as possible on your credit cards and other high-interest loans. The less you owe, the more likely it is that lenders will approve your loan.

2. Don't make a major purchase, such as a car, on credit unless you have little other credit debt. Lenders will be most interested in borrowers who have the lowest debt.

3. Contact creditors who have filed negative reports on you. Something as small as a $5.00 balance on a bill you thought you'd paid off or canceled can result in a bad mark. Send a written request, asking the creditor to remove the unfavorable mark from your record and to send a report to you. This could take up to ninety days.

4. Contact the credit bureau if a creditor has mistakenly or unfairly given you a bad mark. Document the facts and write a letter to be attached to the offending entry in your file.

Discovering Inexpensive Housing

Discovering inexpensive housing is particularly exciting for us Californians who live in areas where costs have soared out of reason. Our mindset is such that we think any house costing less than $350,000 probably has something terribly wrong with its neighborhood or lacks some amenity, such as wall-to-wall floors. When we traveled through the Sunbelt states, places like Louisiana, Georgia, and the Carolinas, we were continually astonished to find nice homes selling for as low as $65,000—in places we would find very comfortable.

Almost automatically, when people think about moving to a new location for retirement, they begin thinking Florida or

California. When a shoestring budget is a major consideration, many will shake their heads and dismiss these states as too expensive. Clearly, many communities in both states will be out of the question, just as some communities in your home state will be too expensive for you. The interesting thing is that many affordable communities can be found in both Florida and California, as well as in Arizona, the Carolinas, and other popular retirement locales.

Although Florida's Jupiter Island is ranked as the richest town in America because of its $3.9 million median home prices, you'll also find some very affordable communities there. According to the most recent cost-of-living survey by the American Chamber of Commerce Research Association (ACCRA), out of sixteen Florida towns listed, fifteen of them had below-national-average home prices. Homes in Panama City (a resort area on the Gulf Coast panhandle) go for almost 18 percent under national market prices. In the Tampa–St. Petersburg area, about 15 percent under. When we were researching Florida, my wife and I were constantly surprised at the low prices and quality surroundings. We visited several places with elegant golf course layouts or beautiful landscaped lakes with homes arranged near the tees so that residents could play golf practically from their backyards, many with prices no higher than you would expect to pay in an ordinary subdivision in other parts of the country. Many Florida communities have homes selling for a median price of $137,000, compared with a national $160,000 median price. Remember, *median price* means that half of the houses in the area sell for *less*, so when the median is $137,000, you can find homes selling in the $80,000 range, perhaps even lower. Furthermore, you'll find inexpensive rentals go with inexpensive home prices. The sixteen Florida communities included in the cost-of-living survey reported that rents average between $522 and $869 a month for quality places.

By the way, I don't want to leave you with the impression that California is an impossible place to retire on a shoestring; there are places in that state that offer an inexpensive cost of living. For example, some parts of the "Mother Lode" country—that picturesque and historic area where the forty-niners first discovered gold—are being rediscovered by bargain-hunting retirees. Property here can be very inexpensive, the climate is mild, and the Sierra foothill country is great for outdoor recreation. In many areas, a house on a large, wooded parcel can be found for $75,000, whereas a smaller home on a narrow lot in one of California's tract-home neighborhoods would cost $250,000. And on the ocean, in places like Eureka—where it never freezes and never gets hot—housing prices are as low as we've seen anywhere.

The point is, do not automatically assume that you can't find affordable housing because nearby communities are super expensive. That could be the case even in your own region. If you now live in a community where the cost of living is significantly above average, chances are you can find less expensive housing not far from where you live. You may have to move to a less convenient location, out of easy commute distance to a big and prosperous city, but you could be reducing one of your major expenditures.

Sharing Housing

Again, to reduce your monthly housing outlay, it's not necessary to move away from your home town. There are several ways to cut costs and stay around family and friends. One way is through house sharing.

In Europe, the concept of more than one family to a home is traditional, as it was in the United States in the early part of the last century. During the depression, people thought nothing of families doubling up to share expenses. A large house can easily accommodate many more people than usually live there. After World War II, a tremendous housing boom made housing readily available and cheap. It then became almost obligatory for every family to own its own little piece of real estate. Shared housing and double-family living became a thing of the past.

Today, with real estate priced out of reach for many people, the concept of house sharing is returning to the American scene. For those who are retired and who don't own a home, or for those who can no longer afford the burdens of home ownership, the notion of house sharing can be enormously practical. If you own a large house that is nearly empty now that the children are out on their own, sharing with another retired couple is one way to cut costs and have income at the same time.

Group living turns out to be a very efficient as well as convenient way to cut living costs. This is particularly true in some of the more desirable but expensive locations. "If we were to rent a home in this neighborhood," said one couple, "we would have to pay at least $1,500 for rent and utilities. That just wasn't in the cards. We found another couple and a single lady to go in with us, and we've cut our rent expense to about $500 a month, yet we live in an elegant neighborhood."

Shared housing is not just for retirement-age people. Many arrangements include multigenerational "families," in which young, middle-aged, and elderly people live as one cooperative unit. Others are organized according to sex; women often prefer to live with other women rather than have disruptive menfolk dirtying up the house. A typical home sharer could be a senior citizen, a person with disabilities, a formerly homeless person, a single parent, a recuperating patient, or simply a person wishing to share his or her life with others. For these people, shared housing offers companionship, security, mutual support, and much more.

Obviously, in order to make a success of one of these situations, the group's members must be compatible. This isn't the place for someone who is rigid, closed-minded, or doesn't like being around people. Making the decision to try a shared-housing lifestyle requires that you not only investigate the situation very thoroughly but also objectively analyze your own personality. Ask yourself some questions: Do noise and confusion disturb you? Would pets bother you? Would you be terribly upset if someone weren't as neat as you are? What if a living companion left underwear hanging on the shower curtain? If these things bother you, or if you are notorious for the offenses mentioned above, you should think things over carefully before making a decision. In any event, see if you can't do a trial month's stay to make sure everyone is like-minded and compatible.

There are other considerations. Will the space be adequate? Besides the bedroom, how much of the house will be yours? Will you have room for your hobbies? Also, how are decisions made in the house? In other words, is it a democracy or is someone in charge—perhaps the owner or the original tenant? Neither arrangement is inherently preferable, but you need to know how the system works in advance. If the person in charge is strict but fair, and if everyone knows where the boundaries are and precisely what the responsibilities are, there should be few problems. But if that person is a tyrant, you may be better off elsewhere. On the other hand, a democratic management—with each resident politicking, lobbying, and arguing heatedly over each and every excruciating detail of life in the house—can be just as bad. A happy medium is always the best path.

There should be sharing of work responsibilities, chores, and perhaps cooking. Often housemates take turns cooking supper, giving the others a welcome break. "There are ten of us living in our house," said one lady as she detailed her experiences in shared housing. "Each of us is responsible for preparing three dinners every month and for cleaning up afterward. That means that except for our three chore days, we have dinner waiting for us every night. We can watch the evening news or read a novel and relax before and after dinner. The dinners are excellent, too, because we cook our favorite meals, and everyone tries to outdo the others!"

Further questions: Will you be close to shopping and transportation? If you have an auto, will you have a parking space? You also need to decide the kind of house partners you'd like to live with. Some groups behave like small, extended families, while others are more formal, with relationships on a neighborly rather than familial level. Note, too, that a larger group gives more of an opportunity to choose friends and to spread expenses over a larger base.

Sometimes a shared housing unit can be quite large, from 20 to 200 units operated as a commercial enterprise. This is called congregate housing. This arrangement is suitable for those in good health who may need assistance in everyday chores, cooking, housekeeping, and shopping, or those who don't want to be bothered with any of the above. The living quarters are small, usually with a tiny kitchen, and there is a group dining room where residents can take meals if they wish. Cooking and cleaning are done by staff. Sometimes these units are federally subsidized and available only to low-income, elderly applicants.

How do you find these situations? The most common source is the classified section of your daily newspaper. The number of "housemates wanted" advertisements grows in direct proportion to increases in housing costs. There are also private and non-profit agencies that specialize in placing individuals in shared housing. Your telephone book's yellow page will put you in touch with these agencies. A great resource is the Eldercare Locator, a nationwide toll-free service that helps older adults and their caregivers find local services. The U.S. Administration on Aging has incorporated this service since 1991. For the nearest source of help, call the toll-free Eldercare Locator service at (800) 677–1116, Monday through Friday, 9:00 A.M. to 8:00 P.M. eastern time. Online contact www.eldercare.gov/default.asp or www.nationalsharedhousing.org/.

Renting a Room in Your Home

You may feel that sharing your home with strangers might take away too much of your autonomy, flexibility, and privacy. After all, the word *share* implies a certain amount of equality among the group, and you may feel more comfortable renting part of your home rather than sharing. This way, you make the rules and set the boundaries of exactly which privileges your paying guests may be entitled to. Many of the same concerns about sharing your home will apply to renting out a room. You must feel prepared physically and emotionally to welcome non-family members into your home and be willing to accept some inconvenience in return for the extra income.

Desirable renters tend to be other senior citizens, serious college students, and young professionals who do not want the expense and bother of owning or renting a home or apartment. When selecting a tenant, you must consider whether you would prefer someone who might keep you company on a social basis or someone who will live privately, who will come and go as unobtrusively as possible, and whose lifestyle will not infringe on yours. Depending on your desires, you can develop a set of "house rules" that outline which behaviors are acceptable and which are unsatisfactory. The rules should clearly cover behaviors such as smoking, drinking, and guests. How often are guests allowed, which parts of the house are off limits to guests, and are overnight privileges allowed? Your renter should have a clear understanding of whether cooking and kitchen privileges are included in the rent, and details concerning space in the refrigerator, cleaning up, and when the kitchen will be available. Other house rules should cover laundry privileges, bathroom policies, use of telephone, a security deposit, and a fixed date for the rent to be paid. It isn't a bad idea to put your house rules in writing and ask the renter to sign in acknowledgement.

It doesn't happen often, but occasionally an unscrupulous con man will answer your newspaper classified ad and try to pull some scam on you. It's recommended that you not give out your exact address (especially if you live alone) until you have confidence that everything is on the up-and-up. In your phone interview, explain your house rules, find out where the applicant is employed or where he or she goes to school, and find out why he or she wants to rent your room. If you live alone, make sure you have someone else with you when you conduct the face-to-face interview. Of course, get landlord and employer references, as well as the applicant's driver's license number and Social Security number. You cannot be too careful in your selection process. After all, it is your house, and you are doing someone a huge favor by sharing part of it. Some communities have a professional agency that goes through this process for you, for a fee. Check your yellow pages for organizations such as Elder Help, or call your local AARP chapter for assistance.

Intentional Community Housing

There is a growing movement toward planned, or "intentional," communities. Though sometimes these are small, family-type affairs, many are larger groups, more like clubs, where people with common interests band together to forge new lifestyles and to share expenses and experiences. The intentional community differs from ordinary shared housing in that there is usually a common goal or special shared beliefs among the participants. They think of themselves as "members" rather than simply "neighbors." For a complete listing of interesting locations, look for a book in your library called *Communities Directory: A Guide to Intentional Communities and Cooperative Living* (Fellowship for Intentional, April 2000). The book contains information on 600 intentional communities as well as 100 overseas locations. (A Web site with detailed information can be found at www.ic.org/.)

A few myths need to be dispelled about the concept of intentional communities. The common belief is that this concept was something that started in the '60s and died out in the '70s. The fact is that many of those communities survived and evolved into more conventional living arrangements. Many new ones have formed since then, as a significant new wave of interest in intentional communities has grown over the last decade.

Another belief is that they are all "communes" in an economic sense—operating with a common treasury and sharing ownership of property—or in a religious sense in that they center around a particular religion or spiritual practice. Some are, of course, but most have the goal of sharing resources, creating an extended family neighborhood, and offering an ecologically sustainable lifestyle. Residents want to share their lives with others who hold similar values. Only 35 percent of intentional communities are explicitly religious or spiritual in nature.

Ecological concerns are a prevalent theme of many intentional communities. Some of these experiments are outgrowths of communities started during the "hippie" era; others are more modern in origin. There are communities for women only, for couples, or for mixed and intergenerational members. Some communities are religiously oriented, often receiving funds from a church. You'll find all spectrums of religious beliefs represented in intentional communities, from conservative Baptists to broad-minded Unitarians. We know of one community that combines feminist witchcraft and Buddhism!

Most intentional communities are owned by members and often provide free room and board in return for a specified amount of work in tasks ranging from cooking and gardening to teaching and housekeeping. Other groups require a stipend or at least a sharing of expenses. Some charge a monthly fee and also require work in exchange for residence and seminars. Some facilities are located on farms, others in forest or desert settings, while still others are urban collectives. About 65 percent of these communities are self-governed by democratic means, with decisions made by some form of consensus or voting. However, a few communities (mostly religious groups) have strict hierarchical or authoritarian rules, so it would be worthwhile to investigate before joining.

Be aware that some communities are in the process of formation and may never get off the ground. So be cautious about investing time and money in a mere pipe dream. Many do not actively solicit new members, so don't think you can simply drop in and take up residence. First you need to contact the group to see if there are any openings and if your interests coincide.

One point to keep in mind: Just because an organization offers inexpensive living doesn't mean you will be happy there. One community listing sounded all right to me until it described member residents as having "undecided sexual propensities." Another group, still in the process of forming, plans on building an undersea village where you will be surrounded by the "awesome beauty of the sea."

Continuing Care Communities

As the retiree population grows, there is a corresponding rise in the number of housing complexes devoted exclusively to senior citizens. An increasingly popular development in retirement communities is the concept of long-range, total-care facilities.

Three conceptual stages of retirement are combined in these developments. First, there are houses, cottages, and apartments for those who want to be totally independent and who prefer to cook meals for themselves. Next, there are facilities for folks who aren't quite up to doing their own cooking (or are fed up with it) or who might have trouble taking care of themselves. These residents live in apartments but take meals in the dining room. Finally, if and when residents become too infirm to take care of themselves, there is a stage in which skilled nursing care and traditional nursing home services are provided in hospital-type rooms.

Some of these complexes are very, very expensive. That's no surprise — just look at the exorbitant cost of medical care in this country. We looked at one place that requires a $400,000 investment (*nonrefundable* on death) and $2,000 a month for expenses. However, because of ever-increasing competition, we're seeing a proliferation of affordable full-service retirement homes. The least expensive place we found charged about $35,000 to enter and a moderate monthly rate for expenses. This was in a small city on Oregon's coast. A monthly income of around $1,500 and some moderate financial net worth would be required. This is not exactly "retirement on a shoestring," but if that's the type of security you're looking for, you can, with some investigation, find a satisfactory place.

One couple who moved into one of these lifetime care units said, "When we retired and moved to this part of the country, our only question was whether to buy a house or to rent. This is a compromise between the two." They bought into this complex ten years earlier, both at the age of sixty. At the time of the interview they were thinking of giving up their villa and moving into the second stage of the complex. "A nice thing about this arrangement is that we keep pace with our friends. The friends we know as golfing or bridge partners will be with us in the next stage. If they aren't ready to move yet, they soon will be. As we grow older and our interests change, we move along together."

Limited-Care Communities

For those who are unwilling or unable to pay the expensive entrance fees of continuing care, there is an alternative more practical for budget retirement: a retirement community *without* extensive health care. These are usually stand-alone facilities and have no medical care of any kind, although in some cases there is a nurse on call. Although each unit—whether an efficiency or a one- or two-bedroom apartment—has a full kitchen, meals are usually served in a dining room. These facilities are becoming competitive, and some bargains can be found. The major difference is that you must be able to take care of yourself without medical supervision. Depending upon location, prices for these places can start as low as $950 a month, including meals, housekeeping services, and all utilities except telephone. This is an ideal arrangement for singles who don't want to bother with full housekeeping.

More than three million Americans now live this way, an increase of 300 percent during the past fifteen years. A boom in new retirement housing of this type is evident throughout the country, with construction not keeping pace with demand. When you consider recent studies showing that the number of Americans over eighty-five years of age will top 24 million in the next half century, the need should be apparent.

Subsidized Housing

Until the 1980s, the U.S. government attempted to do something about low-cost housing through Housing and Urban Development (HUD) programs. Government money subsidized both construction and monthly rentals for qualifying retirees. However, the outlook today is bleak, with continuing cuts in funding. The number of new affordable housing units each year and federal housing assistance continues to plunge despite the growing number of poverty-line retirees. Given the staggering cost of the Iraq War and aftermath, coupled with huge tax cuts granted by Congress, you can be sure that federal housing assistance will continue to decline. In fact, there's a possibility that the entire program could be torpedoed by Congress. There's talk of restricting the program to welfare recipients, and this change could pass through the committees and come to a vote in the fall of 2003.

According to the Retirement Housing Foundation, 250,000 low-income retirees are on waiting lists for low-cost retirement facilities. The odds of being accepted are about one in eight. However, should your local HUD-sponsored facility have a long wait, you might check around with other communities. For example, Audrey W. qualified for low-cost housing, but when she applied at a popular, upscale Pacific Coast town, she was informed that it would be at least six years before her name could possibly come up for a HUD-subsidized apartment. Then she discovered a small town in a beautiful Sierra Nevada location with a waiting list of a few months. She moved there, intending to rent until something opened up, but because she could legitimately plead hardship—with an exceptionally low income and resources well below the allowable amount—Audrey was rewarded with a one-bedroom apartment for payments equaling 27 percent of her net monthly income. After deductions and allowances—according to a complicated formula—her rent came to about $50 per month.

One of the largest nonprofit providers of subsidized retirement facilities, the Retirement Housing Foundation operates 124 retirement communities in twenty-three states. All units are HUD approved, and the tenants' rents are partly subsidized by HUD. In other, non-HUD-subsidized units, residents pay a deposit and competitive rents, although these are somewhat lower than conventional commercial rents because of the HUD low-interest mortgages.

The Retirement Housing Foundation manages a total of 7,918 subsidized apartments and 3,777 nonsubsidized units. These include a few assisted-living and skilled-nursing units. For information, contact the Retirement Housing Foundation, 5150 East Pacific Coast Highway, #600, Long Beach, CA 90804; (310) 597–5541. The other large provider is National Church Residences, 2335 Northbank, Columbus, OH 43220; (614) 451–2151.

Investigate Before Moving In

In any kind of shared or cooperative living, certain conditions must be thoroughly understood. Ideally, there will be a contract, especially if you will be renting from a private or public entity rather than just informal sharing. If you are going to have to put up any money, here are some things you need to know.

How much, if any, of the entrance fee is refundable? Are there additional expenses besides the monthly fees? Should you die, will your heirs receive a portion of your entrance fee or deposit? Suppose you are unable to pay the monthly fee; is any financial assistance available? Are there any controls on how much fees can go up? Under what conditions can the arrangement be terminated by either side? Usually there's a three-month trial period, so you should have the right to cancel and get a refund of your entrance fee. Nonrefundable entrance fees should be avoided. You might want to check with the Better Business Bureau to see if there have been complaints against the facility and whether it is in good financial shape.

An American Association of Homes for the Aging publication, *The Consumer's Directory of Continuing Care Retirement Communities*, lists more than 300 continuing-care retirement communities. Your library should have a copy. For information on shared housing, contact the National Shared Housing Resource Center at (802) 862–2727 or write to AARP Fulfillment, 601 E Street NW, Washington, DC 20049. Another source of information is the National Consumers League, 815 Fifteenth Street NW, Suite 928, Washington, DC 20005; (202) 639–8140.

The Department of Housing and Urban Development Information Center provides pamphlets about the department's programs and free brochures on housing for the elderly. Contact the center at 451 Seventh Street SW, Washington, DC 20410; (202) 708–0408. You also might contact the American Association of Homes for the Aging, 1050 Seventeenth Street NW, Washington, DC 20036; (202) 783–2242 .

Chapter Three
Working and Retirement

Work begins the day we enter kindergarten. That's when our on-the-job training begins (without pay, of course). We quickly learn that we have a solid obligation to get up every morning—whether we want to or not—and that we must appear at a certain place at a certain time. We discover that we have a "boss" (the teacher), and we must please the boss if life is going to be tolerable. Until each long, wearisome school day draws to a merciful close, teachers and administrators direct our souls, control our lives, and limit our leisure time. I'm convinced that the fifth grade is the longest period of time ever measured. (Fifth grade recess may be the shortest time span ever measured.)

By the time we finally finish school and enter the job market, we've learned our lessons well. Get up every day, go somewhere, perform work we may or may not enjoy, and be rewarded with a weekly paycheck instead of a report card. Weekends off, plus a two-week vacation, are the only respite from the grinding schedule. To miss a day's work means losing a day's pay—a serious blow to many budgets—so we go to work even though we feel terrible. Missing too many days' work means losing a job—a disaster.

This process, started in kindergarten, is relentlessly reinforced through the next sixty years of our lives. We sometimes suffer from a mental hang-up called the "work ethic." To have a job is good. Not to have a job is bad. To lose a job is ruinous. Only bums live without working.

Then one day—willingly or not—you stumble into retirement. You no longer have a job, someone to boss you, or a place to be every day at a specified hour—or else. You can get up when you please, take a nap when you please, and you don't have to please anyone who doesn't please you.

For some people, retirement is wonderful. It's the goal they've worked for and anticipated since that first day in kindergarten. School's out! Recess and vacation from now on! When you wake up in the morning, you can roll over and go back to sleep if you jolly well feel like it!

But for others, retirement is a terrible shock. They feel there's something wicked or evil about not having a job. When one of these unfortunate individuals wakes up in the morning without a job to go to, a feeling of guilt sets in. "Something is terribly wrong here," the person thinks. "I should be working, making money, suffering."

This guilty feeling is why many folks refuse to retire, even though they work at jobs they dislike. Others, when forced into retirement, insist on finding full-time or part-time jobs even when they don't need the money. What a tragic waste of a lifetime's goal.

Retirement doesn't necessarily mean the end of a person's working career. On the contrary, retirement means the opportunity to do what you *want* to do rather than what you *have* to do. You now have the time to write a book, join an acting group, become a fishing guide, or turn your hobby into a profitable occupation. No law says you have to suffer while making money.

This may be the time to take up a new hobby, to explore an unlimited range of options. Learn to feel sorry for those who feel forced to work instead of feeling guilty for not being with them.

For those who need to be "doing something" but who can get by without extra income, our recommendation is volunteer work. As a volunteer, you will not only be doing something meaningful and worthwhile, but you will meet other volunteers in your community, widen your network of friends, and lay the groundwork for later years when you may need volunteers to help *you*. You'll also be deeply appreciated for whatever you contribute. We'll discuss volunteer work later.

Expensive Jobs

On the other hand, many retirees truly need extra earnings to supplement their Social Security and other income. Part-time or full-time jobs can mean the difference between bare survival and a comfortable retirement. Yet sometimes the income earned can be costly—in several ways.

One condition that can make a job uneconomical is the government's policy about working while drawing Social Security. To discourage retirees from earning money, the government reduces benefits when you earn more than a certain amount. Fortunately, in 2000, they stopped reducing benefits for those over age sixty-five who work. Before, you had to wait until you were seventy-five to work and collect full Social Security benefits. If you are under sixty-five, in 2003 you are permitted to earn $11,520 a year ($960 a month), then you'll be penalized one dollar for every two dollars you earn over that amount. Once you are over sixty-five, you can earn as much as you like. Those under that age will be penalized.

Let's take the case of Roger, a commercial printer who lost his $20-an-hour job because desktop publishing put his employer out of business. He was sixty-two years old, so Roger applied for Social Security and was entitled to $845 a month (amounting to $10,140 a year or $195 a week). Finding he needed more income, he looked for a job. The best job he could find paid $8.50 an hour ($340 a week). Better than nothing, he thought.

At the end of the year, however, he discovered that he had to repay $3,080 of his Social Security money because at $8.50 an hour he was earning too much! For full-time employment, Roger was only entitled to make $5.53 an hour without penalty; that's just a little more than minimum wage. In other words, Roger worked more than ten weeks for nothing—just to make up for the money deducted from his Social Security! To add insult to injury, he had to pay income taxes on the excess $3,080 that he had earned over the allowable amount. He immediately started looking for a *part-time* job.

Good Jobs and High Prices

Part-time work is, of course, one solution for a shoestring budget. The problem is that competition for these jobs can be fierce and the pay can be minimal. This creates a dilemma: Where part-time jobs are plentiful and pay is good, you'll often find that the cost of living is impossible. A booming economy brings high rents and elevated living costs as well as high wages. It doesn't make sense to retire where living costs are exorbitant in order to find a good-paying part-time job that will only help pay the extra expenses of retiring in a costly area! You're right back where you started.

We have a friend who lived in a nice apartment in Monterey, California. Her rent was $800 a month, but it wasn't a fancy place—it was just in a high-rent area. The high cost of living in Monterey wouldn't permit her to live on Social Security. She found a part-time job in a bookstore that paid $6.25 an hour ($448 a month clear) for working five afternoons a week. If she earned more than this, she would start losing Social Security benefits. When she decided to move to a smaller town in a lower-cost area, she found an equally nice apartment for $350 a month. Part-time jobs there paid about $5.15 an hour, but no jobs were available. At first she was disappointed—until she realized that the $450 she saved in rent made up for the $448 she had been earning at her bookstore job. In other words, she had been going to work five afternoons a week just to pay higher rent! Now she devotes her time to very satisfying volunteer work in the community and takes classes in oil painting at the local community college.

Finding Retirement Jobs

Some retirees have lifetime job skills that make it relatively easy to find part-time work. Although you might no longer have the strength and stamina to handle some of the tougher jobs, your experience and good judgment might qualify you for consulting or supervisory work. Perhaps you have a skill that is in demand for vacation fill-ins or emergency work in case of an employee's illness. Nurses, secretaries, bookkeepers, and others with specialized or professional work backgrounds find themselves in great demand for these temporary positions. For example, I have a brother—a retired veterinarian—who likes to work but not on a regular basis. It turns out that many small veterinary offices are one-doctor clinics, so taking a vacation is out of the question unless another vet can fill in. This works out perfectly for my brother, who schedules his vacations well in advance and limits the number of weeks he works to those he chooses. In other words, he decides when the veterinarian can go on vacation.

Not everybody has high levels of competency at a trade or profession, and many skills have been replaced by computers. So it isn't always easy to find part-time work, especially during the recession that started in 2000. The government officially declared an "economic recovery" a year later, but this had no effect on the millions of workers who have not found replacement jobs, nor has the declaration halted the disappearance of thousands of jobs every month throughout the country. To business, this might seem like a recovery, but to those unemployed it seems like a depression. However, as long as these conditions exist, part-time workers will often be the first to be hired as business picks up.

The yellow pages of your telephone directory will list temporary employment firms, such as Manpower or Kelly (used to be Kelly *Girls*, remember?). They nearly always need temporary or seasonal workers and can usually be depended on to find you a job when needed. These jobs have a way of becoming a regular thing when the employer is pleased with a worker's performance. The good thing about these situations is that it's understood from the beginning that the work is temporary. You aren't embarrassed when you quit if you are under age sixty-five and you've earned as much as Social Security permits.

Another way to look for work is to inquire at the local senior-citizen center. They can direct you to a Senior Citizen Council office (if it isn't in the center itself) where the staff works at placing senior citizens in both permanent and temporary jobs. Of course, the newspaper's help-wanted classified pages carry employment opportunities, but many employers prefer younger applicants. By placing your own ad in the "situation wanted" column, you can put forward your own unique qualifications, job requirements, and preferences. If you have special skills that might be attractive to a particular group of employers, the telephone book will provide a list of companies to whom you can send résumés. As a final resort, there's always the state employment bureau or human development department—whatever it calls itself in your area. There, however, you are competing with unemployed workers who are looking for jobs while collecting unemployment benefits.

The Senior Community Service Employment Program helps low-income persons, age fifty-five or older, find part-time work in community service through the Job Training Partnership Act. This program provides training to individuals who are interested in working in the private sector. To find out the address and telephone number of your local agency on aging, contact the Administration on Aging's Elder Care Locator at (800) 677–1116.

The National Council on Aging attempts to provide part-time employment opportunities for older workers in public agencies, community service agencies, libraries, hospitals, and schools. Applicants must be fifty-five or older and low-income. Participants in the program work twenty hours a week, usually at minimum wage. For information, contact the National Council on Aging, 409 Third Street SW, Suite 200, Washington, DC 20024.

Check with your local American Association of Retired Persons (AARP) office; they often offer career counseling and support a program called Workers' Equity Initiative. AARP has a computer database of employers who need older workers. They can also advise you of your rights under the federal Age Discrimination Act. If you are interested, you might request AARP's free publications, *How to Stay Employable: A Guide for the Mid-life and Older Worker* and *Working Options—How to Plan Your Job Search, Your Work Life.* Contact AARP Fulfillment, 601 E Street NW, Washington, DC 20049.

A well-stocked bookstore will have several books on how to find jobs and how to start your own business. One of the best is Workamper Bookstore, selling books by mail and on the Internet. They carry books on retirement, RV living, finding part-time and full time jobs, and other work-related ideas. Their Web site and monthly publication, the *Workamper News,* have become the clearinghouse for employers seeking help and workers looking for jobs. Workamper is described later in this book. The address is 210 Hiram Road, Heber Springs, AR, 72543-8747. Call (501) 362–2637 for information, or check www.workamper.com.

A mail-order company called the New Careers Center, located in Boulder, Colorado, also has a full selection of these kinds of books. They cover subjects such as finding jobs with a cruise line or in national parks, teaching English abroad, starting a business in your own home, and freelancing opportunities. Don't expect to find any astounding secrets for making money, but these books could be the source of new ideas on work opportunities. Write and ask for *The Whole Work Catalog,* New Careers Center, P.O. Box 339-CT, Boulder, CO 80306.

How would you like to go to Disney World? If you're thinking about central Florida, you might find work at Disney's facilities there. Jobs are often available for park greeters, food and beverage servers, housekeepers, custodians, bus drivers, security personnel, and many more. Call the job line at (407) 828–1000 or drop by the Casting Center in Disney World.

If you are considering moving from your present home and relocating somewhere else, you might look at places where senior citizens get preference for full- and part-time work. For example, seasonal tourist towns like Branson, Missouri, and Myrtle Beach, South Carolina—places where music theaters are big business—welcome older employees to work part-time and full-time jobs. Casinos in Reno and Las Vegas, Nevada, tend to give preference to older employees; they find them more reliable and serious than youngsters.

Sales Work

For the outgoing personality, one of the easiest part-time jobs to land is commission sales work. The reason is obvious: The employer pays no salaries or benefits until you sell something. Automobile agencies typically have half a dozen salespersons lounging about in hopes that a buyer will happen along. Real estate offices can afford to have large staffs because they don't pay wages. Often, the salesperson is obligated to spend some time each week taking care of the office (at no pay) in addition to sales work. The upside is that while you are manning the desk you can pick up leads for listings, and the potential earnings for an effective salesperson can be quite high.

Many sales positions offer little in the way of wages; employees earn the bulk of their income from commissions. If you are successful, these jobs make good part-time occupations and sometimes pay well. The nice part about these jobs is that you needn't invest in any capital except for a few nice outfits. The downside is that when things aren't selling, you not only get nothing for your time, but it can also be boring. Please, before you consider investing any money in a sales business, check very, very carefully; the overwhelming majority of these "money-making opportunities" are scams.

Snowbirds Follow the Weather

People usually think of retirement as a time to travel, to go south for the winter and north for the summer, to enjoy the seashore, breathe fresh mountain air, and live the good life. However, when retirement rolls around, and people find they must exist on a shoestring budget, travel plans often evaporate. "Too expensive," you say. "It's tough enough getting by without quitting my part-time job to spend a winter in Florida or a summer in Wyoming."

Here's the good news: A large subculture of retirees do quite well chasing good weather. They enjoy the best seasons in places where others pay big money for vacationing, yet they do it on a shoestring. How? By working. They call themselves "snowbirds." These happy-go-lucky travelers flock south at the first sign of frost, then migrate north when sultry summer weather sets in. Not all snowbirds work; some just like to be on permanent vacation. Many live in RVs during their travels, using their vehicles as mobile living quarters. Others accept living accommodations such as a small house or apartment as part of their part-time salary. How do they find jobs while following good weather? It's easier that you might think. Seasonal jobs are plentiful; the more popular the vacation spot, the more work is available.

Any time a seasonal migration of tourists descends on a popular tourist area, temporary employees are suddenly in great demand. Business is alive and booming after the doldrums of the off-season. Motels are full, restaurants are busy, services and stores are pushed to the limit. The area's entire economy is positively affected. Businesses of all types need temporary help, especially workers who understand that their jobs cease when the tourists and snowbirds go home.

Almost every business in a resort area needs extra help to handle the increased tourist traffic. From gift shops to garages, restaurants to recycling centers, almost everybody needs temporary help. RV mechanics and repairmen can write their own agendas when thousands of RVs are in town. Temporary jobs in RV parks, motels, and campgrounds are available for assistant managers, clerical staff, housekeepers, and groundskeepers. Ski instructors are needed in mountain resorts for the winter and fishing guides are needed for the summer.

Understand that many if not most of these jobs offer little in the way of salaries, but many provide accommodations and benefits for a limited number of hours worked. Many snowbirds are happy to put in four hours a day cleaning rooms or mowing lawns in exchange for a vacation in a desirable resort. Those jobs that do pay money in addition to benefits often require full-time work, which many people don't need or don't want, preferring instead to have time off to enjoy their surroundings.

It's true that retirees who own RVs have the advantage here because they bring their own housing. They typically receive free hookups and utilities, cable TV, and free laundry as part of their compensation. One of the advantages of RV travel is the ability to take your home with you to the job site. This opens many new work opportunities.

But those without RVs aren't left out of the snowbird picture, not by any means. Many businesses maintain special facilities to house temporary employees. Motels often reserve one of the units for temps, or know of inexpensive housing that can be reserved for the season. Some snowbirds, those who return season after season, make arrangements for renting a house or apartment early, before the rush starts and rents begin to climb into the tourist range.

Seasonal work situations are not confined to tourist resorts. Christmas tree lots love to have commissioned salespeople who can park their RVs in the middle of the merchandise and watch over it at night. Other retirees work as salespeople, following trade shows or shopping-mall promotions, manning booths and selling items to the public. Many of these traveling jobs are best suited for RVers; the work would be impractical if you had to stay in hotels and eat in expensive restaurants.

See Chapter 10 for more information on seasonal jobs in

national or state parks and private campgrounds. Many positions are volunteer and don't pay any cash salaries. The joy of spending a glorious vacation in a natural wonderland is pay enough for some folks.

Finding Snowbird Jobs

At the same time snowbirds are looking for paid or volunteer jobs, employers are seeking workers who are looking for temporary or full-time positions. An excellent publication known as *Workamper News* brings everyone together. The *Workamper News* began a few years ago as an eight-page newsletter to inform RV travelers of both volunteer and salaried jobs available to them. The first issues carried about thirty-five job announcements. Today, *Workamper News* has grown to sixty pages and averages more than 400 listings representing thousands of job openings.

Although the publication was originally directed toward RV owners (and still is to a large extent), the publication lists jobs of all descriptions for people with or without their own housing. The publication has been used by a wide variety of public and private enterprises with great success. The publishers try to weed out phony get-rich-quick schemes, so most of the help-wanted ads are legitimate. Each listing includes information on the job location, duties, benefits, and how and where to apply.

If you have special skills or work situations in mind, you might make your needs known through your own advertisement. The newsletter provides situations-wanted ads (first thirty words free) and a résumé referral system. Résumés from active job seekers are maintained on file and are scanned for those that meet an employer's requirements, based on skills, geographic location, and benefits and length of employment desired.

A new feature, Workamper Hotline, provides 24 hour access to jobs from coast to coast via a voice-mail message and ads posted on the *Workamper News* Web site, www.workamper.com.

The hot line is updated weekly. Job seekers call and hear the voice-mail message or check the Web site, then contact employers directly concerning job vacancies.

The following jobs were advertised in a recent issue: A resort in Maine needed couples for tour guides, clerks, and maintenance duties. Forty Vermont state parks were asking for volunteer help for the summer. A resort in Gettysburg wanted couples for various duties, offering accommodations plus minimum wage. A Montana dude ranch needed cooks, kitchen help, waiters and waitresses, and housekeeping workers. A caravan-tour company wanted wagon masters. Several Sierra Nevada resorts were lining up employees for the coming summer tourist rush. Florida job offerings were numerous. In all, forty-three states and one province in Canada were represented in the job/employee search. Each issue also lists commission jobs, such as working Christmas tree lots, demonstrating computer software, and selling resort lots. The number of job possibilities is impressive.

According to the publishers, Greg and Debbie Robus, there are often more jobs than people to fill them. They also maintain a complete bookstore with books on retirement, work-travel, how to find jobs, and so forth. One popular book they recommend is *Road Work: The Ultimate RVing Adventure* by Arline Chandler. Others include *The Back Door Guide to Short Term Job Adventures* by Michael Landes and *Travel While You Work* by Kay and Joe Peterson.

The address for subscriptions to *Workamper News* is 709 West Searcy Street, Heber Springs, AR 72543-3761. Web address: www.workamper.com; e-mail address: info@workamper.com. For a free brochure, call (800) 446–5627. A year's subscription is $25.

Underground Economy

The Internal Revenue Service is understandably concerned about what it calls the "underground economy." Throughout the country, folks are dealing with each other in cash transactions—or trading goods and services that amount to income— yet they neglect to report these transactions on their income tax forms.

For example, if you do housework for someone in exchange for reduced rent, you are expected to report the rent as wage income, while the landlord reports your labor as rental income. If you sell items at a flea market, you are supposed to report your profits. I don't know if it's ever happened, but that's the way it's *supposed* to be. Without a "paper trail" of transactions, and because individual amounts are relatively insignificant, the IRS finds it almost impossible to track these small-time tax evaders. The IRS seems genuinely surprised and indignant at these transgressions, and it estimates that if everyone paid income tax on all their earnings there would be additional billions pouring into our national coffers every year. (On the other hand, if the wealthy were limited in their loopholes, the amount of additional revenue would be even more staggering.)

But the law is the law, and if you deal in cash transactions, you need to bear in mind that at some date in the future you could face an audit by the IRS. So keep receipts, just in case.

Arts and Crafts

Now that you are retired, you'll have more time to spend on your favorite hobby. When your pastime involves arts and crafts, you may be able to turn it into cash, selling your wares at local craft shows, fairs, flea markets, and by consignment to gift shops. If you have a product that is unique and of high quality, you might find it accepted at a national craft consignment shop. Elder Crafters is one such place. This nonprofit organization accepts hand-crafted work by artists fifty-five years or older. Each submission is reviewed by a committee before being accepted. Out-of-state consignments are common. If customers or other dealers are interested in your work, Elder Crafters will put you in touch with them. A set of color slides of your work, along with a query letter, is recommended. There's a one-time, nonrefundable application fee of $5.00 and a $10.00 annual fee if you are accepted. Contact Elder Crafters at 405 Cameron Street, Alexandria, VA 22314; (703) 683–4338.

Arts and crafts shows are big business in many parts of the country, and some retirees make a good living this way. I interviewed Jean and her husband, Dwan—a Clarksville, Tennessee, couple—who devote much of their spare time to their hobby-business. They travel to craft fairs in several southern states as far away as Florida, selling all the handicrafts they can make.

"Our best time of the year is fall," Jean said, "from Labor Day until the first week in December. The closer to Christmas, the better the sales of lower priced items. Anything priced ten dollars or less sells like hotcakes." Jean specializes in tole-painted objects—shelves, bread boxes, wall plaques, and other small items. "Dwan works with the band saw, and I do the painting," she explained. "From January on through to August we build our inventory, and then we go on the road."

Their net profit averages between $1,000 to $1,500 a weekend, although some of the more successful sellers can take in as much as $15,000 at one of the larger craft fairs, where as many as 40,000 visitors browse the shows. However, getting a booth at one of these high-volume shows requires exceptionally good products (you need to submit good-quality slides and samples of your work), a substantial fee for the selling space, and a long time spent on the waiting list. Jean described one show in Ann Arbor, Michigan, that's reputed to have a waiting list several years long.

To locate these arts and crafts shows, pick up a copy of *Sunshine Artists USA*, a magazine that bills itself as "the Voice of the Nation's Artists and Craftsmen," listing 10,000 arts and crafts shows in the United States. Write to Sunshine Artists USA, 1700 Sunset Drive, Longwood, FL 32750.

Free Flea Market Enterprise

Forty years ago, when I first met my friends Jack and Marie, they were the epitome of early-day "yuppies." Jack had just graduated from a university with a degree in business. Marie was making money hand over fist from a direct-sales enterprise she had started. Clearly, this couple was headed for the top. And that's exactly where they went. Unfortunately, a few years before retirement, a series of accidents and some bad investments seriously diminished their financial portfolio. But not their drive to succeed. Although far from poverty-stricken, Jack and Marie wanted to earn money and decided to use their business knowledge to do it.

"The problem was," said Marie, "we didn't have the 'seed money' necessary to get into a substantial business. Besides, we were retired; we wanted to control our time and not be slaves to business hours. Since we both enjoy meeting the public and selling, we figured that nothing could be more natural for us than working flea markets."

So for the past several years, they've been traveling to flea markets and an occasional craft fair. At times they sleep in their van to save on motel bills. They pick up merchandise to resell from auctions, distress sales, and wholesalers. Garage sales sometimes provide stock, "but we stop at garage sales only if we happen to be driving past," said Jack. "Most of the time, people want more for their junk than we can get for it at the flea market!" Classified ads in the local newspaper are another source of merchandise, especially when a family is moving away and is anxious to get rid of everything.

What's required to become an entrepreneur in the flea market business? You'll need a van large enough to carry your inventory, some folding tables, and a canvas awning to keep off sunshine and rain. And, of course, you'll need to fill your van with interesting items for sale.

To find out where flea markets are, just attend one, visit a few booths, and talk with the proprietors; you'll discover which locations are more lucrative and which to stay away from. Also, most state tourism offices and chambers of commerce list flea market events.

House and Pet Sitting

Remember when you used to go on vacation? You'd load the kids and the dogs into the car, lock the front door, and head for the mountains. If you forgot to lock the front door, no big deal. Probably you paid a neighbor's kid a buck or so to mow the lawn while you were away.

That was before the days of mass burglaries, vandalism, and NO PETS ALLOWED signs at your favorite resort. Times have changed. Many people now insist on a "house watcher" when they go on vacation, business trips, or extended visits. Furthermore, they no longer trust the neighbor's kid to watch over things, not as long as he has access to spray paint and a penchant for graffiti (and it's no longer a dollar a lawn). As a result, many vacationers are willing to pay real money to mature adults in exchange for peace of mind. And they don't expect you to do lawns or windows.

One lady we interviewed managed to build her pet-care and home-watching business into a full-time job. She even has to hire help during the busy season. For $30 a day, she makes two trips to each home. She feeds the pets (walks are extra); waters the house plants as needed; changes the lighting to make it appear that the home is occupied; carries in newspapers and mail; and checks the telephone answering machine for important messages. Total time: two half-hour visits each day. Four customers a day constitutes a maximum schedule, for an average of $300 a week in cash. Her business grew by word of mouth, with no outlay for advertising. "I'm afraid that if I put an ad in the yellow pages, I'd have so much business I'd never get back into retirement!"

Some pet sitters specialize in bringing the pets (usually cats) to their own home so they won't be alone in the house. This arrangement saves driving back and forth to the pet owner's home for feeding.

A friend who lives in upscale Monterey, California, managed to work her pet-sitting business into an unusual lifestyle. She rents a tiny studio apartment as her home base, then specializes in house- and pet-sitting in the exclusive Pebble Beach area. She stays in the multimillion-dollar digs while the home owners are away (in Europe, Alaska, New Zealand, or wherever super-rich people spend long vacations). Marilyn has use of the Mercedes or Jaguar to do shopping. She sleeps in the master bedroom, generally lives in luxury, and gets paid for it. In return, she waters the plants, pampers the dogs and cats, lolls around the swimming pool, and watches over the grounds.

Pet Grooming

This is a business that can be easily conducted in your home with a minimum of capital investment. Because pet lovers spare no expense in caring for their animals, a competent pet groomer can be assured of steady repeat business. Customers realize that grooming is a necessary luxury and schedule it on a regular basis. However, pet grooming is one of those skills that is difficult to "learn as you go." You should take a hands-on class if at all possible. An Internet search using Google will yield hundreds of resources, ranging from in-depth professional training in your area to correspondence courses in the skills of pet grooming. A truly in-depth course could run into money, but the more in-depth you go into training, the higher your skills and earning potential. Local community colleges sometimes offer classes where you can learn the fundamentals. Occasionally, pet groomers learn the trade on their own, by studying books on the subject and by experimentation. (However, I would recommend that you practice on your dog before you begin accepting customers!)

Child Care

This is another business that can done in the home with little investment. This used to be a traditional way for housewives to earn money—taking care of the neighbors' kids. Today, with so many mothers having to work, the demand is higher than ever before. Without someone to care for the children, a married or single mother is out of the job market.

Unfortunately, right at the peak of the demand, the city, county, and state bureaucracies have made it more complicated. Now you have to be certified and licensed in most communities. This is another area in which local colleges come in handy. Ask if they have child care provider classes that qualify you for a license as a day care provider. The courses usually include Preschool Activities, Pediatric First Aid and Safety, and Basic Life Support Strategies for Youngsters. (How in the world did we raise children before the government got involved?) The school can also help with the licensing process.

Licensing laws vary from state to state and provide a baseline of quality below which it is illegal to operate. Before going into child care other than taking care of your neighbors' kids on a casual basis, you should contact your state's child care regulatory agency and see what is required for a professional license. If you don't have an Internet connection, borrow your neighbor's computer and go to: www.childcareaware.org/en/licensing/.

Home Companion

For a single retiree with no resources, an excellent way of making ends meet without spending any of your income is to become a home companion. By watching the classified section of your newspaper or by placing your own ad, you may quickly find a nice home, good meals, and a small monthly stipend. All you do in return is act as a live-in companion to an elderly or infirm person.

Many people in their declining years fiercely resist entering rest homes for the elderly. They see no reason to leave the comfort of their homes, they want to stay in familiar surroundings, and they neither want nor require round-the-clock nursing attention.

This is where the home companion comes in. The home owner needs someone to do the cooking, run errands, do laundry, clean and dust—in short, do light housework as well as provide assistance in getting around when needed. The home companion usually has a private room and run of the house (although some agree to sleep on the living room sofa-bed) and often has weekends off as well as several nights out a week, providing the home owner is capable of being alone. We commonly think of this as woman's work, but single men are in demand as well, particularly when the client is a male who feels intimidated by a female companion. Also, some women prefer to have a man in the house, providing security and not objecting to fixing the garbage disposal when it conks out. We have a friend in Seattle who for several years was a home companion to an elderly college professor. He enjoyed living in a lovely home, attended classes at the local university, and banked most of his Social Security. He earned an AA degree in computer science and at age sixty-eight was probably the oldest of the graduating class.

Obviously, the drawbacks to a job like this are being restricted to the house for long hours at a time and being responsible for the safety and comfort of the employer. Another disadvantage is low pay.

An advantage is that your living costs are totally paid, which permits you to build up a nest egg by banking all of your Social Security money. Also, your duties are usually rather light, with little to do other than light housework. This work can be minimized if you ask that a housekeeper visit once a week or so. You'll have plenty of time to read and watch television.

Part-Time Teaching

Teaching is an excellent (although not always lucrative) way to take advantage of your life experience. Throughout the country, courses in trade schools and adult education classrooms are often canceled because no instructors are available. The problem can be especially critical in smaller towns where qualified craftsmen have forsaken the low wages paid in the community to move to better-paying situations in bigger cities. This means that local students are deprived of the opportunity to learn a trade or a skill—one that you may be able to provide.

The essential requirement to be a teacher in these circumstances is not necessarily a college degree, but often just a solid knowledge of your craft and the ability to pass your skills on to the students. Even in states and localities where academic qualifications are strict for community college and trade schools, adult education instructors seldom have to match the formal requirements demanded of academic instructors.

I once volunteered to work as a teacher's aide in an English-as-a-foreign-language section of the local adult education program. I enjoyed it immensely, but when I tried to quit my volunteer position, the school administrators begged me to stay. They insisted on putting me on a paid basis and granting me a lifetime California teaching credential as a bonus. And all I'd really wanted to do was have fun helping foreigners learn to speak our language.

Teaching opportunities are often advertised in the local newspaper classifieds. A phone call to the relevant school department, especially to the Adult Education office, will verify whether there are any openings. If nothing's available, they'll surely know where to refer you. Some departments will actually create a class to fit an instructor's skills. If they can locate fifteen or twenty students who are interested in your specialty, the school will receive money from the state to fund the class and pay your salary. It's best to prepare a résumé detailing your work experience and what aspects of this experience you are capable of teaching. If you have some college credits, don't fail to mention them.

Many school districts find themselves faced with a shortage of substitute teachers for regular grade school and high school classes (partly because of the low pay scales for substitutes). If you have at least a bachelor's degree, many schools are eager to put you on their substitute list, even if you have no teaching credential. Classroom assistant jobs, almost always part-time, are possibilities for those with little or no experience. Starting off as a volunteer is an excellent way to break in. Private schools don't always demand approved teaching credentials, and because their regular salaries are often lower, they offer a lot of job opportunities. If you have some formal education and feel qualified to teach a subject, you might consider a part-time position in a private school.

A real bonus is that working in a school situation puts you in contact with the community, creating an ideal situation for meeting new people and making friends. If you're a stranger in town, this is the quickest way to lose that status and become known and appreciated.

Beware of Fancy Advertisements

Magazines are liberally sprinkled with ads urging you to start your own business, with the advertiser offering to help you get started. If you've been around long enough to think about retirement, you've also got the smarts to know that these things are too good to be true. The ads claim that you can make $100 an hour cleaning carpets, selling stationery, or engaging in some other scheme, but you end up paying lots of money for nothing. Don't pin your future on a flowery magazine advertisement assuring you that you can make $100,000 a year in your spare time.

Local newspaper ads can also be phony. I had a friend who answered an ad that offered to set up applicants with a free delivery route business, stocking supermarkets with a nationally known product. He should have known there was something wrong when the company insisted that he buy an expensive delivery van from them—at their price. Next, the company "union" demanded a huge initiation fee. It turned out that the union and company were splitting the initiation fees and down payments on the vans. The new "employees" were laid off when new applicants showed up with enough money to buy a truck and pay union initiation fees. To top it off, the company terminated the job but not the payments on the van. Oh, well, he was able to use the van for camping and eventually drove his money's worth out of it.

Taking Inventory of Your Business Skills

Before you think of starting a home business, you need to examine your own personality, ask yourself some questions, and supply some honest answers. From Nancy Olsen's book, *Starting a Mini-Business: A Guidebook for Seniors* (1988), come some of the following ideas on this subject. Ask yourself these questions:

1. Are you a self-starter? If you are someone who hates getting up in the morning and getting after business, being your own boss won't be any fun.
2. How do you feel about dealing with people? You need to like working with people if you are going to get into your own business. Almost all types of businesses require daily contact with others.
3. Can you take responsibility? Are you the type who can forge ahead and get things done, or have you always expected others to do things for you?
4. How good an organizer are you? Running a business means being organized. You're going to have to keep books and records and keep your fingers on all the strings.
5. Can you make decisions? At every turn in the road, there will be instant choices to be made. If you can't, you're going to be paralyzed. Your business will suffer.

6. Can you stick with it? You can't always expect to make money from the very beginning. If you don't encounter instant success, are you going to become discouraged before your enterprise gets the chance to fly?
7. How good is your health? Will you truly have the energy to follow through on your business?

If after assessing your own strengths, you are still assured that you really want to go into business, you might check with your local office of the U.S. Small Business Administration. There are one hundred offices in cities nationwide, offering free counseling, literature, and sometimes financial assistance for starting a business.

For information about where they are and what they offer, call (800) 827–5722. Be sure to ask for a copy of SBA's *The Small Business Directory: Publications and Videotapes for Starting and Managing a Successful Small Business.* SBA district offices are listed in the telephone book under "U.S. Government," or call the toll-free number above for the office in your area.

Volunteer Work

If you don't absolutely have to work to keep bread and beer on the table, why do it? If you feel guilty about not "doing something" or if you get bored hanging around the house, try volunteering. You'll feel good about yourself. A special bonus of volunteer work is that your services will be sincerely appreciated and valued more highly than if you were to work in a fast-food restaurant or some other high-competition, low-pay job, trying to please an employer you don't like in the first place.

Volunteering is also one of the fastest ways of making friends in a community. You'll find yourself rubbing shoulders with genuine people, like-minded folks who want to help others. A dividend is that someday, when you might need help, you will be well-known in the community, and help will be available without asking.

One of the major retiree volunteer organizations is the Retired and Senior Volunteer Program (RSVP), sponsored by the federal ACTION agency. RSVP volunteers provide a variety of community pursuits, helping old and young alike. Services include health care, companionship, security, and education, as well as financial and social services at day care centers, nursing homes, schools, libraries, crisis centers, courts, and other community locations. RSVP volunteers operate runaway shelters, organize widows' support groups, and offer occupational counseling to first-time criminal offenders. RSVP volunteers are usually paid expenses incurred while volunteering, such as transportation and other out-of-pocket expenses. They also receive accident and liability insurance while on service. For further information on the RSVP program, call the National Senior Service Corps at (800) 424–8867.

The federal ACTION agency also sponsors the Senior Companions Program (SCP). SCP volunteers assist mentally, emotionally, and physically impaired elderly individuals by providing companionship, help with errands, financial counseling, health care, and nutritional assistance. The goal of Senior Companions is to help the elderly live independently at home for as long as possible. Senior Companions must be age sixty or older and low-income. In return for twenty hours of service each week, SCP volunteers receive a small tax-free allowance, a meal on the days they work, transportation, insurance, and an annual physical examination. To find out more about SCP, contact your local senior-citizen center or the national ACTION office at ACTION, 1100 Vermont Avenue NW, Sixth Floor, Washington, DC 20525; (202) 606–4855.

Enjoy the outdoors? As a U.S. Fish and Wildlife Service volunteer, you could find satisfying work in a nearby wildlife refuge or fish hatchery. Often it's possible to commute to the job site and back each day. Volunteer positions are often available to match your skills, abilities, and preferences.

If you don't have to return home every afternoon, you might consider volunteering with the National Forest Service. There you will help maintain and improve the nation's forests and grasslands by doing light construction work, maintenance tasks, or clerical work. Depending on the job, you may reside on-site in a barracks, a mobile home, or conventional government housing. Volunteer positions sometimes have a way of turning into paid employment.

To find out about volunteer programs with the Fish and Wildlife Service, call or write the U.S. Fish and Wildlife Service, 4401 North Fairfax Drive, Arlington, VA 22203; (703) 358–2043. To offer your services as a Forest Service volunteer, call or write the USDA Forest Service, Human Resources Program, P.O. Box 96090, Washington, DC 20090; (703) 235–8834.

Chapter Four
Your Tax and Mortgage Investments

In the last chapter we discussed ways to work and earn money during retirement. Now we'll talk about the money you've invested by way of paying taxes all these years, money that finally will be returned to you in one of three ways: Social Security, Social Security Disability, or (for those who are very short of funds) Supplementary Security Income (SSI).

Don't for a moment think of these monthly checks as "charity." Currently, for every dollar you earn, you pay 7.65 cents to Social Security, and your employer matches that. You've invested many tax dollars over your lifetime, money deducted from your paycheck every week, money that has gone to help others before you. Now it's your turn.

We'll also investigate another way to draw down money invested over the years—the equity in your home. The money is just sitting there, fattening up your net worth, but not doing anything for your lifestyle. If your situation is like that of most people approaching retirement, your monthly house payments reduced your loan amount, while steady appreciation increased the value of your home. This locked-up money could help finance your retirement if you could only get at it. This route must be approached with caution; as we shall see, a few potholes can make it a dangerous road for the unwary.

Social Security

Social Security is the key to retirement for the vast majority of workers in our country. Without it, retirement would be impossible for many of them. Two-thirds of today's retirees depend on Social Security benefits for more than half of their monthly income. For millions, that's all there is. Without Social Security, an incalculable number would be forced to continue working until they dropped dead or until their employers decided to replace them with younger employees.

A campaign to privatize this most successful and valued social program has been underway for two decades now. Stockbrokers, insurance companies, and bankers (who stand to make a handsome profit if Social Security is converted to individual investment accounts) have pulled out all the stops to influence public opinion. They've spent millions in an effort to persuade younger Americans that Social Security is going bankrupt and to convince middle-aged Americans that they'd be richer if the money went into the stock market.

This is what Alan Greenspan, chairman of the Federal Reserve Board, thinks of the Wall Street plan: "Investing Social Security assets in equities is largely a zero-sum game," Greenspan said. "Only an increase in national saving or an increase in efficiency with which we use our savings can help us meet the retirement requirements of the coming years."

Attacks against Social Security are not new. Since its very conception in the 1930s, Social Security has been under attack by those who believe that people should save and make investments for their own retirement. (Many cannot, and that's why the program came about.) Fortunately, despite continuing efforts by some congressmen to weaken and even eliminate Social Security, the program survives. These attacks are extremely shortsighted. If Social Security is scuttled, millions of elderly would plunge below the already-low poverty line. The country's economy would suffer irreparable damage, and the extra load on social services would overload the welfare system to the point of disaster. So rejoice that we have Social Security and keep a jaundiced eye on any politician who wants to trash it—and on those who keep saying the system is "bankrupt."

Well, *is* Social Security bankrupt? Of course not. According to the Social Security trustees, the plan is completely funded for at least the next thirty years. It is inaccurate to label as "bankrupt" a program that is secure for at least the next third of a century. Moreover, given Social Security's importance in protecting millions of Americans from poverty, such a label is irresponsible.

Listening to the propaganda would make one think that the Social Security Administration is running out of money and will soon stop sending out checks. Nothing could be further from the truth. The fact is that Social Security is one of the few sectors of government that runs at a *surplus*. It takes in billions of dollars a year more than it pays out. In fact, if Social Security were removed from the budget, the proposed $300 billion deficit estimated for 2003 would double. When we were running a $290 billion deficit, Congress managed to find $300 billion to bail out the savings and loan institutions and doled out billions in aid to foreign countries. Don't worry: They'll find the money to fix Social Security or the voters will find a new Congress.

The economic projection that Social Security will start facing a gap in thirty-four years is based on assumptions that wages will increase about 1 percent a year (adjusted for inflation). However, economists point out that if wages were to grow at their average rate of the last fifty years (at 1.7 percent), then the doomsday scenario is replaced by one that envisions the system in the black for a long, long time, perhaps into the twenty-second century.

Social Security Eligibility

Qualifying for Social Security benefits is straightforward. You need to have earned a minimum amount of money for a minimum number of quarters and paid Social Security taxes on these earnings. The minimum number of quarters needed depends on your age, and the minimum amount of wages depends on the year worked. Before 1977, you needed to earn at least $50 in one three-month period to count that as a quarter. Beginning with 1978, you needed to earn $250, and the amount has increased each year. Currently, earnings of $830 in at least one three-month period are required. The more money you earn, the higher your checks will be. If you work for yourself and have been paying self-employment tax, that can qualify you for benefits.

Generally, anyone who has worked for ten years or more will qualify. Figuring out how much your check will be is not so straightforward. You'll have to ask the Social Security Administration to assist you. The local office can help you make a request for a Personal Earnings and Benefit Estimate Statement. Or you can call the Social Security Administration at (800) 772–1213 and request the form. When you receive your statement, make sure that all of your employers and all of your earnings are included. It's always possible that mistakes have been made. It's wise to check this from time to time, even if you are a long way from retirement, just to make sure you're being credited properly. After all, benefits are based on the highest of the last thirty-five years' earnings, so missing a year's worth of earnings might cause a reduction in benefits of $10 to $15 per month. The form will ask you to make an estimate of your average earnings between now and retirement. Just put down your present earnings. That way you'll receive an estimate in today's dollars, which gives you a better idea of what your retirement picture will look like. Your Personal Earnings and Benefit Estimate Statement will also show you how much you would earn, in today's dollars, if you retired early.

Retirement at What Age?

Normal retirement is at age sixty-five, at which time you'll receive a "full benefit" for your time worked. The earliest you can retire is age sixty-two, but your monthly benefits will be reduced by 20 percent. For example, if you would receive $960 a month at age sixty-five, at age sixty-two you'd be entitled to $768 a month. For each year you wait to retire after age sixty-five, you'll get an additional 4.5 percent added to your benefits. Therefore, if you wait until age seventy to retire, your check would be $1,176 per month.

Those who were born after 1938 will find their checks shorted for early retirement and won't get full retirement credits until they reach the age of sixty-seven, instead of sixty-five. That's one of the ways Congress is dealing with the crisis that could face the plan down the road. That change could very well alienate folks who are rapidly reaching retirement age, so there's a possibility Congress will soon face some angry voters who are just realizing that they are being shortchanged.

So when do you retire? The difference between the $960 you might receive at age sixty-five and the $768 at age sixty-two means almost $200 a month less pension—for the rest of your life. But on the other hand, you'll receive $27,684 during those three years of early retirement. You'll be ahead of your coworker who waits until sixty-five to retire, and you'll stay ahead until he or she catches up with you at age seventy-seven.

For many, the decision about when to collect Social Security is difficult. Obviously, if you plan on working after retirement and earning lots of money, you're going to have to give money back to the government. Remember, if you are under sixty-five, you're allowed to earn only $11,520 before you start paying back one dollar for every two earned. However, if you can work *part-time* without going over the limit, you should come out ahead. Another possibility is waiting until sixty-five to retire—this adds three more higher-income years to your record and gives you a slightly higher benefit check. But you'll miss out on three years of retirement. Decisions, decisions!

The retirement age for those wishing to obtain maximum retirement benefits has been changed, depending upon your date of birth. Those born in 1938 (and who will be sixty-five in

2003) have to tack on two months to their age. That is, they can draw full benefits if they wait two months after their birthdays. That age will gradually increase until it reaches a retirement age of sixty-seven for people born after 1959. Workers who hang onto their jobs after reaching the age of full retirement not only earn more credits but can draw their Social Security benefits and continue working. Also, don't forget that the amount of your benefits increases with each year worked after full retirement age. For example, if you were sixty-five in 2003, for each year you work up until the age of seventy, you'll gain a 4.5 percent increase in your benefit check. For five years of work, your $960 benefit would grow to $1,176, an extra $122.50 a month. On the other hand, had you retired at sixty-five, you would have drawn $34,560 by the time you reached the age of seventy. More decisions!

Social Security Disability

If you are disabled or blind, you don't have to be sixty-two or over to draw Social Security. A doctor must certify that you are "totally and permanently disabled for a period of not less than one year." No matter what your age, you will draw benefits at the same rate as a person who is sixty-five years old who has earned the same amount of credits as you have. These benefits are paid regardless of your financial situation or how much other income you have each month. After two years on disability, you are also entitled to apply for Medicare, just as if you were sixty-five years old.

To encourage you to return to work once you have recovered sufficiently, the government permits you to work on a trial basis, for a limited amount of time, without penalty. That is, you receive your disability payments and your salary for this period.

However, be aware that obtaining disability status is not easy, particularly if your disability is the least bit marginal. Because so many people have faked disabilities in the past, the Social Security Administration takes a hard look at each case and will disallow all but the most obvious disabilities. From time to time they crack down, routinely turning down obviously valid claims and forcing legitimate applicants to appeal the decisions.

To qualify for disability you must prove that you have a severe physical or mental impairment (or combination of the two) and will be unable to do any "substantial gainful activity" for a year or more. Where difficulty most often arises is in interpreting the term "substantial gainful activity." Social Security administrators define this as any work that would pay at least $500 a month.

When a close relative of mine applied for Social Security Disability and was turned down, a caseworker explained it to me this way: "Let's suppose a stockbroker who earns $150,000 a year receives a brain injury and is no longer able to work as a broker. If he were capable of working as a dishwasher, then he could not be considered disabled under our rules. The fact that dishwasher jobs aren't available doesn't enter into the matter. We can only consider the question, 'Is the applicant *capable* of working?'"

The key to qualifying for disability is to have a reputable doctor, and preferably more than one doctor, willing to testify that you have "severe physical impairment that prevents you from doing substantial gainful activity for a year or more." Often, when you apply to a Social Security office for disability, a caseworker will offer to get the medical evidence for you, ostensibly to save you the trouble and expense of going to a doctor yourself. From personal experience, I can advise you to get your *own* evidence from your *own* doctor! To avoid approving the claim, caseworkers have been known to take affidavits from doctors who are sympathetic to the government's side—doctors who hardly know anything about your case—and then ignore your personal physician who could testify that you are disabled. It's not surprising that so many genuinely disabled have to go through the appeal process.

If you feel that you are truly disabled and your application for Social Security Disability is turned down, by all means appeal the decision. Well over half of disallowed applicants win on appeal. You don't need to have an attorney for an appeal, but should you decide that you want one, get a lawyer who works on contingency (if you get nothing, he or she gets nothing).

For More Information

If you would like more information about Social Security programs, you can order any of the following publications by calling (800) 772–1213. You can order some of these publications at night, on weekends, and on holidays, 365 days a year.

1. *Understanding Social Security* (Publication No. 05-10024)
2. *Retirement Benefits* (Publication No. 05-10035)
3. *Survivors Benefits* (Publication No. 05-10084)
4. *Disability Benefits* (Publication No. 05-10029)
5. *Medicare* (Publication No. 05-10043)

People who are deaf or hard of hearing may call a toll-free TTY number, (800) 325–0778, between 7:00 A.M. and 7:00 P.M. on business days.

Are You Missing a Pension?

Many people have pensions coming and don't realize it. Happily, there is a government agency working to locate "missing people" who are eligible for defined-benefit pensions (pensions that assure a fixed benefit) but are not receiving them.

Some are spouses of deceased workers who are entitled to some part of his or her pension but don't realize it. Others know they earned a pension but assume it's lost because their employer went bankrupt. Still others are victimized when companies facing financial difficulties deliberately misappropriate the pension funds in an effort to bail out.

Martin Slate is executive director of the Pension Benefit Guaranty Corporation, a federal agency that insures the private pensions of 41 million workers and takes over when a private pension plan is terminated without sufficient money to pay the promised pensions. Slate says, "Our central mission is to make sure everybody who's owed a pension gets one." The agency recently stepped up its search efforts for missing pensioners. The agency is currently paying benefits to about 160,000 retirees, and they're finding an additional 1,000 "lost" retirees each year.

If you can't locate a former employer who promised a pension, or if you believe your employer may have switched or terminated your defined-benefit plan, you may contact the Pension Benefit Guaranty Corporation for help. The address is PBGC Administration, Review and Technical Assistance Division, 1200 K Street NW, Washington, DC 20005.

Another source of retirement income you may overlook are Social Security benefits based on your ex-spouse's earning records. This is particularly important in the case of divorced women, who typically qualify for much lower Social Security benefits than their higher-paid ex-husbands.

It turns out that you are eligible for benefits based on your ex-spouse's records, even if he is not retired, if you fulfill the following requirements:

1. You are age sixty-two or older.
2. You were married to your ex-spouse for at least ten years, and the divorce is at least two years old.
3. You haven't remarried, or you remarried someone who is receiving Social Security benefits as a widower, widow, parent, or disabled child.

Your monthly check will be the same as if your earning record were the same as your spouse's. Of course, if you earned more than your spouse, forget it.

AARP's Pension Equity Project (PEP) is designed to expand AARP's education and advocacy efforts regarding pensions and employee benefits. It develops programs to promote and ensure retirement security. For more information or assistance, write to Pension Equity Project, Work Force Programs, Department Worker Equity, 601 E Street NW, Washington, DC 20049.

Supplementary Security Income

If your monthly income is exceptionally low and you aren't eligible for Social Security or Social Security Disability, Supplementary Security Income (SSI) can come to your rescue. To qualify for SSI, you must be sixty-five or older *or* disabled *or* blind, and you must have little or no income. It's important to note that SSI isn't just for the elderly, it can be paid at any age as long as the applicant meets the disabled or blind standards. *Blind* doesn't necessarily mean totally blind; very poor vision will sometimes qualify you. *Disabled* doesn't mean confined to a wheelchair, either. If doctors agree that you have a physical or mental problem that keeps you from working and that is expected to last at least a year or to result in death, you may qualify. The rules are similar to Social Security Disability.

The basic SSI check is $530 for a single person and $796 a month for a couple. Some states add money to that amount. In addition, folks who qualify for SSI usually also qualify for Medicaid and food stamps.

The financial qualifications vary from state to state, but basically your total income must be less than $700. Some items of income don't count against you, including, for example, the first $65 of your earnings every month; food stamps; food, clothing, or shelter provided by private, nonprofit organizations; and most home-energy assistance. There are other exemptions that your local welfare office will explain to you. You also cannot have assets that exceed $2,000 for singles or $3,000 for couples. Some assets are exempt; these will be explained to you when you apply.

Reverse Mortgages

The idea of a "reverse mortgage" started in California, where highly inflated property values shelter huge sums of untouchable equities. Many folks who bought their homes thirty years ago for

$30,000 are still living in the same home, but it's paid for and it's worth $450,000.

When retirement rolls around, unless your income is adequate, you could be "house poor." Some decisions need to be made. You could sell the house and pull down the equity for retirement. But then where do you live? You could take out an equity loan, but then you'd be back to making monthly mortgage payments. Should you move to a less expensive, but less desirable neighborhood? Or do you move to a lower-cost part of the country altogether? If you like your neighborhood and love your home, it might *not* make sense to sell and move away.

An alternative for those with huge equities is to take the value built up in their homes and turn it into a reliable monthly income through a "reverse mortgage." Instead of paying a monthly installment payment to the bank, the bank sends you a monthly check, adding that amount to the total debt, or mortgage, against your home. These payments aren't taxable income, and they do not affect your Social Security benefits in any way.

A reverse mortgage promises you a stipulated monthly payment based on several factors. The amount of cash you can borrow depends on the amount of equity held in your home, the property's value, and its location. The cost of the loan and the annual percentage rate applied against your equity also affect the cash payment. Your life expectancy enters into the equation, as well. That is, the largest cash amounts usually go to older borrowers who live in homes of higher values.

Typically, a reverse mortgage loan requires no repayment for as long as you live in your home. But the loan must be repaid in full—along with accumulated interest and any other charges—when you sell the home or move away permanently or when the last living borrower dies.

As you receive monthly repayments, the amount you owe grows larger; therefore, the amount of money that you or your heirs will receive upon selling the house and paying off the loan correspondingly shrinks. Of course, if local real estate prices increase the value of the house, there may well be more cash for you or your heirs.

Because you continue to own your home, you are still responsible for property taxes, insurance, and repairs. If you don't fulfill these responsibilities, the loan could become due and payable in full.

To qualify for a reverse mortgage, both you and your spouse must be at least sixty-two, and the home must be your principal place of residence—where you spend the majority of each year. Lenders usually accept only single-family, one-unit dwellings for reverse mortgages. However, some will accept two- to four-unit owner-occupied dwellings as long as all owners are borrowers. Some condominiums and manufactured homes may also qualify. Mobile homes and cooperatives are not eligible for reverse mortgages.

Be careful, though—a reverse mortgage isn't a simple solution. You'll need to be quick with your calculator and be aware of sharks feeding in this huge pool of home equities, an ocean worth an estimated $800 billion. Before taking such a big step, you should discuss your plans thoroughly with family members, your attorney, or other trusted advisers.

Essentially, there are three kinds of reverse mortgage loans:

1. A "tenure plan," which pays a fixed monthly cash advance for as long as you live in your home. You can stay until you die, the home is then sold, the bank takes its money, and the remainder, if any, goes to your heirs. By the way, this mortgage bears a compound interest rate, with interest being charged on accumulated unpaid interest.

2. A "term plan," which pays a fixed monthly cash advance for a specific time period. The cash advances stop when the term ends, but you are not required to repay the loan until you die, sell your home, or move permanently away. Short-term mortgages are practical if you plan to live in your home for five or six years and then move to a retirement community. You can then sell the house, pay off the loan, and have something left over for your new lifestyle.

3. A "line-of-credit plan," which lets you decide when to

draw advances and how much of your home equity to use. Interest accumulates only on the money you draw.

The difference between regular home-equity loans and reverse mortgages is that home-equity loans usually require proof of a certain amount of income and require installment payments over a specified length of time, usually ten or fifteen years. With a reverse mortgage, lending institutions are secured by a first trust deed on the home, so they don't care about your income. They're protected because a typical reverse mortgage loan pays out considerably less than the market value of the house. When the borrower moves or dies, whichever comes first, the house is sold and the mortgage is paid off with the proceeds of the sale. Interest on the reverse mortgage is debited from the equity.

As in any financial transaction of this complexity, you'll find lenders all too willing to take advantage of our ignorance. They may come up with outrageous calculations based on unrealistic life expectancies, or they may try to saddle the home owner with high interest rates that quickly eat up the equity. In some cases, the borrower finds his home drained of value, with zero equity, by the time the agreed-upon term is up. This can be serious; you'll have no equity in your home to pay for your spouse's nursing home care—or your care—and nothing to leave your grandkids.

Don't let anyone talk you into signing a "service" agreement to help you get a reverse mortgage. You can get all the help you need for little or no cost from a HUD-approved housing counseling agency or your nearest HUD office. Your out-of-pocket expenses should be no more than the cost of an appraisal (maybe $300 or $400) and a credit report (about $50). Another trap is a clause that the lending institution is entitled to 50 percent of any appreciation in your property over the term of the loan. Don't go for this.

If a reverse mortgage sounds like the answer for your situation, take steps to protect yourself. First, request the free forty-seven-page booklet *Homemade Money* by mailing a self-addressed postcard to AARP Home Equity Information Center, 601 E Street NW, Washington, DC 20049. This will give you an idea of how to shop for a reverse mortgage.

Wait! Before you start signing papers for a reverse mortgage, you need to realize this is a big step, and you need to take a close look at all your options before making such a major financial decision. Let's review your alternatives to see if you can find a less costly or better way to meet your needs.

Selling your home and buying a less-expensive home. If there is a possibility that you might consider selling and moving anytime soon, you need to think twice before taking out a reverse mortgage. These loans are expensive when repaid within a few years after closing because of substantial start-up costs, mortgage insurance, and "risk-pooling" fees. You pay these fees to guarantee that you can stay in your home for as long as you need to. But if you end up selling a couple of years after closing, you will be paying for a guarantee you won't need.

To decide whether to sell, you need to compare the cash you can get from the sale with the cost and maintenance of buying a newer, but less expensive home. Also, how much money will be left over after you buy the new home, and how much income will you derive from that investment?

Selling your home and moving to a rental or apartment. Will you be satisfied living in a rental after all those years as a home owner? Again, how much money will be left over from the sale of your home, and can it be put into a safe investment?

Renting your home and using the rent money for a rental house or apartment. This can work in an area where the rental potential is high, yet property isn't moving very quickly. You would need the option of low-cost rentals not too far away or would need to be moving to another part of the country. This way, you can hold onto your equity until the home can be sold.

Also, be aware that there are government-backed reverse mortgages that originate under a Department of Housing and Urban Development program. HUD loans carry no appreciation clause.

In addition, closing costs on a HUD reverse mortgage are generally lower—about $4,000 as compared with $5,000 or more for conventional loans.

If you are sixty-two or older, check with the Federal Housing Authority (FHA) to see if it will insure your reverse mortgage. If available, the insurance may guarantee payments even if a lender goes bankrupt or if the home's market value falls below the loan balance. For more information about insuring a reverse mortgage or to find a reverse mortgage lender in your area, call the FHA at (800) 732–6643. The FHA can also refer you to a HUD-approved independent counselor who can check the terms of a reverse mortgage, analyze your financial situation, and advise you about whether or not to proceed. The counselor can also give you a list of HUD-approved lenders.

Single-Purpose, DPL, and PTD Loans. Another type of reverse mortgage is called a single-purpose loan. These reverse mortgage loans, when available, are granted for one specified purpose, for example, to repair your home or to pay your property taxes. These loans are the lowest-cost reverse mortgages you will find, and they are usually offered by state or local government agencies. Thus your dealings with the lender will be straightforward, with no hidden catch phrases.

A variation of this plan is a deferred payment loan (DPL), which also can be used for repairing or improving your home or paying back taxes. This type of public sector reverse mortgage provides a one-time, lump-sum advance. Some agencies forgive part or all of the loan if you live in your home for a certain length of time after taking out the loan. If you find and qualify for one of these "forgivable" loans, you'll probably have more equity left at the end of the loan than you started out with.

A final option, available from some state and local government agencies, is a property tax deferral (PTD) loan. This is a reverse mortgage that pays your property taxes with yearly loan advances. No repayment is required for as long as you live in your home. Like other reverse mortgages, PTD loans are generally paid off from the proceeds of the sale of your home.

1998 FEDERAL POVERTY GUIDELINES: ANNUAL INCOME IN DOLLARS

FAMILY SIZE	STATES & DC	ALASKA	HAWAII
1	8,050	10,070	9,260
2	10,850	13,570	12,480
3	13,650	17,070	15,700
4	16,450	20,570	18,920
5	19,250	24,070	22,140
6	22,050	27,570	25,360
7	24,850	31,070	28,580
8	27,650	34,570	31,800

Programs using the federal poverty guidelines to determine eligibility include the Food Stamp Program and the Low-Income Home Energy Assistance Program. Note that in general, public assistance programs (Aid to Families with Dependent Children and Supplemental Security Income) do not use the poverty guidelines in determining eligibility. The Earned Income Tax Credit program also does not use the poverty guidelines to determine eligibility.

Single-purpose loans, DPLs and PTDs aren't available everywhere and can be difficult to find. You'll need to query your city or county department of housing or community development agency. You can also search online at www.homemods.org/linked-frameset.htm. Eligibility criteria will vary from program to program, and loans are limited to home owners with low or moderate incomes. Many lenders place a limit on a home's value or lend only in defined areas. Some have a minimum borrower age or a disability requirement. Sometimes community agencies that do not offer single-purpose or deferred loans offer other low-cost home repair programs with affordable monthly payments.

Other Ways To Tap Equity

More conventional ways to spend some of your home equity are refinancing your home, taking out a second mortgage, or taking out a home equity line of credit. But remember that all three of these strategies require that you make monthly installment payments on your loan. And because the loan is secured by your home, you could face foreclosure if you can't make the payments for any reason. If you're on a shoestring budget, you may rightly be hesitant to do this. You are also responsible for loan fees and for points charged by the lender.

A more creative way of drawing your equity and staying put in your home is through a "sale leaseback." The idea is this: You sell your home to an individual for a substantial down payment and monthly installment payments over the term of the mortgage. In return, you receive a lease for the term of the mortgage. Your lease payments will be much less than the house payments you will be receiving because the purchaser will be paying interest on the loan.

Normally this type of sale leaseback transaction is done between parent and adult offspring. Let's suppose you sell your house to your daughter. She knows she will be getting the property anyway, but in the meantime, she can be taking deductions on interest, taxes, property maintenance, and depreciation. These breaks, along with the rent you pay, make it painless for her to help you because it won't cost her any money. (In order to do this, the sale price of the home should be at a fair market value, and your rent should be a fair market rent.) Should you die before the mortgage runs out, she will inherit the property and the mortgage is moot. By that time there's probably been appreciation, so your daughter will make money on the deal.

Another way to work this is to have the buyer take out a conventional loan through a bank to purchase the property. In this case, you would receive all the proceeds from the sale and can use this money to invest in a safe, income-producing investment to help out with retirement expenses.

You'll need a family lawyer to make out the papers and ensure that both parties are protected. You'll want to be sure you have a lifetime lease with full rights to share the house with whomever you please. The contract must have a clause requiring subsequent buyers to honor that lifetime lease. You'll also want a rent-control clause that limits rent increases to the cost-of-living index, as well as a clause that makes the buyer responsible for taxes, insurance, and repairs.

Chapter Five

Now It's Your Turn!

All your working life you've paid federal income tax and probably state income tax, as well. Maybe you've even been nicked for city or county income taxes. If you own property, you don't have to be told that you've paid a wagon-load of dollars to city, county, and state governments over the years. If you didn't own property and just rented a house or apartment all your life, don't feel smug and think that you've avoided paying property taxes. Actually, you've graciously included taxes in your monthly rent payments. The landlord simply paid the money over to the government for you and took a tax deduction for his trouble. When his taxes went up, so did your rent.

Now, to this amount add the state, county, and city sales taxes you've paid over your lifetime, as well as miscellaneous hidden taxes and fees, and you begin to get an idea of how much money you've paid to keep your government in clover. You'll never know for sure because every time you buy something from the store, the cost of the manufacturer's taxes—corporation taxes, sales taxes, property taxes, import duties, payroll taxes, and who knows what else—are passed along to you as part of the purchase price.

You've wondered what the heck they do with all this money, haven't you? (If you haven't, you must have an exceptionally high pain threshold.) We often hear politicians taking cheap shots at food stamps, Medicare, Social Security, and other programs as being wasteful. If you listen carefully to their solutions, you'll find that we could solve all our budget problems simply by cutting back on programs that help the elderly, the needy, and the unfortunate, while decreasing taxes for the well-to-do. Congress doesn't hesitate to spend our money to bail out wealthy corporations, bankroll foreign dictators, and provide ever-increasing benefits for its members. They take our surplus Social Security money and spend it on current budget items to reduce the deficit and then advocate cutting back on benefits and cost-of-living increases for retirees because "we can't afford it."

Although an enormous amount of tax money is wasted, we have to recognize that a great deal of money is prudently spent. Without police and fire protection, highways, libraries, schools, and health services, our lives would be very different. Without Medicare, Social Security, and other programs for senior citizens, prospects for retirement would be very grim. We can probably agree that not all tax money is spent on boondoggles. This brings us to the focus of this chapter: What government and private services are out there for senior citizens and how do you get your share?

"Wait a minute," I hear you saying, "some of those services sound like charity. Charity is for losers, not for me!" Well, perhaps some of this *sounds* like charity, but the cold fact is that you have paid for these services all your life. You've paid through taxes, club dues, United Way contributions, and money in the Sunday collection plate. All these years you've subsidized tasty meals at the local senior-citizen center, paid for card tables and bridge prizes, and home care and meals-on-wheels for invalids. If you don't participate when it's your turn, it's like putting money in a bank and failing to take it out when you most need it. Now *that's* being a loser!

It is of utmost importance that those forced to retire on limited budgets participate in these worthwhile services for senior citizens. It makes retirement on a shoestring much easier.

Food Stamps

The Food Stamp Program is one of the tax-funded services designed to help low-income citizens. Yet many folks look down their noses at food stamps. They feel as if food stamps are a form of panhandling or charity. One reason for this negative impression of food stamps is the continual harping by political opportunists who see this as a way to increase their popularity with middle-class voters. Some politicians love to suggest that food stamp recipients are guilty of crimes or immoral conduct when they receive stamps from the government and then use them to buy food for the table. They link food stamps with welfare.

The fact is, the funding for food stamps comes from the Department of Agriculture and has nothing whatsoever to do with welfare, which is financed largely by property taxes. Some of these same Department of Agriculture funds go to wealthy farmers who receive payments for raising certain crops and for *not* growing others. Huge corporate farms collect millions of dollars of Department of Agriculture money in the form of crop insurance and assistance of all kinds. At one point, dairy farmers received millions to slaughter milk cows so the government could cut down on the amount of surplus milk it has to buy from farmers in order to keep prices up. These same funds are used lavishly to pay subsidies to gentlemen farmers who grow tobacco for cigarettes and chewing tobacco.

We rarely hear criticism of Agriculture Department subsidies for the wealthy. But we hear plenty about "welfare queens" who drive Cadillacs and buy groceries with food stamps. Well, it turns out that if a person owns an automobile that's worth more than $4,700, any value over that is counted against the food stamp applicant as cash assets, which affects eligibility. So don't be upset when some out-of-work housewife happens to drive a beat-up old Caddy to the supermarket.

Food stamp eligibility requirements change with the Consumer Price Index. According to the latest available regulations, the rules go something like this: For folks over sixty, a single person can have no more than $905 a month in *gross income*, and a couple no more than $1,219 per month. Gross income includes all sources of income, including Social Security payments. If you have enough expenses to deduct from your gross income figure and if your net worth is low enough, you may qualify for food stamps.

You are allowed a standard deduction, plus 20 percent of the family's gross income, child or dependent care, and certain medical expenses. You can also take a deduction for a combination of rent or mortgage, utilities, taxes, and insurance that totals more than 50 percent of your income after other deductions have been subtracted (up to a maximum of $250).

After all this figuring, you can qualify for food stamps only if your net income is less than $696 for one person or $938 for a couple. Can we agree that if a couple has less than $938 net income a month, including their Social Security benefits, they deserve all the help they can get? (Remember, this money comes from the same funds that pay farmers for not growing crops.)

But just a low income may not qualify you for assistance. You must prove that you have no more than $3,000 in allowable assets ($2,000 for those under sixty and not handicapped).

A home is not counted as a cash asset, but an automobile is, as noted above, if it is worth over $4,700. The excess value over $4,700 is counted against the $3,000 in allowable assets. Licensed vehicles are *not* counted if they are used over 50 percent of the time for income-producing purposes or if they're needed for long distance travel for work (other than a daily commute), to transport a physically disabled household member, or to carry most of the household's fuel or water. Your reportable assets include money you have in savings or checking accounts, money market funds, certificates of deposit (CDs), credit-union savings plans, Christmas clubs, cash in hand, stocks, bonds, mutual funds, and the cash value of any collection (stamp or coin collection or other collectible that's worth money). It's noteworthy that a motor home or a travel trailer is not considered an asset when valued over $4,700—as long as you live in it! Then it's considered your residence and doesn't count against food stamp eligibility. But you have to live in your rig for more than half the year.

The amount of food stamps you receive depends on your income and assets. The formula is rather complicated. A one-person household could receive up to $120 in food stamps per month; a two-person household will receive up to $220. To apply for food stamps, be prepared to show lots of proof to the food stamp office. Besides your personal identification, you'll need Social Security numbers for everyone in your household, bank books, pay stubs, payroll check receipts, and copies of checks or benefit statements from your Social Security, pension, SSI, or any other earned or unearned income. Never lie or withhold information! Everything is checked against other government records; you could lose your benefits for a long time if you give false information. *Sign the application on your first visit!* The thirty-day (maximum) wait for your food stamps starts the day you fill out your application and sign it. You don't need all the information or all the documents on your first visit; you don't even need to have your formal interview the first day. The important thing is to get the process started. Insist upon signing and dating your application the very first day!

Emergency food stamps are available from your county human services, welfare, or social-services department. If you have no place to live or if you have less than $150 monthly gross income and no more than $100 in ready cash, you may be able to get emergency food stamps in three days or less. If your rent and utilities for the coming month are more than your income and the cash you have on hand or in the bank, you can ask for emergency food stamps. The department must act by the third calendar day. Migrant farmworkers, homeless individuals and families, and persons whose shelter and utility costs exceed their income have additional exemptions that may qualify them for action by the third day. If you feel that you have not received a fair shake or if you have been denied food stamps, you have the right to request a fair hearing. Contact your legal services office or other community group that has trained advocates for help.

If you are not receiving food stamps, feel fortunate that your income is large enough that you don't qualify, but please don't look down on those who are not so fortunate. If you must be angry with someone, take it out on wealthy agribusinesses that lobby Congress and the Department of Agriculture. Should you qualify, by all means, demand your rights. You've always paid your share, and now it's your turn to benefit.

Senior-Citizen Services

Some communities have highly successful programs that can make a world of difference in people's lives. For many retired folks, a well-run senior center is their focal point, a place to enjoy free medical services and nutritious meals, as well as social activities and a host of other free benefits. Senior-citizen centers help make shoestring retirement possible.

The surprising thing about these community services is that so few retirees take full advantage of them. Recently, when doing research at a particularly attractive senior center, we asked the director what she considered to be her biggest problem. She replied, "Getting the news out that we exist! Folks just have no idea of what we offer. We send out mailings, and we ask our people to spread the word among their low-income neighbors. Many of our services are free, some have a nominal cost, others have a sliding fee, according to the ability to pay. Some items are limited to lower-income folks, but most are available to everyone. We just can't seem to spread the news!"

She then began listing the things senior citizens are entitled to in her area and the surrounding region, most of them just for the asking:

- *Adopt-a-senior programs* provide social and transportation assistance for those who are socially or geographically isolated and need assistance to meet daily living needs.

- *Adult day care programs* provide volunteers to visit the homes of full-time caregivers to provide respite care and assistance as needed. This service is a lifesaver for a spouse who is tied down while taking care of his or her invalid partner. It provides the caregiver a chance to go shopping or to enjoy a movie or some outside recreation without having to worry about the partner.
- *Adult family homes* offer room and board in a licensed residential environment for seniors who require some assistance with daily living tasks. This is also an option for single persons who are unable or unwilling to enter a nursing home.
- *Adult protective services* investigate elder abuse, neglect, exploitation, and abandonment, and provide short-term emergency support to adults in need of protection.
- *Advocacy programs* provide assistance for low-income seniors to cut through red tape. They receive help with forms, applications, and appeals, plus advice on how to handle government bureaucracy.
- *Alzheimer's support groups* provide counseling, information, and support for families. This service is very important for those frustrated by an inability to get help.
- *Blind or impaired-vision services* offer assistance to the blind of all ages. "Talking books" are featured as a part of this program.
- *Chore and in-home care services* provide assistance with household tasks, shopping, meal preparation, personal care, and transportation to medical appointments. Sliding fees make this service affordable and help keep folks out of expensive health-care institutions.
- *Clothing banks* provide suitable clothing for senior citizens. Donations come from the closets of well-off members of the community, so the quality of the clothing is very good.
- *Companion programs* provide social contact and support for elderly persons who show signs of confusion or weakness.
- *Dental care* is available to low-income seniors at reduced costs.

- *Educational opportunities* include classes that are available to seniors free or for a nominal fee. Course offerings include not only classes in traditional subjects, but also classes in aerobics, art, health and nutrition, water exercise, and driver's education.
- *Employment programs* especially for seniors provide on-the-job training, part-time employment, and job-search assistance.
- *Energy assistance programs* inform seniors about utility discounts and rebates to which they are entitled and administer a federally funded program designed to assist low-income households during the winter months. These programs help pay heating bills and assist homebound seniors in completing applications.
- *Financial assistance counseling* is available for seniors dealing with Medicaid, Social Security, and other financial-assistance programs for folks who are on low incomes or are elderly, disabled, or blind.
- *Food banks* provide food to elderly folks in need or in emergency situations. Some of the food comes from government surplus commodities, some from donations by local businesses, and the rest from community funds. USDA food surplus and donated food are distributed to needy low-income people.
- *Food stamp assistance* offers help to low-income seniors who need help obtaining food stamps.
- *Guardianship programs* provide advocacy services for those who are no longer able to make decisions or access essential services for themselves.
- *Health care services* include immunizations; screenings for diabetes, hearing loss, and blood pressure; tuberculosis clinics; and low-cost programs for foot care. Financial assistance is available for those who need hearing aids.
- *Home-delivered meals* are provided by the famous Meals-on-Wheels program for home-bound seniors over age sixty. A donation of $1.50 per meal is suggested, but only if the person can afford it. Care is taken not to embarrass those who cannot pay. In addition, the senior center provides lunch at noon, Monday through Friday.

- *Home health care* is available from skilled nurses and physical therapists who visit the home. Costs are covered by Medicare, Medicaid, private insurance, or on a sliding-fee scale for low-income people.
- *Hospice programs* enable terminally ill patients to stay in their own homes, and provide education and emotional support both for the patient and the patient's family.
- *Legal services* are provided to older persons regarding their civil rights, benefits, and entitlements. There are reduced fees for simple wills and community property agreements. Free civil legal services provided by volunteer attorneys are available to eligible low-income clients. Child custody, criminal, or litigation cases are not usually accepted.
- *Low-rent housing* in this particular town includes more than 300 units, ranging from efficiencies to small houses, that are managed by the county housing authority. Residency is limited to low-income adults aged sixty-two or older or senior couples, at least one of whom is sixty-two or older. There is currently a waiting list for vacancies, but mortgage assistance is also available.
- *Medical equipment* is available for loan to eligible individuals.
- *Recreational opportunities* include arts and crafts, card games, senior dances, and an almost unlimited number of recreational programs.
- *Rent assistance* is available in emergencies to help low-income elderly when an eviction notice has been served and when all other state and local resources have been exhausted.
- *Telephone reassurance programs* provide volunteers who talk with homebound seniors at prearranged times daily. This service helps many invalids live independently and gives them confidence that someone in the community cares about their well-being. There are no fees for this service.
- *Transportation* door-to-door is available for eligible seniors. Volunteers provide transportation to shopping, libraries, doctors' offices, therapy sessions, hospitals, and other places. There are also regular van and bus services available.

- *Travel clubs* for seniors provide day trips, overnight getaways, and longer excursions at very low cost.

Finding Services

Where are these senior-citizen services located? Depending on the community, you can locate senior services at senior-citizen centers, community or civic centers, the local park district, colleges and universities, the YMCA or YMHA, YWCA or YWHA, and churches and synagogues. Your telephone book's yellow pages are a good place to start. Sometimes your town's city hall or county offices can help you locate senior services.

The Eldercare Locator is a good source, no matter where you live. Eldercare Locator is a public service of the Administration on Aging, U.S. Department of Health and Human Services, and was created for the purpose of locating local support resources for aging Americans.

Anyone can call the Eldercare Locator on the toll-free number, (800) 677–1116, Monday through Friday, 9:00 A.M. to 11:00 P.M., eastern time. Be ready to provide your county and city name or zip code, as well as a brief description of the problem. If you are unsure about what kind of service is best for your situation, Eldercare's staff can direct you to a source that can answer your questions.

You can get information on how to locate a wide variety of services, such as housing alternatives, meals, home care, transportation, recreation, social activities, legal assistance, and other community services. The Eldercare Locator can also direct you to an office of the Senior Community Service Employment Program, if there's one in your area. This program helps low-income persons over age fifty-five find part-time work in community service. Often there's a job-training program involved for those who want to find employment in the private sector.

All Centers Are Not Equal

The senior-citizen programs listed above are all splendid examples of a community in action, providing quality services for its retired and elderly citizens. But be aware that these services are not available everywhere. Before making a decision about where to retire, I recommend that you pay a visit to the local senior-citizen center. Talk to the director and staff and see what is provided and the spirit in which it is offered.

During our research, we were continually surprised at the wide differences between senior centers in the towns we visited around the country. In some places the level of interest and quality of services were excellent—in others, next to nothing was available. The lesson is simple: Not all senior-citizen centers are equal.

For example, one center we visited served free coffee and doughnuts in the morning, while arts and crafts programs were getting underway. Daily meals were delicious and tastefully served, with cooking done on premises by a staff of paid senior-citizen workers. At least ten rooms were devoted to activities, including a library, a conference room, and exercise rooms. Enthusiastic senior citizens worked on volunteer or self-help programs, while city, county, and federal government funds paved the way for success.

Another center, in a town of similar size, consisted of nothing more than a small room furnished with a few shabby card tables. The door was open for just a few hours every afternoon, mostly for poker games. As for meals, we were told that two churches served lunch—one day a week each—as did the local Elks Club and Lions Club, making a total of four meals during the week. Nothing was provided by the center itself; you had to go to the club or church to be served. In addition, an automobile was required to get to the meals, which had the unmistakable aroma of charity. Instead of enthusiastic, caring staff members, we found a senior-center manager who resented our taking up her time with an interview.

If, God forbid, you have health problems, volunteer in-home care workers may be available to perform household tasks necessary to keep you in a clean, safe environment. They will prepare meals, vacuum, change linens, do laundry, mop floors, and clean sinks. In addition, they may well be able to provide transportation and escorting to all types of medical services when public transit isn't available, and they may even do shopping and run errands when necessary. In-home care programs mean being able to remain at home during convalescence instead of being forced into expensive care facilities not covered by Medicare. These in-home care programs are funded by federal, state, and local taxes. Most of these programs aren't limited to low-income senior citizens, by the way. Folks at all income ranges are eligible, although higher-income individuals are sometimes required to contribute toward the service cost based on a sliding-fee scale.

An additional benefit, of particular interest to senior citizens who are in need of part-time work, is that the paid in-home care employees are often senior citizens themselves.

Volunteering

The most successful and energetic senior-citizen centers all seem to have one thing in common—a large number of volunteers. Folks at centers with high levels of service don't just sit back and wait for things to happen or for the government to do something for them; they get out and *make* things happen! Their enthusiasm is catching. It spreads to local officials and to local citizens and businesses, bringing everybody into the act. They get involved in local politics and let their voices and needs be known. Politicians listen when voters speak!

The best way to help yourself in a senior-citizen center is to volunteer in helping others. I mentioned this earlier, but it can't be stressed too strongly. By volunteering, you gain a deeper sense of self-respect and well-being, and you build up a store of gratitude and good will that may well be repaid someday—when you need it most. Somewhere down the line, when you need help, you'll feel free to call in your debts.

Volunteer jobs have a way of developing into paid positions. You will widen your network of friends. And, finally, you'll know that you aren't receiving charity because you are giving just as much as you are receiving.

Medical Care USA

Thank heaven for Medicare! For years, insurance companies, medical practitioners, and health service organizations fought tooth and nail against health-care reform in general and the principle of Medicare in particular. Then, back in 1965, a surprisingly courageous Congress succeeded in making medical care for the elderly a *right* rather than a privilege. Medicare at last! Since that time, it's saved millions of elderly couples from disastrous poverty.

If you do qualify for Medicare—either because you are over sixty-five or because you qualify under permanent disability provisions, consider yourself lucky. At least that part of your retirement will be taken care of. Unfortunately, some 42 million U.S. citizens must do without health coverage. It's embarrassing that among the community of industrialized nations, only the United States and communist China stand out as countries who deny universal health care to their people. Even most third-world nations consider health care to be a human right and provide citizens with the best medical care possible. Obviously, America cannot afford tax cuts, world domination, military excellence, *and* decent medical care for all.

The important point here is that you need to carefully analyze Medicare coverage, decide what is in your best interest, and keep abreast of rule changes. Insurance companies have convinced the government that money can be saved by moving retirees out of the regular Medicare program—which is funded by the government—into private insurance plans known as HMOs (health maintenance organizations). It works this way: Medicare turns over your financial entitlement to the HMO and has no further obligation. Private enterprise is in charge from then on. The HMO gives you a big "come on" by enticing you with offers of free prescriptions and zero monthly premiums.

One problem with this: Once you drop out of Medicare and fall into the grasp of a profit-oriented insurance company, management can decide that prescription drugs are too expensive and cancel that benefit. They can decide that monthly premiums are necessary. The worst scenario is, after an HMO lures thousands away from Medicare and later determines that the community isn't returning a satisfactory profit, everyone's coverage is canceled, casting policyholders adrift with no medical insurance. This can be disastrous for those with preexisting medical conditions, which most insurers refuse to accept.

This is not to imply that all HMOs are devious or that ordinary Medicare is a better choice. Many health-care organizations offer perfectly satisfactory care with very low costs. (The author belongs to an HMO, and although the policy is somewhat expensive and without prescription benefits, the quality of care and services are superb.) The lesson is that you have a duty to investigate local HMOs before dumping traditional Medicare.

Medicare Eligibility

Below are the current ways you can become covered by Medicare and Medicaid. Remember that the rules change from time to time. Be sure to obtain up-to-date information when applying.

First, how do you qualify for Medicare? Three conditions make you automatically eligible:

1. When you reach the age of sixty-five and are receiving Social Security retirement benefits or railroad retirement benefits, you are automatically entitled to Medicare.

2. When you turn sixty-five and your spouse is receiving Social Security, or you turn sixty-five and your

deceased spouse had worked enough quarters to qualify, you are also automatically eligible.

3. At any age after you have been eligible for Social
   Security Disability payments for twenty-four months
   you automatically qualify. Note that the twenty-four-
   month waiting period begins the date you were *disabled*, not when you first started receiving disability
   checks.

If you fall into one of these three "automatic eligibility"
groups, you will be enrolled in the Part A Medicare program
without filing an application or paying a premium. Part A benefits cover hospitalization, skilled nursing facility services, home-
health-care services, and hospice care.

Three other groups are entitled to enroll *voluntarily* in the
Part A Medicare program by filing an application:

1. If you are age sixty-five or older and would be eligible
   for Social Security but are not drawing benefits—that
   is, you're still working or are not ready to retire for any
   reason—you can voluntarily enroll in Medicare and
   not pay any premium.

2. At any age if you, your spouse, or any of your depen-
   dents has permanent kidney failure, that individual is
   also eligible for Part A Medicare without premiums,
   starting from the third month of dialysis, or from the
   first month if you participate in a self-dialysis program.

3. Anyone over sixty-five who doesn't qualify for Social
   Security benefits can enroll and pay a premium for
   the Part A coverage. However, this coverage is fairly
   expensive; you might be better off with a private plan.

Note that if you don't fall into one of the "automatically
qualified" categories, you must take it upon yourself to enroll.
Even though you automatically qualify, don't wait for the government to act. To make sure you are protected when you
retire, apply for Medicare three months before your sixty-fifth
birthday. That way you'll be covered the month you turn sixty-
five. If you don't enroll within three months after your birthday, you can enroll later, during the first three months of each

year, but any premiums you pay will be 10 percent higher for each twelve-month period that elapses after the time you first could have enrolled.

Two Parts to Medicare

Medicare comes in two segments: Part A and Part B. One part covers you while in the hospital, the second part takes care of you outside the hospital. When you qualify for Medicare, you are automatically covered for hospitalization. But the outpatient portion of Medicare—the part that pays doctor bills, medicines, and items of that nature—is optional. To make sure you receive all benefits possible, sign up for Part B as well. They'll deduct a small premium from your Social Security check, but it's worth it.

Everyone who qualifies for Medicare automatically receives Part A benefits, which help cover hospitalization, skilled nursing facility services, home-health-care services, and hospice care. This coverage is financed by the payroll taxes you've paid during your working life, both before and after you become eligible for benefits. There's a deductible of about $800 for each benefit period and a co-payment of around $200 per day for the sixty-first through the ninetieth day of your stay in the medical facility.

Part B is called Supplementary Medical Insurance and it helps cover the costs of physician and outpatient services. While Part B coverage is optional, 95 percent of those eligible choose to participate in Part B. When you become entitled to Medicare, you will be asked if you wish to enroll in Part B or to decline it. If you decline Part B and choose to join later, your premiums may be higher. Part B is financed by your monthly premiums of about $45 and partly by general revenues of the federal government. There's a $100-per-year deductible, with a 20 percent co-payment. That means that after your deductible, Part B takes care of 80 percent of doctor bills, outpatient hospital services (such as emergency room visits), diagnostic tests, ambulatory surgery, laboratory services, and pap smears. It also pays 80 percent of approved charges for occupational and speech therapy services and durable medical equipment and supplies. Items not covered are things like eyeglasses, hearing aids, dentures, or routine physical exams.

It's important to remember that you must *apply* for Part B. It isn't automatic. And it isn't unlimited coverage.

Part B pays all *approved* charges for medically necessary home health care. The catch here is what Medicare considers to be approved and what it does not approve. Doctors often have different notions about their worth than Medicare officials do.

Uncovered Expenses

Medicare Plan A doesn't cover telephones or televisions, private rooms, or private-duty nurses, and it won't pay for staying in a nursing facility if it is mainly for personal care, such as help in walking, getting in and out of bed, eating, dressing, bathing, and taking medicine.

Something you need to pay attention to is whether or not a hospital "participates" in Medicare. Participating hospitals are under contract with the government to accept Medicare reimbursement. Most hospitals do participate in Medicare, but you should confirm this with hospital admissions or the administrative office.

There is one situation in which Medicare will cover you even if you receive care in a nonparticipating hospital. That is when you receive emergency care. This coverage is good only if going elsewhere would risk death or serious bodily harm, and only until the emergency passes. When the emergency is over, you must transfer to a participating hospital or you'll pay your own bills.

With two exceptions, Medicare insurance does not cover care in foreign hospitals. Hospital services may be provided in Mexico or Canada *if* you live closer to one of these hospitals than you do to a participating American hospital. This assumes that comparable services are not accessible in your U.S. neighborhood. Also, emergency care in Canada is covered, but only while traveling to or from Alaska.

The rules change from time to time, with deductibles and limits continually going up with inflation and the whims of Congress. Therefore, you might want to order a copy of *The Medicare Handbook*, Publication #HCFA 10050, from the U.S. Department of Health and Human Services, 6325 Security Boulevard, Baltimore, MD 21207. Also, AARP can supply you with information on the nearest Medicare/Medicaid Assistance Program. Write or call AARP at 601 E Street NW, Washington, DC 20049; (202) 434–2277. Be sure to order the free booklet, *Guide to Health Insurance for People with Medicare*.

Medicare strategies

• If you are retiring early (or about to be laid off) and you are covered by a company health policy, try to make arrangements for continued insurance coverage (if you can afford it). This is especially important should you or a family member have an "existing condition" that could make it impossible to find a company willing to insure you. A federal law known as COBRA guarantees the right to continue on your company health plan for up to eighteen months at your own expense.

• In some cases, your spouse and children are also eligible for COBRA coverage, sometimes for as long as three years. However, individual plans that you buy on your own, rather than through work or an association, are not subject to COBRA laws. If you have used up your COBRA benefits and attempt to buy new coverage within sixty-three days, you are eligible for a policy regardless of any health problems you have.

• Use generic drugs and don't demand the latest drug you see advertised on TV or in a magazine. Also be cautious of HMOs that feature full prescription drug coverage to lure you away from traditional Medicare coverage. They have the right to change the coverage when a drug becomes too expensive.

• If you're in a low-income bracket, be sure to investigate state programs that help patients pay for drugs. Also ask your doctor about pharmaceutical assistance programs offered by drug manufacturers.

• If you're eligible for Medicare and have trouble paying the Part B premium and the coinsurance, see if you are eligible for the Medicare programs that will help you pay these costs. Your state insurance counseling program will tell you how to apply.

• If you are eligible for health care through Veterans Affairs, look into it. It may be a way to get coverage for prescription drugs. Also, the VA's electronic medical record system is said to improve the quality of patient care.

• If you do not qualify for Medicare and have too much income for Medicaid, you might consider relocating to a place where medical costs are not so high. For example, the average daily cost for a hospital room in Middlesex, New Jersey, is $2,032; in Sacramento, California, $1,700; and in New Haven, Connecticut, $1,224. However, a hospital room in High Point, North Carolina, is only $259; in Ocala, Florida, a room costs $320; and in Mobile, Alabama, it's only $290. Now, don't think you have to move to the South for lower medical costs, because in Holland, Michigan, a hospital room will cost $282; in Appleton, Wisconsin, the average cost is $352; and in Great Falls, Montana, it's $521.

How about doctor's visits? An office call in Lansing, Michigan, averages $41; in Danville, Illinois, only $48; and Las Cruces, New Mexico, $50. These costs are roughly half of places like Las Vegas, Nevada ($91), Bakersfield, California ($86), and Stamford, Connecticut ($78). Why the differences in hospital and doctor office visits? I haven't a clue, but I do know why most hospitals in Canada charge less than $70 a day. Like all other modern nations in the world (with the exception of the United States), Canada provides universal medical care coverage for its citizens.

Medigap Insurance

As you can see, Medicare has some big gaps, holes that can suck up savings accounts in a hurry. Most people purchase additional coverage if they can afford it. This supplemental insurance is known as "Medigap," and it is supposed to cover some or all of your extra medical costs. Medigap policies come in the form of Medicare supplements and major medical policies sold by private insurance companies.

Be very careful when purchasing Medigap coverage. This has been a fertile field for con artists working for unscrupulous insurance companies. They pressure clients into buying more insurance than is needed or policies that don't pay off as advertised. Don't let a fast-talking salesman scare you into a policy that isn't right for you. One comprehensive Medigap policy is all you need. Some low-income people don't need Medigap at all. However, be sure that the policy you buy to supplement your Medicare coverage does exactly that. Policies that pay only for hospitalization or for a specific disease are not substitutes for comprehensive health insurance. Premiums may be small, but so are the benefits.

Follow these recommendations when you are buying extra insurance:

1. Choose from reputable companies and do comparison shopping. There can be big differences between one company and another.
2. Resist pressure to buy and don't let anyone sell you more than one Medigap policy. Ask friends and your doctor for advice. You needn't change policies if you are satisfied with the one you have.
3. Don't buy a policy by mail, at least not before checking with your state's department of insurance or consumer protection agency.
4. If you aren't satisfied with your new Medigap policy, by law you have thirty days to demand a full refund. If they give you a hard time, call your state department of insurance.

Medigap benefits are divided into two categories: core benefits and optional benefits. According to the law, only ten standard plans can be sold, and every insurer that sells Medigap insurance must also offer the basic plan. The basic plan includes:

1. Coverage of Medicare Part A co-insurance expenses for hospitalization to the extent not covered by Medicare from the sixty-first day through the ninetieth day in any Medicare benefit period
2. Coverage of the Medicare Part A co-insurance amount during use of Medicare's sixty lifetime non-renewable hospital inpatient reserve days
3. Upon exhaustion of all Medicare hospital inpatient coverage, including the lifetime reserve days, coverage of the 100 percent Medicare-Part-A-eligible expenses for hospitalization subject to a lifetime maximum benefit of an additional 365 inpatient hospital days
4. Coverage for the reasonable cost of the first three pints of blood unless replaced in accordance with federal regulations
5. Coverage for the co-insurance (generally 20 percent of the approved amount; 50 percent of approved charges for outpatient mental health services) of Medicare-eligible expenses under Part B regardless of hospital confinement, after the Medicare Part B deductible is met

Optional Benefits

In addition to the core package of benefits that Medigap insurers are required to offer, there are ten other packages of benefits that companies can sell. The other ten packages include various combinations of the following benefits:

1. Skilled nursing facility care: $95 daily co-insurance for days 21 to 100
2. Part A deductible

3. Part B deductible
4. 100 percent of the Part B Excess, that is, the difference between the doctor's bill and the Medicare-approved Part B charge (not to exceed the limiting charge)
5. 80 percent of the Part B Excess, or the difference between the doctor's bill and the Medicare-approved Part B charge
6. The cost of medically necessary emergency care while in a foreign country
7. An at-home recovery benefit (up to $1,600 a year, $40 per visit, for care in addition to Medicare's home-health-care benefit)
8. An extended prescription drug benefit (50 percent of drug expenses after a $250 deductible up to $3,000 per year)
9. A basic prescription drug benefit (50 percent of drug expenses after a $250 deductible up to $1,250 per year)
10. Preventive medical care (up to $120 per year for certain preventive tests and screenings)

Medicaid: The Second-Level Safety Net

The unfortunate fact is that not everyone who retires—voluntarily or involuntarily—qualifies for Medicare. Or suppose, for example, you qualify and your spouse isn't old enough? It takes only a few trips through the medical system to wipe out that nest egg you've worked so hard for all your life.

Fortunately, there's a second-level "safety net," a public-assistance program that provides medical benefits to people who cannot afford to pay for their own health care. It's called Medicaid. This is a joint federal-state medical-assistance program that squeaked through Congress along with Medicare. Medicaid (called Medi-Cal in California) pays benefits to people who are blind, age sixty-five or over, or disabled—but not eligible for Medicare—provided they meet certain strict financial eligibility requirements. Medicaid should not be confused with Medicare,

which is a federal health insurance program for aged and disabled people administered by the Social Security Administration.

It isn't only the indigent and elderly infirm who need to be
aware of the Medicaid program. Even those who think of themselves as financially comfortable should know about steps they
can take to protect themselves and shelter their life savings in the
event they or their spouse require long-term care.

If you are retiring on a shoestring, perhaps you'll be eligible
immediately for Medicaid. However, even if you're in the fortunate position of having too much income to qualify, the huge
holes in Medicare's safety net can quickly make you eligible for
Medicaid.

The largest hole in Medicare's safety net is nursing-home care.
Because Medicare was designed to cover "skilled" medical care, it
won't pay for "unskilled" or "custodial" care. Furthermore,
Medicare covers the costs of skilled care in a nursing home only if
the patient enters after hospitalization. Less than 30 percent of
nursing home patients enter that way. But it's these unskilled and
custodial services that disabled patients desperately need—things
like dressing, bathing, and cooking. Expenses for at-home care
that are not covered by Medicare can easily exceed $2,000 a
month, and nursing care can cost $3,000 to $5,000 a month. It
doesn't take long for your life savings to disappear. This is where
Medicaid becomes essential. It turns out that Medicaid has
become the major provider of long-term care for older Americans.

This all sounds very well and good, but Medicaid's future isn't
as bright as it used to be. It finds itself under a cloud of uncer-
tainty and lowering funds. Under current law, the federal government matches a state's spending on Medicaid patients. Since
most states are currently undergoing financial crises, they will
not be able to continue funding at former levels, resulting in less
state and federal money. To compound the problem, the present
administration is pushing for cuts in its portion of the funding,
which could conceivably reduce or eliminate future care. Let's
hope these cuts do not get through Congress!

Unlike Medicare, which is relatively uncomplicated—either you qualify or you don't—Medicaid requires recipients to show a definite financial need. The ground rules to qualify are different from state to state, but all fall within general federal guidelines. If and when you qualify, Medicaid pays for prescription drugs, unskilled long-term care, and many other items normally not covered by Medicare.

Who Is Eligible for Medicaid?

Medicaid eligibility is complicated. Because Medicaid is a state and federally administered program, each state interprets and applies the rules differently. Unless you fall into the class of very poor, you may need expert help in figuring out whether you are eligible for Medicaid. Even if you don't appear to qualify, the experts may be able to show you how you can be covered. They can also tell you how to appeal an unfavorable decision.

In general, three categories of individuals may qualify for Medicaid. The first category includes aged, blind, or disabled people who are receiving federal Supplemental Security Income (SSI) payments. They automatically qualify for Medicaid assistance. Some states, however, place additional restrictions on SSI recipients. If you live in Connecticut, Hawaii, Illinois, Indiana, Minnesota, Missouri, Nebraska, New Hampshire, North Carolina, North Dakota, Ohio, Oklahoma, Utah, or Virginia, check with your local social-services office for limitations.

The second category includes individuals who are on Medicare but who are financially unable pay the premiums, deductibles, and co-payments. All states are supposed to pay for Medicaid coverage in these circumstances, provided the recipient qualifies under the Medicaid limits. But you have to request payment. We'll discuss this at greater length below.

The third category includes the medically needy—aged, blind, or disabled patients—who have income in excess of the Medicaid limits but not enough income to pay their medical bills. However, many states won't pay if an applicant receives as little as a dime above the Medicaid income limits. The states that do *not* provide Medicaid coverage to "medically needy" applicants are Alabama, Alaska, Arizona, Arkansas, Colorado, Delaware, Florida, Idaho, Iowa, Kansas, Louisiana, Mississippi, Nevada, New Jersey, New Mexico, Oklahoma, Oregon, South Dakota, Texas, and Wyoming. In the states not listed, recipients must "spend down" their excess income on medical bills; Medicaid benefits kick in when the recipient's income falls below Medicaid income limits.

Qualifying Medicaid Income Limits

The following explanation is necessarily complicated. If you have any questions about your eligibility, consult your local Medicare/Medicaid Assistance Program office.

To qualify for Medicaid, all of your income from all sources is counted against your eligibility except the following: half of all *earned* monthly income, plus $65, plus $20 of all *unearned* monthly income (money from Social Security, pensions, interest, and so forth), and infrequent or irregular income. In effect, a single person can earn up to about $834 a month (or $1,105 for a couple), depending upon individual state regulations, and still qualify. Limits are higher in Alaska and Hawaii.

If you live in one of the states not listed above, you can "spend down" your income on medical expenses. For example, if you are single and go over your Medicaid income limit by $300 a month, you can qualify for Medicaid in any month during which you spend more than $300 on medical bills.

So far, the income limit seems fairly straightforward. But if you are married and your spouse needs Medicaid, the rules become more complicated. It turns out that if the disabled spouse lives at home, a fairly low earnings limit applies, but if your spouse is in a nursing home, then your limit may be larger. The limit in this case could range from $1,200 to $1,800 a month, depending on the state and several other factors. All of this seems bizarre because in most states Medicaid coverage of home-care services is virtually nonexistent. And even in states where Medicaid covers home care, you're often better off paying for your care at home privately for as long as possible. Why? Because in order to be covered you must go to a nursing home that accepts Medicaid, and you must accept whatever care is offered.

Actually, the whole matter of Medicaid income limits is so complicated that those who are on the verge of qualifying are urged to consult the local Medicare/Medicaid Assistance Program office. To find the office nearest you, contact AARP, 601 E Street NW, Washington, DC 20049; (202) 434–2277.

Medicaid Resource Limits

Another complicated matter that may require expert help is determining whether your assets are near or over the limits. The amount of cash and property you can possess varies with individual state regulations. Depending on the state, you generally are permitted to hold cash and property not to exceed $2,000 to $4,000 for a single person and $3,000 to $6,000 for a married couple.

Items that do not count against your eligibility are:

1. Your home, which must be your primary residence
2. Your household goods and personal effects
3. An automobile up to a value of $4,500
4. Life insurance with a face value of up to $1,500
5. A cemetery lot and $1,500 for burial expenses
6. Income-producing property, such as land you use to grow food for personal use

These exempt resources are subject to some conditions that may or may not be to your benefit, depending on how you handle your affairs. For example, your home is exempt, even if you move out of it, as long as it remains occupied by your spouse or if you plan to return home after your illness. Yet sometimes state Medicaid officials add a qualification: that you realistically will be *able* to return.

Several strategies exist for qualifying for both Medicaid and SSI—maneuvers for bringing assets and income down that sound devious yet are perfectly legal. You'll probably need a Medicaid legal practitioner or an attorney who specializes in Medicaid before you take any such steps. Your senior-citizen center or local bar association can refer you to such a specialist. If you're entitled to it, go for it; your taxes paid for it.

Qualifying for Medicaid When You Aren't Poor

The one major health-care item that Medicare does not cover is long-term nursing care. For many families this could be the most devastating medical expense of all. The thousands of dollars a month needed for nursing care can wipe out lifetime savings, leaving a couple penniless, just when money is needed most. Medicaid does cover nursing home care, but you must qualify by being almost poverty-stricken. Those with more than a minimal amount of resources cannot qualify for Medicaid.

However, even if you have a comfortable net worth and you see long-term care problems on the horizon, there's a little-known way to qualify for Medicaid. You must plan in advance, and perhaps be prepared for a short-term outlay of nursing care expense until you qualify.

The key is to reduce your net worth to the allowable limits by placing your assets into an "irrevocable trust." (A financial adviser or attorney can help you here.) Your children or other trusted relatives become beneficiaries of the trust, and technically you are broke, even though you still are in control while you or your spouse are alive. After a three-year period of having assets in a trust, you may then qualify for Medicaid and long-term nursing care. If there's any chance that you or your spouse could be headed down that road, try to prepare for that three-year wait or get started early. One thing you might consider is disability term insurance that covers you for those first three years, until Medicaid kicks in. Of course, these policies can be expensive and possibly out of reach for a shoestring budget. This makes it doubly important to plan ahead.

Free Medicare?

More than two million Medicare beneficiaries are paying too much for their Part B premiums. They don't take advantage of some benefits intended for low-income retirees, usually because state governments keep these benefits quiet and so save money by not fulfilling their obligations under law.

You should know that Congress enacted a Qualified Medicare Beneficiary program (QMB), which requires states, through their Medicaid programs, to pay Part B premiums for financially needy individuals who are on Medicare but who cannot pay the premiums, deductibles, and co-payments because of low income. The earnings limit is $1,194 for a single person (with assets under $4,000) and $1,603 for a couple (with assets under $6,000). In some cases the states will pay for co-payments and deductibles. That is, if a patient qualifies, he or she isn't billed for some or all of the excluded charges. However, if you don't apply for this assistance, the state won't pay. The state government has no way of knowing your economic situation unless you speak up.

There are other Medicare and Medicaid benefits that accrue to very low-income patients. If you are in this category, you should inquire at the Medicaid office of your local department of human welfare or social services. The local senior-citizen center can supply you with directions. Should you have problems getting information, check in the phone book in the government section and look for the local office of your state or local agency on aging. For a pamphlet describing eligibility, an application, and other detailed information, send a self-addressed, stamped envelope to Families USA, 1334 G Street NW, Washington, DC 20005.

Discount Medical Care

No discussion of low-cost medical care is complete without mentioning what's happening along the border of the United States and Mexico. Medical, dental, and optical practitioners are luring patients with cut-rate services and low-cost prescription drugs. It could be argued that the quality of the medical and dental care may not be up to U.S. or Canadian standards. I'm in no position to judge something like this. I can only observe that the prescription drugs come from the same manufacturers who sell on this side of the border. Also, most patients return enthusiastic about their treatment. And there's no question that the fees are affordable.

A dramatic example of this is found in the Mexican border town of Los Algodones ("the cotton fields"). For several years, this quiet community has been drawing thousands of people from all over the United States and Canada to take advantage of unbelievably low-cost dental, medical, and optical care. You'll find $135 root canals, discount eyeglasses, and hormone pills selling for a fraction of the cost charged on this side of the Mexican border. Los Algodones is also popular with those seeking alternative medical treatments that aren't available on this side of the border, especially restricted cancer drugs such as laetrile.

Discount medical care is nothing new in Mexican border towns. But nowhere else has medicine taken over the economy as it has in Los Algodones. Doctors and dentists are big business here. Although the town has fewer than 10,000 residents, you'll find fifty dentist offices, fifteen doctors' offices, almost thirty pharmacies, twenty optical shops, and many related businesses. On the other hand, you'll find only ten restaurants. Thousands of visitors cross the border every single month of the year, looking for low-cost medical care. The fierce competition for patients and customers helps keep costs down.

Dentistry is especially popular with visitors. Because neither Medicare nor Canada's government-sponsored health system covers dental care, many patients journey to Los Algodones in search of affordable dentures, root canals, bridges, and implants. People claim they save two-thirds of normal dental bills by having their teeth fixed in Mexico. Eyeglasses, frames, and contact lenses are well crafted, supposedly using materials identical to those used in the States, but at drastically reduced prices. Because Los Algodones is only a short drive from Yuma, Arizona, it isn't even absolutely necessary to stay there overnight.

How does the quality of care stack up against the care you'll find north of the border? As you might guess, U.S. dentists caution that low-cost dentistry could be accompanied by substandard care, and of course it's difficult to lodge a complaint within Mexico. And naturally, U.S. medical doctors abhor the unconventional treatments for everything from cancer to arthritis that attract visitors from all over the country, particularly those who are searching for cures to "incurable" problems. In short, the American medical and dental establishments discourage patronage of professionals on the Mexican side of the border.

As an uninformed layman, I'm obviously not qualified to make judgments about the quality of care served up in Los Algodones or the advisability of going there. My only observation is that we've interviewed many people who see doctors and dentists across the border, and they've enthusiastically endorsed the treatment and products they receive. We may simply have missed folks who have had bad experiences.

Understand, the people we interviewed are low-income retirees who are not covered by private dental plans; some are not even covered by Medicare. They have two options: either Mexican dental and medical care at one-third the regular cost, or no treatment at all. For some folks, places like Los Algodones are the only option.

Across the Canadian Border

For years, folks living in the northernmost part of the United States have been aware of the bargain prices for prescription drugs in Canada. People make regular bus trips to save 25 to 50 percent and more on lifesaving drugs. Now a new twist has cropped up: Internet prescription sales. More than 80 Web sites provide this service. A recent article in the AARP *Bulletin* profiled a Maryland Social Security recipient who used to spend a third of her monthly check on medications, at the cheapest pharmacy she could find. Then she discovered Canada and began buying over the Internet. Her drug costs dropped to $160 a month from the U.S. price of $430. The yearly savings come to $3,240.

As you can imagine, the pharmaceutical companies are furious about this trend and are lobbying Congress to not only stop Internet sales but also to prevent patients from crossing the Canadian border. At this point in time, we don't know how successful they will be. There's an old saying, money talks, and the pharmaceutical corporations (who make billions of dollars in profits every year, enough to pay their CEOs $20 million a year or more in bonuses) have plenty of money to talk loudly.

AARP recommends that if you use the Internet for your prescriptions, make sure you are dealing with a legitimate pharmacy. This would be one that has—besides an e-mail address—a postal mailing address and a telephone number so that patients can talk to a pharmacist, and will prominently display its license number and name of the authority that granted the license. Be skeptical of a Web site that says prescriptions aren't necessary.

Chapter Six
Moving Away for Retirement

If you plan on moving to a new community when you retire and if you feel that you must own a house, the best strategy is to think small town. Property away from the bustle and economic grind of a city is always less expensive. Because of lower labor costs and low demand, buying a home in a small community can save you as much as 60 percent over a similar house in nearby metropolitan areas.

The well-known advantages of small-town living are low crime rates, the affordable cost of living, and the absence of congestion. The downside is a lack of good restaurants, stores, convenient public transportation, and access to medical care. Not all small towns are inexpensive, however. If you live in an urban area where housing costs are exceptionally high, such as California's Silicon Valley, you'll find people commuting to work for an hour or more just to find affordable housing. Naturally, this bumps up prices in small towns that are within commuting distance of the metro area. As a result, you may need to move several hours away from your city home to find a small town that's affordable. If this is the case, you might well consider moving out of state—perhaps to a better climate and certainly to a place where homes are affordable.

In general, homes in the southern states, the Ozarks, and the Appalachian states are excellent buys. Real estate is also often bargain priced around military bases. This is partly due to ongoing military cutbacks, with early retirement incentives thinning the ranks.

Any number of economic factors coming together at one time can seriously depress the market. A perfect example of this was Bisbee, Arizona. This is a small mining town, with old brick Victorian buildings in a picturesque canyon setting. The town's prosperity came to an abrupt halt when the Phelps-Dodge Corporation decided to close down the local mines. Without employment, families began leaving Bisbee, selling their homes when they could, abandoning them when they could not. At one point you could buy a *furnished* home for $4,000 or less. Some changed hands for as little as $500, albeit with a mortgage involved.

Naturally, when the news got out, retirees began taking advantage of these bargains. Today, Bisbee is regaining its prosperity because of this influx of retirement money. Ajo, Arizona, also a mining town, underwent the same experience. Six hundred houses went on the market almost overnight! In a town of 3,500 inhabitants, you can imagine what this did to prices. Again, the bonanza days are gone, but there are still bargains to be found.

A slump in the mining economy also enhanced retirement possibilities in the coal-mining areas of Appalachia in Virginia and West Virginia. In this case, the mines didn't close. Operators automated the mining process with labor-saving machinery. Thousands of workers whose jobs were eliminated placed their homes on the market for whatever they could get for them and moved on. Today, more than a decade later, the housing market is still depressed. But there's nothing at all depressed about the communities the miners left behind. It turns out that coal miners were unionized and earned good wages (about equal to middle management employees elsewhere). Because they could afford any kind of housing they wanted, they built high-quality homes with lots of landscaping. The communities are prosperous looking and welcome newcomers to replace the ranks of those who left.

These kinds of giveaway prices don't last forever; they gradually move upward to a more sensible level. But bargains pop up any time a local economy collapses. Future bargains will predictably occur any time the government closes a military base or cancels a multibillion-dollar defense contract. For inexpensive housing, keep your eye on news stories and look for newly depressed areas.

Prices also drop when one or more industries fall on hard times and suspend operations. An example of this is Aberdeen, Washington. Here is a town that depended on fishing and lumber for its livelihood. Both occupations paid good money, and the area prospered. Then foreign boats, with their 30-mile-long dragnets, began cleaning out the fish. Japanese factory ships started buying raw logs, processing them with low-paid Filipino workers, then selling finished lumber products to our consumers. Aberdeen's economy sputtered to a standstill. Fishing boats stayed in port. Lumber mills closed down. As people left the area, houses went on the market—but few buyers were interested.

Many towns in Washington and Oregon have been hit hard by the lumber industry's decline, and most are suffering economic doldrums to one degree or another. I use Aberdeen simply as an example. A few years ago, we saw houses offered for as little as $20,000. We don't know if they were selling. We talked to a couple who had just moved there from California. They were thrilled with their home purchase. "It sits on three acres on a hill overlooking the bay and the ocean," the husband said. "It has four bedrooms, each with its own fireplace, and a huge fireplace in the living room. It's a regular mansion, and we only paid $85,000!" In their California neighborhood, that wouldn't have bought a two-car garage.

Try Before You Buy

Should you decide that moving to a less expensive community is your best strategy, you need to do some in-depth exploration of possibilities that will suit your needs. Your first step is to determine what kind of lifestyle changes you might want to make.

This is your chance to be creative and find your unique retirement niche. Of course, if you are a couple, you need to match each other's needs and desires.

It might be helpful to make a list of the conditions most important to you. Many people will place a mild climate at the top of the list. Others give priority to recreation, hobbies, or sports. Your final decision should be based, however, on all of the items on your wish list. After you've done your research and narrowed your choice, try to spend a vacation visiting your dream community. Rent an apartment for a couple weeks—a month is better—and see if you fit in. See if this is what you really want.

Some time ago, while doing research in the Midwest, we stopped over in a small town in the Ozarks, one that had been praised highly as a retirement paradise by popular retirement guides. It was indeed a pleasant place, with a friendly, small-town atmosphere and several excellent fishing lakes nearby. The scenery was gorgeous.

Most of the folks we interviewed seemed to love the town. Property was inexpensive, the climate relatively mild, and the bass fishing was fantastic. An added bonus was low property taxes. Retirees who had moved there from elsewhere were almost unanimously pleased with their decision. Then we happened to meet a man who had retired there and hated it. He was in the process of moving away. I asked why.

"I was born and raised in Philadelphia," he explained. "I've always been used to the city. I like to sleep late in the morning and stay up late at night. In the city, if I wanted a snack at midnight, there was always a restaurant open, or if I needed something from the grocery store, there was always one nearby open twenty-four hours. But here, everything shuts down early. I tried to learn how to fish, but I've never been able to get the hang of it. I just don't fit in here."

When asked why he made the decision to move here in the first place, he replied, "Well, I learned about this town in a retirement guide, and I read several magazine articles about it. According to the writers, this is one of the top-rated retirement places in the country. I had just gone through a divorce and decided this would be a great place to start over. It sounded pretty good on paper, but nobody mentioned anything about this being a dry county. I was used to having a couple of drinks after work and mingling with friends in a corner tavern. And I like to order Cabernet Sauvignon with my prime rib, not Pepsi-Cola. To order a drink here, I have to drive 35 miles to the next county, go to a liquor store, bring it home, and mix it myself. I hate to drink alone!"

It turns out that a few weeks previously he received an invitation to a party from one of the few friends he had been able to make. His first social event. The party was in the next town, about 15 miles away, and he felt comfortable having a few drinks because a "designated driver" had volunteered to drive everyone home after the party. Unfortunately, on the way home, they were stopped in a police roadblock. Even though the designated driver hadn't had a drink, the whole lot of them were tossed into jail. The passengers were accused of being "intoxicated in public," and the designated driver was charged with "transporting drunks." "I just don't fit in here," the retiree repeated sadly.

The lesson is, *try it before you buy it.* This unhappy man could have saved himself a lot of time, money, and effort had he done some investigating on his own and not blindly accepted someone else's statistical evaluation. A trip to this dream town and even a few nights in a motel would have told him everything he needed to know.

What Magazine Articles Don't Tell You

Many magazine articles and guidebooks that recommend retirement locations are written for an audience of fairly affluent people. Retirement writers tend to assume their readers live in an ideal world of country clubs, fancy restaurants, and split-level ranch homes. Some do, others don't. The guides count the number of museums, operas, theaters, and symphony orchestras in a city and use them as criteria for a good place to retire. Of course, these amenities add a touch of class to your retirement, but how many times a month will you be going to the opera, a symphony performance, or a museum? Some retirees would consider the number of municipal golf courses, bowling alleys, or public libraries far more important.

Retirement writers sometimes judge the quality of medical care by counting the number of doctors in the area, the amount of money invested in hospitals, and the number of CAT scanners available to physicians. Special praise goes to communities with a medical school. Frankly, I'd be more interested in whether doctors are accepting new patients. Do they accept Medicare? What's the cost of an office visit? How much will I pay for a hospital room? And what's this nonsense about a medical school? I'd rather have my vasectomy done by a journeyman doctor than a nervous student, thank you very much.

Favorable ratings are often awarded on the basis of conditions that don't affect retirees. For example, good schools, high employment, and a booming business climate lead writers to boost a town's popularity rating, while horrible weather and high taxes are often ignored. Quality elementary schools and good recreation programs for kids matter less to retirees than quality senior-citizen centers and safe neighborhoods. The problem with full employment and thriving business conditions is that they usually result in high prices and expensive housing.

The bottom line is this: By giving the same weight to concerts, museums, and medical schools as to climate, reasonable housing costs, and personal safety, many retirement guides paint a picture that's simply unrealistic for all but the affluent.

Of course, the better retirement guides are excellent sources of data on towns and cities that would otherwise be difficult to find. Guides can present a world of information that can help you decide whether a place is a viable candidate for retirement. But in the final analysis, you have to go there and see for yourself. You have to see what the retirement guide cannot tell you — will you love it or will you hate it?

What To Look For

Following is a list of requirements my wife and I personally consider essential for a successful retirement relocation. Your needs may be different; feel free to add to or subtract from the list, and then use it to measure communities against your standards.

1. *Safety.* Can you walk through your neighborhood without glancing fearfully over your shoulder? Can you leave your home for a few weeks without dreading a break-in?

2. *Climate.* Will temperatures and weather patterns match your lifestyle? Will you be tempted to go outdoors and exercise year-round, or will harsh winters and suffocating summers confine you to an easy chair in front of the television set?

3. *Housing.* Is quality housing available at prices you're willing and able to pay? Is the area visually pleasing and free of pollution and traffic snarls? Will you feel proud to live in the neighborhood?

4. *Nourishment for your interests.* Does your retirement choice offer facilities for your favorite pastimes, cultural events, and hobbies? If you fish, are there accessible lakes and streams? If you're an art buff, are there art centers or museums?

5. *Social compatibility.* Will you find common interests with your neighbors? Will you fit in and make friends easily? Will there be folks who share your own cultural and social background?

6. *Affordability.* Are goods and services reasonable? Can you afford to hire help from time to time when you need to? Will your income be high enough to be significantly affected by state income taxes? Will taxes on your pension make a big difference?

7. *Medical care.* Are local physicians accepting new patients? Does the area have an adequate hospital? Do you have a medical problem that requires a particular kind of medical specialist nearby?

8. *Distance from family and friends.* Are you going to be too far away or in a location that nobody wants to visit? Would you rather they wouldn't visit?

9. *Transportation.* Does your new location enjoy intercity bus transportation? Many small towns have none, making you totally dependent on an automobile or taxis. How far is the nearest airport with airline connections? Can friends and family visit without driving?

10. *Senior services.* Senior centers should be more than merely places for free meals and gossip; there should be dynamic programs for travel, volunteer work, and education. What about continuing education programs at the local college?

Use Your Vacations To Investigate

If you decide to move away for retirement, then ideally you'll start your retirement search long before your employer shakes your hand and says good-bye. Instead of going to the same old place for vacations, try to visit someplace different each time. Look at each location as a possible place to live.

Even if you are already retired, you need to do some traveling if you plan on moving somewhere else. Your travels needn't be expensive. Pick up some camping equipment at the next garage sale in your neighborhood—a tent, sleeping bags, and a cooking stove. Just about anywhere you want to visit will have either state parks with campgrounds or commercial camping places—like KOA—where you can pitch a tent. Many RV parks have special spots for tent camping. Your local library will have a campground directory to help you locate a place in or near your target town.

Check out real estate prices. Look into apartment and house rentals. Does this town offer the kinds of cultural events you will enjoy? A cultural event could be anything from light opera to hoisting a glass of beer at the corner tavern; the question is, will you be happy you moved there? Just looking closely and imagining that you truly intend to move there will tell you a lot.

While you are there, be sure to drop in at the local senior-citizen center. Talk to the director and the members of the center to see just what services will be available should you decide to move there. A dynamic and full-service senior center could make a world of difference in your everyday life. Don't take it for granted that the senior center will have everything you need. Some are very dreary; others are exciting places to visit.

A very important consideration is public transportation. Over the years, a large number of smaller towns in the United States have been stripped of intercity bus service. The Greyhound Corporation was permitted to buy out its major competition, Trailways, and shut down the least profitable runs. If you choose to live in one of these towns, you ought to be aware that you will be totally dependent upon an automobile. If at some time in the future you are without a car—because you've become unable or cannot afford to drive—you'll be trapped. Your grandkids can't visit you by bus, and if the nearest airport is 100 miles away, you'll not be able to meet the incoming flight. They'll have no way to get from the airport to your home. Yes, you could take a taxi, but places that don't have bus services may not have a fleet of taxis at your disposal, either. Besides, by the time you make a few 200-mile round trips by cab, you could have purchased your own taxi. These conditions are something you probably wouldn't notice on a regular vacation. But you can pick up on them if you pay attention and ask the right questions.

When you're investigating a town, one of your first stops should be the local chamber of commerce. A world of information can be found there. The level of enthusiasm and retirement advice offered by the chamber staff clearly tells you something about the town's elected officials, the business community, and their attitudes toward retirees.

Most chamber offices love to see retirees move into their towns; they recognize the advantages of retirement money coming into the economy and the valuable contributions retirees can make to the community. These offices will do just about anything to help you get settled and to convince you that living in their town is next to paradise. However, don't be surprised if the person behind the counter isn't the least bit interested in your idea of retiring in the town. My experience has been that some chamber of commerce offices are staffed by minimum-wage employees who seem to resent folks coming in to ask questions and interfering with their reading. When this is the case, you can guess that the level of services and senior-citizen participation in local affairs could be inadequate. This is not always true, but the local chamber of commerce generally reflects the business community's interest in retirement attraction.

Newspaper Research

Between periods of travel, you can do your research at the local library or by mail. Almost all libraries have out-of-town newspapers. The larger the library, the wider the variety. If you live in a small town where your library can't provide the newspapers you want (particularly those from another state or smaller towns some distance away), one way to obtain them is to write to the chamber of commerce in the place you are interested in and explain that you need a copy or two to make decisions about retiring there. You can also write to the newspaper office (look in the phone directory section of your library for the local phone book and the name of the paper). Some real estate brokers will gladly mail you copies of the local newspaper because they know you will probably use their services when and if you decide to buy. We once had a real estate office send us a three-month subscription to the local paper to help us make up our minds.

A newspaper is a very valuable research tool. The most important section in an out-of-town paper is always the classifieds. Here you can check the prices of homes, rentals, and mobile home parks. Compare them with those in your hometown newspaper, and you begin to get a picture of relative costs. Look at the help-wanted ads and compare them to the work-wanted ads. You can see what the offered wages are, as well as the wages people are asking. This gives you an indication of what kind of earnings you can expect should you look for part-time work, as well as what kind of competition you will have for jobs. Some classified pages have a special "managers wanted" section, where you'll find positions managing apartment buildings, motels, or trailer parks. Typically, these jobs offer free rent and perhaps a salary in return for a minimum amount of management work. Be careful, however, that you don't end up working full-time just for rent!

If mobile home parks advertise spaces for rent, you know that the situation should be okay for buying a mobile home. If there are no rental spaces available, you might find conditions where mobile homes will depreciate sharply. Compare the prices of used items—furniture, appliances, automobiles—to prices listed in your local paper's classifieds. If prices are much higher, you can figure the cost of living is also higher.

Check the rest of the paper to get a sense of what the town is like. See if supermarket prices compare to those at home, particularly if the same national chains operate in both places. Sometimes identical specials will be priced differently; this comparison also tells you something about the cost of living.

Look at the newspaper's editorial pages to observe the publisher's political stance. It's very interesting how this can influence the thinking of a community. Look over the news stories to see if they are heavily slanted politically or if they strive for a neutral position. Particularly revealing are campaigns for or against services and spending for senior citizens and low-income residents. If you are uncomfortable with the direction of the political slant, this may be something you can investigate when you arrive in the town. It's impossible to tell for sure how local people think or vote by the way a newspaper presents its opinions, but often—when this paper is the only source of local news—these opinions are accepted locally as fact. If you have strong political views, you might feel uneasy in a community where you are in a tiny minority. Check to see how crime is reported; the way a paper reports crime news tells you about a town's safety.

Newspapers should announce senior-citizen activities, cultural events like lectures and free concerts, and news of community college classes open to seniors. Look for this menu of activities. See which ones are free, which ones cost money, and which activities might interest you. A newspaper with a large section devoted to senior-citizen news indicates a high level of interest in the well-being of retirees. Look for retiree political action groups. Wherever senior citizens band together to vote, the level of senior services and benefits rises proportionally.

Out-of-town telephone books are valuable adjuncts to newspapers for information. You can check for retirement homes and apartment complexes that cater to seniors and get the address of the local housing authority office. If there is subsidized housing available, the housing authority can tell you how to find it and how to apply. A telephone book's yellow pages can give you a picture of the business life in town. The number of banks, supermarkets, shopping centers, and other commercial entities tells you something about the vitality of business. This is where you check for bus service and taxi companies. Look at the listings under "airlines" or "airport" to see if there is a local airport and which airlines service it. A telephone book also gives you an up-to-date listing for the chamber of commerce office and the senior-citizen center. A letter to each of them could yield valuable information about the locality. A non-reply also tells you something.

After you've researched a community thoroughly by library research, you still need to visit in person.

Internet Research

The newest craze is the Internet. More than a craze, it's a valuable tool for research. If you don't have access to the Internet, you should visit your grandkids and ask them to do some research for you.

The procedure is to use one of the "search engines" (don't worry, your grandkids will understand) and to enter the name of the town or city you need to investigate. Like magic, a long string of Web pages that refer to your query will appear. Virtually every town or city in the country that has retirement possibilities will have one or more Web pages to tell you about the community. Usually there are dozens to look at. Type in the name of the community and add the word "retirement," and you'll find the list narrows down, but each item has more pertinent information.

You can learn about the town's history, culture, cost of living, real estate market, rentals, climate, recreational opportunities . . . and on and on. When you encounter a particularly interesting page, you simply press the "print" button, and your grandkids' printer spits out a page that you can put in your file.

The amount of Internet information about most communities is truly staggering. Some of it is fluff, of course; every community wants to put its best foot forward. But the hard facts and details are there for you to absorb. Most pages will have e-mail addresses inviting you to ask questions. Real estate companies always have e-mail addresses that you can use to ask detailed questions. E-mail is a great way of communicating without the cost of postage or telephone rates. E-mail is virtually free.

Here's a tip: Ask your grandkids to help you learn about getting your own access to the world of the Internet. Used computers today are so cheap that they are practically free. In fact, many people give away their old computers as they are outmoded by faster machines. Understand, the speed of a computer has nothing to do with the speed of browsing the Internet or the speed at which you send and receive electronic mail. The speed at which the Internet runs is determined by your modem, an item that costs about $20 for the fastest transmission you will use when connected through a telephone line.

By having a computer in your home, you can keep in touch with family and friends no matter where you live or where they live. Messages travel across the street, across the country, or around the world with equal, blazing speed. And they cost nothing beyond the fixed monthly cost charged by your Internet service provider. Most people pay nothing extra for the phone connection, because local calls are usually unlimited for a fixed monthly fee. You can connect to the Internet free by signing up with a service such as Juno or similar servers. Instead of collecting a monthly fee, they earn income by posting a few ads on your pages. But the service is free.

And, of course, you'll take your computer with you when you move. When you are miles away from your kids and grandkids—who are scattered all over the map anyway—you'll enjoy keeping in daily touch with them. The more you use the Internet, the more you'll communicate with the world and the less you'll spend on postage and phone calls. E-mail is an astounding bargain, with free Internet connections from companies like Juno.com, Bluelight (Kmart), Ace Hardware, and dozens more. They'll give you free disks for going on-line and toll-free numbers to get you started. There's hardly a reason to use a stamp anymore.

Can't afford a used computer? Check with your local library. Today most libraries offer Internet service.

Chapter Seven
Weather, Crime, and Your Budget

For many people, retirement means moving to a warmer climate. After experiencing a lifetime of freezing winters, they dream of living someplace where they won't have to shovel snow or change to special tires every November and back to regular tires in March. They know they'll love warm winters because they've occasionally managed to spend a week or two of their precious vacation time in Phoenix or St. Petersburg during the dead of winter. Expensive, but worth it for many folks.

Before retirement, they knew they'd love to live in the Sunbelt full-time, but finding a good-paying job in a desirable, warmer climate isn't always possible. Job competition can be intense, and working conditions and wages are often substandard. As a result, people tend to postpone moving to that idyllic climate until retirement.

But when that day finally arrives, unless retirees have a more-than-adequate retirement income, many abandon that dream of Florida, Arizona, or California retirement. They remember those high-priced vacation interludes, with expensive time-share or high-priced motels. "I can't afford that," they say, as they make plans for toughing it out every winter for the rest of their lives.

However, if you consider the facts carefully, you might discover that suffering through cold winters isn't necessary after all. The interesting thing is, depending on how you do it, retirement in a benign climate can cost far less than staying at home in a cold climate. There's no reason you can't enjoy a shoestring retirement *and* mild winters. You just have to find an affordable location.

Shoestring retirement is possible in milder climates for several reasons. For one thing, heating costs—one of the biggest budget-busters—are much lower in milder climates with short winters. Furthermore, low wages don't matter to retirees who don't have to work. On the contrary, smaller paychecks for those who do work tend to keep prices down for everyone. When incomes fall below the national average, the cost of living usually follows suit.

Another cost-cutting factor is that many low-cost, warm-weather communities have unusually economical real estate and rentals. This is partly the result of a wave of overbuilding during the easy-S&L-money era of the late 1980s. Even today, in some areas of the nation you can find a buyer's market for real estate with low rents due to high vacancy rates. While you might pay $800 a month for an apartment in Dayton, you could be spending $500 for the same quality rental in Daytona Beach. That gives you $300 to put toward groceries and the electric bill. This savings alone is reason enough to pull up stakes from a frigid winter zone. (If you can get the stakes out of the frozen ground.)

This isn't true *everywhere* in warm climates. The same pleasant weather that draws ordinary working people quite naturally brings in the big money, as well. Cities like Palm Beach, Scottsdale, and Palm Springs aren't exactly places where you might expect to live on a shoestring. But you'll encounter other places, not too far from these luxury neighborhoods, where prices are reasonable and where living without snow shovels is possible on a restricted budget.

Saving on Utilities

If you live in a cold climate, you don't have to be reminded how much it costs to heat a home in the winter. We've talked to many couples who commonly spend as much as $250 a month on their winter heating bills. In really cold climates, like Minnesota, Montana, or the Dakotas, $400 a month isn't unusual. Now, in some sections of the country, $250 pays most of the rent for an adequate apartment or a small house, or it can buy groceries for an entire month.

As you will see later on, there are inexpensive places to live in this country where air conditioning is unnecessary and heating systems are limited to plug-in space heaters. We've interviewed folks who seldom pay more than $50 a month for utilities year-round, usually far less than that in the summer. This means a savings of $200 a month on utilities. Add that $200 a month to the $300 a month you've saved on rent, and you are bringing your budget down to the point where you now have money to spend on yourself instead of blowing it on your home and its greedy furnace.

Do You Need Air Conditioning?

Okay, I hear you protesting, "But what about air conditioning in the summer? If I move to a warm climate, I'll have to spend as much to cool my house in the summer as I used to spend heating the house in the winter. Where are the savings?"

Air conditioning is a wonderful invention, something that many people cannot conceive of doing without. Yet think back a few years. When we were kids, nobody had air conditioning, did they? Yet we survived just fine. Remember when the only air-conditioned building in town was the local movie theater? Remember those signs painted like icicles on the movie marquee that announced, "air cooled inside"? In the "good old days," when thermometers topped 90°F, our parents used to string a hammock in the shade, relax, and sip a cool lemonade or iced tea. Temperatures today haven't changed. Unless you suffer from a medical condition that demands otherwise, you seldom *have* to turn up the air conditioner full blast. I know friends who keep their thermostats set at 78°F in the winter, then turn them down to 70°F in the summer. Are we surprised that their utility bills are so high?

On the other hand, when below-zero temperatures settle in for the winter, you don't have the option of lighting the furnace or not. If you don't, you'll die. Winter heating is a matter of life and death, whereas summer air conditioning is a matter of relative comfort.

If you hate the thought of hot summers yet still want no-frost winters, there are many places in the country, mostly on the West Coast, where air conditioning is unknown. While writing this book, I am living in a California coastal town. None of the houses has air conditioning because it never gets hot. When temperatures climb into the 80s, our local newspaper reports the event with headlines. Our electric blankets go on every night of the year without exception. On the other hand, in the dead of winter, should temperatures fall low enough for frost to damage our jade plants or fuchsias, you can be sure of more banner headlines. As a matter of fact, we don't even have a furnace; a single gas space heater takes the chill off our large, two-bedroom apartment. You'll find many similar locations along the California, Oregon, and Washington coastlines. We've talked to folks who seldom spend more than $50 a month on utilities. The best part is that some of these places are affordable: They have some of the lowest costs of living in the country and real estate prices approaching rock-bottom.

Where we live, it's shirtsleeves in the afternoons but sweaters after dark, year-round. Nobody here owns an overcoat; when it's necessary to travel east in the winter, we have to scout around for one we can borrow. My wife absolutely adores this kind of a climate; she's a cool-weather person.

On the other hand, many people love hot weather. There's something special about a real summer—with backyard barbecues, good, honest sunshine that makes a cold drink sound like heaven, and balmy evenings that invite a dip in the swimming pool. This is my kind of climate; I'm a warm-weather person.

The Perfect Climate ⸶

Everyone seems to have a different definition of a "perfect climate," but the truth is that there's no such thing. Folks in Maine dearly love their summers but complain that winters are cold and dreary. Their neighbors who retire in Florida adore Miami winters, but complain because summers are too muggy. Hawaii has near-perfect weather, but you'd better take a shopping bag full of money if you expect to stay very long. The nice thing about retirement is that you finally have a variety of choices for your weather.

Personally, I consider parts of California, inland Oregon, and Washington to have the best overall climate in the nation—sunny summers with low humidity and relatively free of bugs. (You almost never see a cockroach there.) Winter days require nothing more than a sweater or windbreaker, with little frost or snow—sometimes none all season. Many residents of the West Coast have never experienced cold weather. In the winter of 1990 we were living in Grants Pass, Oregon, when an unusual cold snap burst water pipes throughout the area. Residents here do not customarily protect their pipes from freezing weather. Extreme cold spells are so rare that it isn't worth the bother. But when we lived in Michigan, we not only wrapped exposed pipes in insulation, we also used electric warmers—or else.

Cold Weather Robbery

Readers will have little trouble detecting a definite bias in my writing, a bias against winter ice, dirty snow, and slush. I fully realize that not everybody is trying to escape snow shovels. Many folks sincerely enjoy winters, with ice fishing, skiing, and lovely Christmas card scenery. Therefore, I'll try to be careful not to make this book sound like a chamber of commerce advertisement for Florida or Arizona. But the fact is that cold weather can be very detrimental to your pocketbook—partly because of heating bills and partly because of the extra wardrobe required for cold weather, with down jackets, padded boots, and long underwear adding to the seasonal expenses.

One unrecognized cost of cold weather is the subtle destruction of your automobile. Batteries deteriorate quickly in cold weather. Cold-weather starts wear out engine cylinders by dragging moving parts against each other without the benefit of free-flowing oil for lubrication. Antifreeze and snow tires also batter away at the budget. Unlike winter clothing, auto repair and maintenance are ongoing expenses that cannot be put off until next year.

The truly vicious damage comes from the effects of road salt. If you live where roads must be salted to clear away ice and snow, you must deduct years from the useful life of your car. Salt destroys steel and body sheet metal faster than termites could ever attack a house! It's interesting to note that in the colder parts of the nation, you rarely see an auto more than ten years old. That's because older cars have long ago dissolved in the salt solutions that slosh around the roads in the winter. When you move to a salt-free environment, your car's life expectancy depends on the number of *miles* you drive, not on the number of *winter months* you drive. When you need to buy another automobile every three or four years, your shoestring budget gets stretched to the breaking point.

Climate, Exercise, and Health

The other way cold weather can be costly is in terms of doctor bills and shortening of your life expectancy. Medical and health experts agree that one of the biggest dangers to retired folks' health is inactivity. Many medical researchers, cardiologists, and scientists are coming to the conclusion that exercise is *the* key factor in health and long life. Exercise, they believe, may be much more important than diet.

Unquestionably, people living in warm climates tend to spend more time outdoors. They get out and exercise, doing healthful activities instead of huddling next to the fireplace with eyes glued to the television set. Bicycling, swimming, tennis, and daily walks for your health and recreation can add years to your life. In mild winter climates these are year-round activities. In cold weather climates folks generally exercise only occasionally during the winter, if they exercise at all.

Some of you will say, "Yes, it would be nice to escape winter, but have you ever tried taking a brisk walk or playing tennis in the South during August?" They have a point. Although it is clearly possible to get the exercise out of the way early in the morning or to wait until after sundown, many people just cannot stand the muggy humidity of the southern states and yet don't care to move to the low-humidity western states.

For some folks, the solution to the climate problem is to become "snowbirds" and enjoy the best of all worlds. Snowbirds are those free spirits who choose to escape winter's anger by flying south for the season. When summer's heat threatens to become oppressive, it's back to a kinder, gentler climate. Snowbirds luxuriate in balmy Phoenix winters and enjoy springlike summers in Montana. Those who choose RV retirement epitomize the snowbird lifestyle. There is an in-depth discussion of this lifestyle in Chapter 10.

Some escape winters by going south of the border, choosing an inexpensive, part-time retirement in Mexico, Guatemala, Costa Rica, or other countries. Personally, my wife and I choose to do our snowbirding in Costa Rica. We've also fled to Mexico, Guatemala, and South America to avoid winter.

Snowbirding is also possible through creative housing schemes. Many retirees make regular arrangements to work at a resort motel, a state park, or a lake marina—with free rent as part of the arrangement—thus enjoying summer resort weather while their neighbors shiver through the season back home. Some people rent their homes or apartments for a nominal income while they are on "vacation." Others take similar positions in popular winter resorts in Arizona, Texas, or other warm winter retreats. These jobs are easier to find that you might think. In Chapter 10 we look at strategies for finding these kind of seasonal jobs.

Finding a Low-Crime Area

Locating a crime-free area is an important objective for anyone searching for a new retirement home. Unfortunately, as you might guess, there is no such thing as a totally "crime-free" community. There are, however, many "low-crime" areas around the country, and they are relatively easy to locate—easier if you're rich.

Why rich? Because it turns out that the *lowest* crime rates in North America are found in the most affluent neighborhoods! I discovered this fact while studying the FBI's crime statistics for cities in the United States with populations over 10,000. Until then, I had always assumed that most burglaries and robberies would naturally take place in the wealthiest neighborhoods. Not so; the *richest* neighborhoods generally have exceptionally *low* rates of burglary, larceny, and robbery. This is true for several reasons. First of all, law enforcement in wealthy neighborhoods tends to be more efficient than in poor neighborhoods. Also, these locations tend to have fewer teenagers in residence—the presence of young people is a basic factor in the number of burglaries. And finally, strangers with criminal intentions tend to "stand out" in wealthy neighborhoods and can be reported to police before they get a chance to commit a crime.

None of the foregoing will be of comfort to those who are looking for economical yet safe retirement neighborhoods. However, many low-cost places to retire are just as safe as such expensive spreads as Palos Verdes and Palm Beach. Read on, and we'll explain how to find them.

Although crime rates in the United States are decreasing dramatically throughout the nation, many areas are still plagued by crime and violence. We're suffering in a way that we didn't dream of back in the 1930s, when the country was in a deep depression, when unemployment was 20 percent, and when soup lines were common sights. If you are old enough to remember, you'll recall that many folks never bothered to lock their doors at night, and we kids played outside until long after dark. Crime rates then were much lower than today. So it isn't necessarily poverty or unemployment that creates crime, it may be that stealing is a lot easier and more profitable than working, especially for those who are supporting a drug habit and must turn to crime.

What's the answer? Some say we need to get tougher on criminals. But how do we do that? We already have a higher percentage of our population locked up than any other civilized nation in the world. Recently, the United States passed the two-million mark for prison inmates. That means one out of every 147 Americans is in prison! We can't build prisons fast enough; prisoners are being kicked out of jail before their terms are up in order to make room for more criminals! The truth is that you and I can't do much about crime except to look for a safer place to live.

Why Some Places Are Safer

The number of police officers does not determine low-crime areas. Some large, crime-ridden cities have so many cops patrolling the streets that they get in each others' way. Nevertheless, the crime rates remain high. On the other hand, some communities have only part-time police protection, yet burglars are as scarce as honest lawyers. A large police force is usually a *response* to crime, not an indication of a town's safety.

As a rule, the larger the city, the higher the crime rate. But even in large cities you'll find areas of tranquillity, often not too far from the problem areas. When checking out a neighborhood for possible retirement, look for mature, low-turnover neighborhoods where residents know each other and the average resident is at or near retirement age.

The age of neighborhood residents is important. When a working-class neighborhood is overrun with young people—particularly males between the ages of fifteen and twenty-two, most of them underemployed—you are looking at a troubled neighborhood. When seeking a rental or a home to buy, cruise the neighborhood and look for teenagers hanging out on the street corners. Try to find a neighborhood with older, mature residents; your chances for peace are better there.

It's also important to avoid places where drug addiction is a large problem. Whether drug addiction is a cause of crime or merely a symptom of an underlying problem is hard to say, but we do know that wherever we find high crime rates, we also find a high incidence of drug use. Criminologists estimate that as much as 80 percent of property and violent crimes in our country are drug related. The point to remember is that drug addicts pay for their expensive habits through crime. Burglaries, muggings, and robberies are the quickest and easiest way to get money. Therefore, when you live in an area of high drug use, your chances of being victimized by robbery or burglary are well above average.

One way to identify high-crime areas is by studying the local newspapers and seeing how crimes are reported. You can tell how safe a town is by the importance accorded various crimes. When murder, robberies, and burglaries in an area are reported routinely or not at all, you can be sure that the place has a high crime rate. But when a bicycle theft makes headlines, you've found a safe community.

You can't blame the newspaper; murders are so common in some cities that if all of them were reported on the front page there wouldn't be room for other news. The victims aren't newsworthy enough to have their names published, so their murders are reported as casually as a stock market report in my hometown newspaper.

The lesson is this: When murders and rapes are reported on page 23, if at all, you can assume that violent crime is epidemic.

On the other hand, if a burglary makes front-page headlines, then burglaries can't be all that common. If a newspaper publishes a detailed police log, read it over carefully. In towns where police are involved in important cases such as rescuing a cat from Mrs. Smith's tree or recovering a bicycle stolen from Jimmy Jones's front yard, it's likely that crime isn't exactly out of control.

Safety Tips

Your local office on aging, and the police department, can help you make your home or apartment more secure. In most communities these organizations sponsor crime prevention projects and work together to publish educational materials about crime prevention.

Often your police department will be happy to make a free "burglary audit" of your home. They'll send a police officer to your home to check on your home security and make suggestions for your safety. Some of the more common security recommendations include:

1. Always lock your garage, even if you are at home or are just stepping out briefly.
2. When you are out of the house, lock your windows as well as your doors.
3. Cut back bushes near doors and windows.
4. Install dead-bolt locks and night chains.
5. Install and use a peephole in your door.
6. Keep outside areas well illuminated.
7. Keep valuable personal property in a safe deposit box rather than at home.
8. Do not keep large amounts of cash in the house.
9. Do not hide an extra set of keys to your home in an obvious place, such as under the doormat, on the ledge above your door, in a planter box, or in the mailbox.

If you go away on a trip:

1. Use timers to keep lights on inside and outside the house in the evening.
2. Stop mail and newspaper deliveries and ask a neighbor to pick up circulars and packages from your driveway.
3. Hide your empty garbage cans.
4. Arrange for someone to maintain your yard.
5. Turn your telephone bell down.

FBI Statistics

Over the years I've used the FBI's *Uniform Crime Report* to analyze various cities as to the crime rate, but there were several things that puzzled me. Towns that I knew to be exceptionally peaceful often showed up on the charts as terribly crime ridden. Other places where I wouldn't park my car overnight looked exceptionally safe! Part of the explanation is the method individual police departments use to report crime. Some departments don't bother reporting crimes such as rape and arson, only extra-serious crimes. Not wanting to make themselves look bad, some police change the results to make crime rates lower than those in neighboring communities. Other departments report the theft of a tricycle and fist fights between town drunks as crimes.

The FBI warns about this inconsistency in the report, so none of the above is a surprise. But what seems curious is that some places, especially towns with large tourist populations in the season, would appear to be exceptionally dangerous, with murder, assault, rape, and robbery at high levels. It turns out that when you lump 50,000 tourists with a year-round population of 20,000, you end up with an exceptionally high level of incidents. The FBI takes the crime statistics of 70,000 people and divides it into the 20,000 regular inhabitants, and it looks bad.

A second flaw in the FBI's statistics is that they do not show the *nature* of crimes reported. When a town shows several murders and many assault cases a year, the report doesn't indicate whether these incidents were the result of holdups, burglaries, or other crimes against ordinary citizens, or whether they involved youth gangs fighting over turf and their share of the shrinking drug market. Very few senior citizens will be involved in drive-by shootings because of a bad drug deal. What might be dangerous for a gang member is perfectly safe for a senior citizen.

Example: According to FBI statistics, our California hometown is one of the safest in the country, because of the low number of crimes reported. And we feel very safe. Yet not 20 miles away is a small city with a very high murder rate. Why? Drive-by shootings. Do the retired people who live in that city feel safe? Yes, they do. The problems do not happen in their neighborhoods, nor do they occur in the city's downtown area—only in the neighborhoods where retired people wouldn't live anyway. In fact, this city was called one of the country's "top retirement destinations" by a leading retirement magazine about two years ago. The lesson here: Do not rely on statistics as to whether or not a community is safe. Do your own analysis as I pointed out above, then ask the folks living in your target neighborhood how they feel about crime.

Chapter Eight
Mobile Home Living

Some folks, when they near retirement, begin thinking of selling their home and "drawing in their horns" by buying a mobile home. Many consider this an ideal way to live in comfort and convenience and on a minimum amount of money. Approximately four million mobile homes in the United States house more than eight million people, the majority of whom are retired. Many of the better parks are exclusively inhabited by retirees. Those who choose the mobile home lifestyle point out that this is one option for home ownership without the high investment and real estate taxes that go with conventional property. As one couple said, "It costs us only $175 a month to live in our own home. And that includes water, garbage, and sewer. We don't pay property taxes; instead we buy a license plate." (Of course, this will depend on the local tax structure–some states tax mobile homes the same as conventional homes.)

Not all mobile home parks are inexpensive, of course; some charge as much as or more than apartment rentals in the same neighborhood. In most communities you have a wide range of costs and luxuries from which to choose.

Generally, space rents depend upon the facilities and scarcity of mobile home spaces in the locality. The least expensive place we found was in the California desert near the Salton Sea. It was an 8-foot-wide, 32-foot-long Vagabond (1952 vintage) for $800, with space rent a mere $50 a month. You probably wouldn't want to live there. The most expensive mobile home housing we've heard of was a used 1,000-square-foot, metal-sided home priced at $350,000, with a space rent of $1,180 per month. You probably wouldn't want to live there, either—at least not on a shoestring.

Mobility

Mobile homes today are anything but mobile. Most are so wide and so long that only specialized companies attempt to move or install them. The manufacturers are trying to change the term to "manufactured" homes, yet the buyers insist on the term "mobile."

Once installed on a site—sometimes three- and four-bedroom units, complete with everything but a basement and swimming pool—mobile homes are permanently in place. Then how did they get the name "mobile"? It started during World War II, when they actually were mobile—only 8 feet wide and rarely more than 35 feet long. The living units were popular with war workers who needed emergency housing that could be moved on a moment's notice from one production site to another. Because of a severe postwar housing shortage, hundreds of thousands of house trailers were built, and young families lived in them as they traveled to booming job locations. Construction workers found house trailers indispensable; they were easily towed behind the family car, and they could be placed near, or sometimes on, the job site. Although they were the size of today's recreational vehicles, their purpose was housing, not recreation.

As these homes became larger and more elaborate, folks who lived in these sometimes luxurious housing units felt embarrassed at the concept of "house trailer." It was reminiscent of prewar days, when depression-bruised families were forced to live in dilapidated trailers because of economic necessity rather than for temporary convenience. To put a more positive spin on the situation, house trailers became known as "mobile homes." And today, quite often, "manufactured homes."

For Retirement

The lingering memory of the early days of house trailers, when they were considered suitable only for vagabonds and losers, combined with the presence of many run-down, dreary trailer parks, gives mobile home living an undeservedly poor reputation. Many people picture mobile home parks as full of poor, underemployed welfare families with herds of grimy children roaming the premises. In some cases this picture is fairly accurate, but these parks are probably not where you would want to live, anyway. Especially not with herds of noisy, destructive children around.

The category of mobile home living that you'll probably choose is totally different. These can be upscale parks that cater to middle-class, often affluent retirees. Facilities are tailored to couples or singles who want exceptional personal safety, friendly neighbors, and a clublike atmosphere. This lifestyle attracts a great number of retirees who could afford more expensive housing but who prefer to place their home-sale profits into income-producing investments. The nicer locations are restricted to those over fifty-five years old. (Try to avoid parks that accept youngsters and teenagers. They can make mobile home living a nightmare!)

Many benefits accrue to this lifestyle besides low-cost, carefree living, not the least of which are friendly neighbors and park clubhouse social activities. The better parks will have a large recreation and social hall, usually next to the swimming pool, where dinners, club meetings, bingo, and dances are regular activities.

Some luxury mobile home parks offer amenities such as Olympic-size swimming pools, hot tubs, Jacuzzis, tennis courts, spacious clubhouses, and just about everything you expect to find in expensive apartments and luxury condos. Many in Florida feature eighteen-hole championship golf courses! You don't have to worry about landscaping or maintenance of anything but your own small plot of ground. Even individual landscaping chores are sometimes taken care of by the park management. And because mobile home communities are enclosed by fences and have limited outside access, they are exceptionally safe places to live. Some of the more expensive places have security guards posted at the entrances around the clock. In any case, because the homes are close together and because residents know each other far better than in traditional neighborhoods, criminal activities are rather quickly noted.

The standard width of a mobile home today is 12 feet, with lengths up to 70 feet. Many are 14 feet wide. When two of these units are joined together, forming a "double-wide," you end up with a large home. The square footage is sometimes larger than the retiree's original home. If you've ever visited one of the expensively furnished display models at your local mobile home sales lot, you've probably been dazzled at the luxury and spaciousness.

What does it cost to live in a mobile home? That's like asking what it costs to live in a house; it all depends on the cost of the house and the neighborhood. We've seen acceptable park spaces renting for as little as $100 a month, and others for much, much more. For example, we looked at a park near Sarasota, Florida, that featured a landscaped lakefront, a clubhouse and tennis courts, plus the inevitable swimming pool—all for around $300 a month. Used two-bedroom mobile homes were priced at $14,000 to $25,000, with new units starting at $35,000. A social director arranged a full schedule of activities for the park residents. We visited a generic mobile home park in St. Petersburg, a nice place, but without the upscale items such as lakes, golf courses, and the like. The only facility besides a clubhouse was a small pool. A couple had just recently purchased a unit with one bedroom and a small office for $6,500. "We could have bought for as low as $4,500," said the wife, "but that was a little too downscale for me." They retired from northern Illinois, drawing down a small equity in their home "Not enough to do much more than make a good down payment on a Florida condo," the husband added. "So when we found this place, with a mobile costing about the price of a used car, we bought. Now we have our own place plus a nice bank account." The monthly mobile home lot rent was less than the condo maintenance fee would have been.

Another park just a few miles away was full of older units, many ten to twenty years old, more closely spaced. The major facility was the laundry room, which traditionally serves each park as a place to meet, socialize, and exchange gossip. According to residents, all of whom were retired, there was a satisfactory level of social activities, which were organized by residents on an informal basis rather than by the park management. It was quite pleasant and peaceful, with mature trees for shade. A few homes displayed FOR SALE signs, including a single-wide, one-bedroom place for about $8,000. Park rent was $195 a month. Space rent farther out in the country was even less expensive, as low as $165 a month according to some park managers. Yes, that's in Florida.

It's interesting to note that many parks—particularly the higher-quality ones—prohibit posting FOR SALE signs on homes. You might drive through a park and conclude that there is nothing for sale. When you don't see any signs, simply inquire at the park manager's office. The rule forbidding the posting of signs is partly just to keep things uncluttered, but I suspect that another motivation is the management's desire to filter out undesirable tenants they do not want buying into the park.

Purchase Prices

Prices of mobile homes vary widely, depending on the newness of the mobile home, the condition of the park, and—most of all—the scarcity of park spaces in the area. Bear in mind, you are paying for the location rather than the actual value of the home. A mobile home located in a city where spaces are scarce could sell for $50,000, whereas the identical make and year, located in a town where mobile home lot vacancies are plentiful, might be worth only $15,000. Mobile home salesmen are quick to claim that this difference in value is appreciation. Appreciation has nothing to do with it; the extra money simply reflects the scarcity of park spaces. When land is valuable, fewer entrepreneurs are willing to devote it to mobile home parks unless there is a good return on the investment. That's why in smaller towns, where land is cheaper, mobile home prices and park rents are far lower.

We recently looked at a large, two-bedroom, two-bath mobile, with new appliances, washer and dryer, and a storage shed, situated on a large fenced lot, for $18,000. In a similar park in a large city the unit would sell for closer to $40,000. Another two-bedroom, one-bath mobile home in a marginal park was listed at $10,000, but the owner hinted that he would take much less on a cash sale. Had this been in a nice park and in a tighter rental market, it would probably sell for at least $28,000. Remember, selling prices often depend more on the scarcity of land and competition among parks, and don't necessarily have anything to do with the value of the mobile home itself. The fact is that mobile homes depreciate, just like automobiles. Don't let salesmen try to tell you differently.

Pitfalls for Mobile Home Buyers

It's true: A mobile home can be an excellent way of cutting back on living costs. On the other hand, if you're not careful it could turn out to be a seriously costly and risky investment. Some hazards lurk out there to trip up unwary buyers. A few missteps, and mobile home living becomes far more expensive than owning a conventional home. Some problems can be avoided if you can keep from being blinded by the beautiful furnishings or a dealer's glowing sales pitch. Other important conditions require close investigation.

I personally would hesitate to purchase a new unit and have it set up in a park. Sometimes it makes much more sense to buy one already in place with the costs known—landscaping, carport, storage shed, and so forth—all in place and ready to use. If the unit is used, so much the better, because, again, despite what a salesman might tell you, mobile homes do *not* appreciate in price as ordinary real estate does. They *depreciate*. The older the unit, the less you should consider paying. Let's examine why.

Although you own your mobile home, the land it's sitting on belongs to someone else. Obviously, you are simply renting a patch of land from month to month. A problem arises when the park is in an area of rapid development. You could suddenly find that the owner of the property wants to kick everybody off and sell the land for a shopping mall or an industrial park. The land has become too valuable to be kept as a mobile home park. This happens all too frequently. When a developer offers big bucks, the park owner can easily succumb to the temptation to get rich quick instead of depending on your monthly rent.

A situation like this is much more serious than simply the annoyance of having to move your home to another location. Moving one of these so-called "mobile" homes is not a job to be taken lightly. You are at the mercy of professionals who may take full advantage of your plight. That's bad enough, but when all mobile home parks in the area are full, and there is no place to move, your valuable home suddenly becomes all but worthless. Even when spaces are available, many parks refuse to accept any unit that is over five years old. The better parks accept only brand-new mobile homes. Worse yet, some parks accept only homes they sell themselves. An out-of-town dealer might offer you a pittance for your unit; he will haul it to some other part of the state where park spaces are abundant.

Scope out the mobile home park situation in the area thoroughly before making any decisions. Talk to park residents where you are thinking of buying. Go to the laundry room and start asking questions. This is easy to do because the laundry room is not only the nerve center of a mobile home park but also a place where folks are unusually friendly and talkative. While waiting for their clothes to dry, they happily talk each other's ears off. Ask residents if they have worries about the park's future.

If you ask about the park's management or the owner, be prepared to hear all the good and bad things about living there. Too often, park managers, poorly paid and spiteful, find a sense of power in their jobs and can become virtual Napoleons. I know of one place where a new manager forced everyone to get rid of all the landscaping shrubs alongside their mobile homes by treating the soil with something like Agent Orange and then covering the sterile ground with decorative white rock. "If you don't like it, you can just move," he warned. The next manager decreed that the white rock had to go and grass and shrubs had to be replanted in the now-dead soil—or else. You don't need a situation where tenants are continually skirmishing with management. An aware and caring park ownership rarely hires this kind of employee. When they do, you can guess that the owners are *not* aware and caring.

Check the local classifieds and see if mobile home spaces are listed in the "For Rent" columns. If they are, you can assume that park openings are plentiful. Look at the "Mobile Homes for Sale" columns to check prices, and visit nearby parks to see where you might move if you have to. Do this even if you are buying a new unit. You never know.

Another consideration is that a scarcity of mobile home spaces usually causes space rents to escalate far faster than the rate of inflation. My wife and I lived in a mobile home park in San Jose, California, for several years. When we moved in, our space rent was a delightfully low $95 a month. Seven years later, when we moved out, the rent was $395! However, that was not the reason we sold our mobile home; it was because of the dreaded "fifteen-year rule."

The Fifteen-Year Rule

This is the biggest zinger of all. Many mobile home parks around the nation try to maintain a spiffy image by continually upgrading the homes in their developments. Replacing older units with glitzy new models keeps the park looking new, thus justifying higher rents. Managers can't go around evicting older units, but when possible they invoke a "fifteen-year rule." That is, whenever a mobile home more than fifteen years old is sold, it must be removed from the park. If spaces are at a premium in the area, the mobile home becomes practically unmarketable. Most buyers of used mobile homes want a place to *live in*, not a mobile home that they have to *move*. In this type of situation, depreciation accelerates rapidly, and your investment fades as your unit approaches the magic fifteen-year limit. Some parks have a twenty-year limit, but the end results are the same.

It is therefore essential to know management's policy on older homes, particularly if you are thinking about saving money and purchasing one that is thirteen or fourteen years old. A few states, like Florida, and some cities have laws prohibiting this age discrimination. A mobile home there can only be evicted for unsafe or unsightly conditions. That's not to say that some park managers won't look for ways to get rid of older mobile homes one way or another. Folks in the laundry room will tell you about this. So if a mobile home unit is kept in good condition, one fifteen or twenty years old *can* be an excellent buy, provided it isn't in danger of eviction.

A final caution is against moving into a "family" park—particularly one of the older, run-down parks. Young, low-income families who live in these parks, often on welfare, will crowd into a small trailer with three or four youngsters. Keeping the kids outside, playing in *your* yard, is the only way the parents get any peace and quiet. Too often they exert no control and don't show any serious concern for their kids' behavior. When you have a gaggle of children trooping through a park in search of entertainment, you not only have noise but you are also bound to have vandalism. Youngsters cease to be cute when they start unplugging your electricity, drawing pictures on your automobile, or picking your flowers to take home to mommy. Adult parks are customarily quiet, and chances are much better that you and your neighbors will have something in common.

Having said all of these negative things about mobile home buying, let me say that of all the retired folks we've interviewed, some of the happiest are those living this lifestyle. It's economical and practically worry-free, as long as you make sure that's the way it's going to turn out. Keep your eyes open, heed the advice in this chapter, and you'll be okay.

Buying Your Own Lot

Some mobile home developments *sell* lots rather than simply renting them. This is usually a package deal; they sell you a mobile home as well as the land. One park we visited in Texas offered a $38,900 package (including taxes and fees) for a lot and a two-bedroom mobile home with a carport, utility room, and screen room. The development had a twenty-four-hour guarded gate, a swimming pool, and tennis courts.

When buying into a development, make sure you actually hold title to the land and not just a revocable lease. A good salesman can make a lease sound exactly like an iron-clad deed. Also be aware that even though you own the lot, you will be liable for monthly maintenance and membership fees. These could be as high as rent in a similar-quality park.

Rock-Bottom Mobile Home Living

Many of those older, 8-foot-wide units that were popular before the wider ones came into vogue are still around and still in livable condition. In their heyday, they were built for full-time living instead of just summer vacations. They are solidly built, sometimes of galvanized steel, and well insulated. Instead of small space heaters, they usually have oil or gas furnaces with forced-air heat. Because they have only a small interior space to heat in the winter or cool in the summer, utility bills are almost a joke. The units that survive make excellent, inexpensive living quarters, and if push comes to shove, they can be moved easily. A pickup or an old Cadillac with a good equalizer hitch can zip them away—no problem—with no special permits or WIDE LOAD warnings front and rear required.

Because these survivors are old-fashioned and clumsy-looking, with birch-finished interiors instead of today's plastic and simulated-wood panels, these older units often go for incredibly low prices. You won't find them in newer mobile home parks because they've long since been kicked out to "upgrade" the park. But they make comfortable living quarters and have surprisingly efficient interiors for storage and everyday living. Beds and living room furniture are usually built in, so you won't have to buy furnishings. You do need to inspect these units carefully for water damage and dry rot, however, and you must make sure that the undercarriage is sturdy and not rusted through.

The next step up from the 8-footer is the 10-foot-wide mobile home. These are more spacious and often have 8-foot expansion rooms, which make the living rooms or bedrooms a spacious 18 feet wide. When both living room and bedroom are expanded, the home is called a "double expando." You don't feel as if you are in a trailer when you're in one of these. They sell for a bit more than the older units, but far less than the newer 12-footers.

An Affordable Winter Home

Older, inexpensive mobiles are ideal for summer homes in the mountains or winter retreats for escaping freezing weather and outrageous utility bills. For example, we looked at one park in Yuma, Arizona, that caters exclusively to retired folks who live elsewhere but enjoy the warm Arizona sunshine for the winter. Almost all units are about twenty years old, but in good condition and furnished.

The landscaping features natural desert plants, so there is virtually no upkeep problem for the winter residents. Space rent in this seniors-only park, with a pool and spa, is $245 a month including utilities. When residents go home for the season, they pay $50 a month for the space through the summer (when the place is abandoned except for the park managers). It's a good deal for the park owners, because for half the year they don't have to bother with tenants, and it works out well for the winter residents because they don't have to tow an abode back and forth every season. They would have to pay $50 a month for RV storage back home anyway. In the spring of 2003, one of these units was for sale: a 12-by-56-foot two bedroom for $8,500.

The winter visitors start arriving at this Arizona park around the middle of November. When they have a quorum at the clubhouse, they elect officers for the season, appoint committee members, and decide on a calendar of events. A recent calendar included trips to nearby Mexico, Las Vegas, and Disneyland. Dances, potlucks, and card games completed the social schedule.

"We can't afford to stay home," one lady said. "In our Wyoming home, we would be spending at least $400 a month to heat our place. And when the north wind blows, nothing will keep the house warm." She was wearing shorts and a halter as she rode a bicycle around the park. Her husband was out playing golf.

We asked what she figured for a budget during the winter months. She replied, "With $180 for rent, about $250 for food, $100 for entertainment, and $200 for miscellaneous, we manage everything on my husband's Social Security check."

Try Before You Buy?

Ordinarily, I'd advise you to rent before deciding to buy. However, for mobile homes, this usually turns out to be impractical. That's because all but the most humble (sometimes sleazy) parks strictly prohibit residents from renting out their mobile homes. This is an almost universal rule: no rentals. Places where renting is permitted are generally places you wouldn't want to live anyway. This isn't always true, of course, but don't count on finding anything you might like.

We have found one exception to the no-rental policy. It's an interesting concept in mobile home living—one we've seen in some Florida parks and that may possibly be available elsewhere. It's called a "try before you buy" plan. A park near the town of Hudson, Florida, is an example. Average-looking, well-kept, and nicely landscaped—but without a golf course or lake—this park has a limited number of two-bedroom, furnished mobile homes for lease. The minimum stay is three months, the maximum six months. The manager of the park told us, "We don't make money on these leases, but after folks spend a month or two here getting acquainted, they usually buy. This is our best sales producer."

The manager pointed out that this is an excellent way to discover three things about yourself. First, you will find out whether or not you like Florida well enough to retire there. Second, you will learn whether you like that particular part of Florida. And third, you will discover whether you like mobile home living well enough to retire in one. The monthly charges are stiff, starting at $1,200, but this includes linens, dishes, cooking utensils, unlimited use of the clubhouse and pool, and lawn maintenance.

Instant Housing

For inexpensive, quick housing on your own land, you can't beat a mobile home. All it takes is someone to move it onto your lot, and you have plumbing, electricity, and a comfortable place to live. By the way, the best way to buy a mobile home for your property is to look for one of those distress sales mentioned earlier, one of the fifteen-year-rule disasters that must be moved at any price. When a mobile must be moved, you can cut the asking price drastically.

You will, of course, need to check local regulations very carefully before placing a mobile on your lot. Many localities absolutely prohibit them on private land. In addition, you need to investigate several other things, particularly if you plan on buying property out in the country. The following items must be considered.

1. Are electricity and telephone services available? If you have to pay to install telephone and power poles several miles to your place, you might end up paying more for that than you did for the land and mobile home combined.

2. A good water supply is essential; if city water isn't connected to the property, you'll need to know how much it will cost to bring it in. The alternative is a well, which could be expensive, depending upon the locality. Even if a well is possible, you need to be assured that the water is drinkable. I have a friend who spent several thousand dollars drilling a well through layers of hard rock, only to find that the water tastes like sulfur and smells like rotten eggs. Makes for unpleasant showers, to say the least.

3. If a city sewer hookup isn't in the picture, you'll likely need a permit for a septic system. Sometimes this is impossible to obtain. Percolation tests may be required, and if your property can't qualify, you could end up using the bathroom at the nearest filling station. If your luck is *really* bad, it will be a pay toilet, so keep a plentiful supply of coins on hand.

4. If your land is truly out in the country, you must be sure that you have access easements across other people's property to reach your land. This is not only important for a road or driveway but also for stringing power and telephone lines. If your neighbors aren't friendly, the only way to reach your property could be by parachute.

5. Check your deed for timber and mineral rights. Usually these aren't important, but if your land is in a mining or timber-harvesting area—as parts of the Ozarks are—you could find bulldozers strip-mining your front yard or chain saws rearranging the landscaping.

Buying a Mobile Home *and* Land

The total investment in a mobile home on private land can be quite minimal, but it does entail a bit of work to get set up. Sometimes the obstacles are much more formidable than meet the eye. Frankly, I believe it's better to let someone else do the work; I'd prefer to buy something already set up and ready for occupancy.

During our research travels, we found exceptional buys in mobile homes on their own lots. For example, how does $25,000 sound for a double-wide, two-bedroom unit sitting on ten acres of wooded land? Or a single-wide on a riverside lot for $15,000? These are common prices to be found in the Ozarks area of Missouri, Arkansas, and Oklahoma. One lovely place was a five-minute drive from a boat ramp on Lake Tanycomo. The double-wide mobile home was set back among a growth of pine trees, almost hidden from the road and surrounded by more than ten acres of wooded solitude. Of all the landed mobile home setups we've seen, the Ozarks offer the best bargains.

It should go without saying that you need to be positive that country living is what you really want. If your spouse craves fishing, hunting, and communing with the outdoors, but you can't stand the sight of dead catfish or the thought of doing without HBO on cable TV, it may be time to talk about a compromise.

Chapter Nine
College Town Retirement

Fifteen years ago, when my wife, Sherry, and I began doing research for a book on retirement, we began the first of many trips across the country. We looked at hundreds of small cities and towns—evaluating them as possible places we could recommend as retirement destinations. After a while, we discovered something curious. It turned out that most of our favorite towns and smaller cities seemed to have one feature in common: most had a college or university with a large number of students and faculty in residence. At first we thought this a coincidence. After all, how could a school affect a community for anyone but those connected with the college or those retirees who are interested in higher education? How could the mere presence of a college make a town a better place to live?

After much puzzling over why our favorite towns were different from the others, we finally stumbled upon the key. College towns are dinosaurs—suspended in a time warp. Prove it to yourself: Walk into the downtown section of a typical college town, and you'll feel like you are stepping back in time. You're looking at the way our hometowns were forty years ago! Remember how it was then? The center of town was alive. It was the place to shop, have lunch with friends, browse the bookstore, or take in a movie. Something was always happening downtown. You couldn't stroll through the town center without seeing a half-dozen friends and acquaintances. Drivers would honk at friends as they passed by. Downtown was the social focus of the entire community. That's the way it used to be. That's what retirees today are looking for.

Starting about forty years ago, Small Town U.S.A. began undergoing profound changes. Large shopping centers began opening up out on the Highway 161 bypass, cutting prices until the small stores and businesses in the town itself couldn't compete. They either joined the movement to the strip mall or they closed their doors. Today many of these towns are hollow shells. The downtowns are deserted. You'll see little more than abandoned buildings, deserted storefronts, empty sidewalks. Stroll through the town center, and the only people you see are those patronizing the secondhand stores—the only businesses left. The one positive thing you can say is there are plenty of parking spaces.

But this didn't happen in most college towns. Why? Because students and faculty simply are not going to hang out at a strip mall. They want a lively, user-friendly downtown within walking distance of their dorms and offices. Yes, when they shop for groceries or a refrigerator, they have to go to the strip mall. But when they want to buy a sweater, have lunch with friends, or listen to a jazz combo in a pub, they think "downtown." With several thousand students, faculty, and school employees as customers, this means plenty of traffic in the town center. As long as there are people downtown, there will be stores, shops, and businesses downtown. And as long as there are stores, shops, and businesses, the other residents of town go there as well. You'll even find the old-fashion single-screen movie theater—showing foreign or classic movies perhaps—but it's still named the Bijou or Rialto! It's like going back in time forty years.

A university not only influences the intellectual atmosphere, but indirectly affects the business, entertainment, and dining traditions of the area. A university lures intellectuals from all over the country, creating an air of sophistication unknown in most towns of moderate size. Yet when you stroll along a downtown street, strangers are likely to nod and say hello as they pass. After all, this is not just a small town, it's a *college town*. Most people are connected with the university. We're all neighbors.

Although some university towns boast expensive and exclusive neighborhoods, they also provide neighborhoods with reasonably priced to inexpensive real estate. There is always a demand for affordable housing to meet the low-budget needs of students, employees, and beginning faculty members. Living costs are usually no higher than those in other similar-sized towns in the area. After all, as many as half of the community's residents are students who don't hold steady jobs, so there aren't a lot of extra wages bidding up rental and real estate costs.

Any time you combine a large number of university students with lots of retired folks, local businesses naturally respond with reasonably priced services, nicer shopping facilities, and good but affordable restaurants. Neither students nor retirees are over-burdened with money, but they do appreciate quality at afford-able prices.

For retirees operating on a shoestring budget, one of these towns can be the doorway to an exciting new lifestyle, as you make new friends who share your interests.

Even if you have no intention of going back to school, you'll discover many benefits of retirement in a university setting. Most institutions provide the community at large with a wide selection of social and cultural activities. You don't have to be a registered student to attend lectures and speeches (often free) given by famous scientists, politicians, visiting artists, and other well-known personalities. Concerts, ranging from Beethoven to boogie-woogie, are presented by guest artists as well as the university's music department. Stage plays, from Broadway musicals to Shakespeare, are produced by the drama department, with season tickets often costing less than a single performance at a New York theater. And of course there's football, basketball, base-ball, and other sports with low-cost or even free entrance. Some schools make special provisions to allow seniors to use their recreational facilities. Art exhibits, panel discussions, and a well-stocked library are usually available to the public.

College towns usually have at least one large bookstore where you'll enjoy one or two free events each week. Often you'll have the opportunity to meet a best-selling author and listen to her discuss her latest work. In some bookstores, you can sip a coffee and listen to a string quartet while you browse.

Because of the high level of sophistication, most college towns support bars and restaurants that feature entertainment, often well-known talent. Ordinary towns nearby seldom have this attraction. Throughout the southern states, where some of the more delightful college towns are located, "local option" has "dried up" surrounding counties, but most college towns have managed to reject the notion of prohibition. After all, what is a college experience without beer?

There is one economic downside to retirement in a college town: vigorous competition with students for part-time work. Unless you have a special skill or can do some teaching, you may have plenty of spare time to enjoy retirement by taking free classes and doing volunteer work. That's not so bad. On the other hand, students have a tendency to drift in and out of jobs, often quitting during summer vacation. Some employers prefer steady employees.

When choosing a college town for retirement, there are several items to look for. Of course, in any town, you'll need to check out medical care, transportation, and personal safety. College towns usually rank high in health care; many have a university hospital and sometimes a medical school. Because so many people travel to and from college towns, they almost always have intercity bus service such as Greyhound or Trailways and commuter airports nearby. Since many students don't own automobiles, there's usually local bus service, too. And as in most small towns, crime rates are usually very low.

You also have to ask yourself, "Is this really a college town?" Sometimes a school is basically a technical or religious institution that doesn't interact with the community. The important thing is whether the school reaches out to the community, inviting residents to events such as plays, concerts, lectures, and sporting events. A good school will offer free or reduced tuition for seniors and will have noncredit classes tailored for mature students.

Taking College Classes

Scientific research shows that we don't necessarily lose our capacity to learn as we age. Furthermore, the common belief that memory fades with each passing year is simply not true. Numerous psychological experiments prove that those who regularly exercise their minds hold up quite well.

You don't have to go back to school, but as long as you're retiring in a college town, why not give continuing education a try? More and more, dynamic seniors with active lifestyles are enjoying the pleasant, invigorating mental exercise of part-time classes. And this time around, they sign up for subjects they want to study, rather than what's required to get a degree!

More than two-thirds of all colleges and universities offer reduced rates or even free tuition to mature citizens. Many communities have special centers, schools, and programs tailored to older adults' needs. You won't feel like the proverbial sore thumb when you're in a setting where many students are your age or older.

Nervous about going back to school? Never been in a college classroom? Don't worry. For a mature adult, it's a snap. Professors are usually much closer to your age than to the age of other students. They'll tend to treat you as an equal but will talk down to younger students. Most schools allow you to audit courses, which means you take the class but don't have to worry about tests, finals, or term papers. You get the benefits and fun from the course without the tension. Below are some courses selected at random from a schedule offered by Valdosta State University in Georgia:

Home Fruit Growing
Instant Piano for Hopelessly Busy People
Basic Watercolors
Early Twentieth-Century Artists
Starting a Home Business
Creative Ideas for Filling Your Memory Book

If a university classroom seems a bit much for your ambitions, then try adult education classes. They're usually offered in the evenings, often in the local high school or community college buildings. You'll find a broad assortment of offerings—everything from philosophy to auto repair. The bonus is that in many college towns, you'll find that the adult ed instructor is also a university professor, moonlighting for extra money or simply because he enjoys sharing his special expertise.

Don't overlook your local two-year community college. Most towns either have a school or have one within driving distance. Although some are specifically for trade and entry-level professional training, others have wonderful offerings of low-tuition or tuition-free classes especially oriented toward mature students. Many community college classes are noncredit, mostly for personal improvement or hobbies, with subjects such as flower arranging, fly-fishing, cooking, book discussions, or woodworking. But you'll also find practical courses that could be useful in starting a home business, such as income tax preparation, dog grooming, and child care certification. University level or adult ed—it doesn't matter. You'll find yourself among a group of lively, interesting people. Just the kind of folks you would like for friends.

University Retirement Sampler

Following are some places I particularly like, towns where folks retire primarily because of the university setting. Of course, many other college towns throughout the nation offer everything that my favorites do. Doing your own investigation could turn up a setting that better suits your taste in climate, recreation, and location. You can take advantage of continuing education just about anywhere you choose to retire. As mentioned, most small cities without a university will usually have a two-year community college. It's just that in some towns, the university is the centerpiece of local attention, the focus of social and cultural

activities. This creates a situation in which everyone can participate in the excitement generated by the university. The following places are my personal favorites:

Oxford, Mississippi Stately antebellum mansions, enormous magno-
lia trees, live oaks and flowers in profusion, an ancient court-
house with a statue of a Confederate soldier—all of these
combine to make Oxford a model of a gracious university town
in the Old South. This is my all-time favorite college town. A city
of 20,000—half of them students—Oxford is large enough to
provide quality services but small enough that you'll meet
friends just about every time you go to the supermarket or walk
to the library.

Although upscale homes have soared in value in the past few
years, there are plenty of affordable neighborhoods with inexpensive prices and rents. A nice mixture of Yankees and Deep
South natives adds spice to the flavor of retiring here; if you're
not from the South, you won't be a stranger because your neighbors come from everywhere in the world. The 140-year-old university also lures intellectuals from all over, creating an air of
sophistication unknown in most isolated southern towns.
Retirees find Oxford a wonderful place for education; everyone
over the age of fifty-five can take three hours of classes tuition-
free per semester and can audit as many classes as they care to.

Columbia, Missouri This is more than a "college town"; it's more
properly called a "university city." Much larger than Oxford,
Columbia blends the sophistication of a small city with an exciting academic environment. Instead of just one university, three
well-known institutions of higher learning make education a
major industry here. Some programs offer free tuition in return
for volunteer work after graduation. Kansas City and St. Louis
are two-hour interstate drives in either direction for those who
can't live without major league sports or other amenities of big-
city life.

Making the decision to retire in Columbia is made easier by
a unique chamber of commerce program. Retiree volunteers

greet visitors and take them on a "windshield tour" of the city. They drive you through neighborhoods ranging from economical to deluxe, past the town's colleges, golf courses, and hospitals.

Ashland, Oregon Couples with mixed interests, who want more than intellectual stimulation, might check out Ashland. Set in southern Oregon's gently rolling hills, Ashland is an excellent retirement choice for outdoorsy, sports-oriented people. Great hunting, fishing, and skiing are available in the nearby Cascade Range, with crystal-clear rivers teeming with world-class salmon and steelhead trout. White-water rafting on the wild and scenic Rogue River draws adventurers from all over the country. One of the best climates in the nation makes outdoor sports enjoyable year-round; Ashland's 20 inches of yearly rain is a third to half that of most popular midwestern and southern cities. It's wonderfully sunny here most of the year.

Ashland offers all the usual cultural amenities of a small college town (it is home to Southern Oregon University) and more. Its renowned Shakespeare festival draws thousands every summer, and year-round community involvement in the college's activities keeps retirement interesting. A charming downtown offers excellent restaurants and shopping. As a final incentive, real estate costs are typical Oregon, ranging from cheap to affordable, although—as with Oregon real estate in general—prices have risen somewhat in the last few years.

Auburn-Opelika, Alabama Eastern Alabama's rolling hills and forests provide a good setting for college town retirement. Low property taxes are a bonus. The adjoining towns of Auburn and Opelika, with a combined population of 57,000, are centered around Auburn University and draw a diverse mixture of retirees from all over the nation. In fact, a third of all Auburn-Opelika residents come from other states.

In addition to the university, there's a two-year school, Southern Union Junior College, with about 1,400 students, and Opelika State Technical School, which offers extended day programs. Because of the university's top medical school and the

East Alabama Medical Center, health care here is superior. Nearby Fort Benning, Georgia, has medical facilities for military retirees, as well as a commissary and post exchange.

One of the famous Robert Trent Jones Golf Trail courses is located here, offering top country-club quality at public-golf fees. Great fishing is enjoyed at any number of sparkling lakes around the countryside. The climate here is mild, with a brief winter, early spring, and late fall.

Gainesville, Florida Home of the University of Florida, Gainesville is a culturally stimulating city of 90,000 inhabitants in a state famous for its culturally unstimulating cities. It doesn't look like Florida, either. Were it not for an occasional palm tree, Gainesville could easily be mistaken for a college town anywhere in the Midwest. Old-fashioned residential areas with tree-shaded streets justify Gainesville's official nickname, "the Tree City."

You needn't be a student to participate in the many activities connected with the university. A cultural complex with museums of art and natural history and a performing arts center serve the public at large. There is also an excellent two-year college that accepts most students over age sixty tuition-free. The extensive curriculum covers classes like dog training, computers, and antiques collecting.

If a town of 90,000 is too large for you, the nearby communities of High Springs and Archer are a fifteen-minute drive away. Housing costs less here, and small farms are affordable.

For outdoors types, there's plenty to do. A dozen nearby lakes invite anglers. Golf and tennis facilities abound, and beach fun at either the gulf or the Atlantic is a short drive away. The closest saltwater fishing is in Cedar Key, a 49-mile drive.

Chico, California Only a twenty-minute drive from tree-covered mountains and excellent fishing and hunting, and just a little farther to winter skiing, Chico is the site of a California state university. This is a typical Sacramento Valley town, with live oaks and huge ash trees shading quiet streets on topography as flat as a table. The thing that lifts Chico above most small, agriculturally centered valley towns is its university and vibrant academic timbre. Like all California state universities, Chico State encourages senior-citizen participation with free and reduced tuition rates. Cultural events, such as concerts, plays, lectures, and foreign films, are plentiful and usually free.

Chico weather, as in all Sacramento Valley towns, is both a blessing and a drawback, depending on your opinion of how hot summers should be. You can find days on end with temperatures in the 100-degree range. Balance that against the warm, seldom-frosty winter days with almost no snow, and Chico's weather comes out a winner. After all, when the summer gets going, that's the time for you to head for the nearby mountains for a picnic beside a cool stream or a day's prospecting and panning for gold in the Feather River.

Chico is an example of a California location that hasn't seen real estate go bonkers. Nice tract homes can be found for $85,000 and up. A twenty-minute drive takes you to the Feather River Canyon mountain country, where homes are hidden by huge pine trees.

Danville, Kentucky One of the prettiest towns in Kentucky, Danville is home to Centre College, an outstanding school that consistently receives high academic ratings. Located in a historic part of the state, Danville is just a few miles from Harrodsburg—the birthplace of Abraham Lincoln—and several Civil War battlefields. Incidentally, both Abe Lincoln and his Confederate counterpart, Jefferson Davis, were born in Kentucky, less than 100 miles apart.

Danville was named one of "Six Great Low-Cost Towns for Retirement" in *Where to Retire* magazine (winter 1999 edition). The magazine took into consideration culture, entertainment, beauty, safety, climate, medical care, and cost of living.

Danville has a population of 17,000, but it is only 35 miles from Lexington, a city of 350,000. The town is located in the famous Bluegrass country, known for rolling farmlands, horse farms, and pleasant rural scenery. Danville is a place where people are friendly, the streets are safe, and citizens are committed to keeping it that way.

Senior citizens are a vital part of the Danville area community. A well-equipped senior center provides activities that include lunches, speakers, shopping excursions, day-long outings, dancing, and fitness sessions. The center also provides periodic health screenings and transportation for elderly persons.

Fayetteville, Arkansas Up in the northwest corner of Arkansas, the college town of Fayetteville consistently receives favorable publicity as a great place for retirement. Its low cost of living, nearby outdoor recreational opportunities, and a community-friendly college are all part of the attraction. Not exactly a small town, Fayetteville has a population of 50,000, plus almost 15,000 students at the University of Arkansas.

This part of Arkansas has some of the most beautiful Ozarks scenery in the entire region, starting just a few miles from downtown Fayetteville. In the foothills is Beaver Lake, with 28,000 acres of fishing and boating.

The University of Arkansas is Fayetteville's heart and soul. The school, its students, and the faculty add excitement and vigor to the city. To savor fully the magnetism of the community, you must visit Dickson Street, near the campus. This colorful, entertaining street is filled with bistros, restaurants, and art galleries.

The university is ranked as one of the top schools in the country in the number of chief executives produced for major U.S. companies. (Bill Clinton taught law at the university before he entered politics.) The nearby town of Rogers is the home of Northwest Arkansas Community College, with 2,600 students to add to the educational scene.

Aiken, South Carolina Although the university here is small and doesn't impact the community like schools in some other college towns, Aiken is still a good candidate for retirement for a number of reasons, not the least of which is its beautiful, gracious setting.

Huge antebellum mansions and cute little cottages are shaded by enormous trees on meticulously landscaped lots. The natives are ingrained with notions of politeness and southern chivalry, all adding immeasurable charm to the setting. However, Aiken is different from many Deep South towns in that so many out-of-state people have moved here that distinctions between natives and newcomers have blurred. About thirty years ago, the DuPont Corporation developed a high-tech complex in Aiken and imported engineers, physicists, technicians, bricklayers—you name it—from all over the country. At the project's peak, more than 13,000 people were employed. These newcomers severely strained Aiken's housing market; so DuPont built a large number of single-family dwellings for employees.

When the energy project was finally up and running, most workers moved elsewhere to new jobs, and DuPont was stuck with hundreds of homes. Naturally, this sent the real estate market into a spin. Word soon got around about this beautiful little town with mild winters, friendly people, and fantastic real estate prices. This brought even more outsiders into Aiken. Bargain-basement real estate days are over, but the eclectic collection of people from all over the country remains.

Athens, Georgia Here is a prime example of how a university can shape a town's architecture, business structure, and social ambience. Downtown Athens looks exactly as a university town should look. Its main street is arched over by large trees and lined with old-fashioned cast-iron lampposts with glass globes. Sidewalk tables and chairs in front of cafes invite residents to linger over a cup of coffee. Students, residents, and tourists stroll the streets, browse stores and shop, or simply sit on wrought-iron benches, observing the passing world with an unhurried casualness only students and retirees can afford.

It's obvious that the downtown isn't just for the university's 26,000 students. Residents as well as visitors from nearby communities come to browse bookstores and specialty stops for articles not normally found in small Georgia cities. They love to dine in downtown Athens's exotic restaurants serving not only traditional southern-style cooking but also wood-fired pizza, Mexican enchiladas, Indian tandoori, and Japanese cuisine. This is one of our favorite college towns.

Tuition Breaks

Many states have legislation granting free or reduced tuition to senior citizens. Here's a list of retirement-destination states and their policies. Some states are considering liberalizing these regulations, so check locally for up-to-date facts. The information comes from a report by the U.S. Senate Special Committee on Aging.

Alabama:
: Most colleges and universities in the state offer free or reduced tuition to residents age sixty or over. Some private schools offer tuition discounts, special classes, and access to recreation and cultural programs for retirees.

Arkansas:
: State schools waive general student fees for credit courses for persons age sixty and older on a space-available basis. State vocational and technical schools also waive fees.

California:
: Depending upon space, many state colleges waive application and regular-session registration fees for regular credit courses for persons age sixty or older.

Florida:
: Waives application, course registration, and related fees at state universities on a space-available basis for residents age sixty or older.

Georgia:
: Waives fees for courses scheduled for resident credit for persons age sixty-two and older on a space-available basis.

Hawaii:
: Waives tuition or fees for credit classes at the University of Hawaii to persons age sixty or older on a space-available basis.

Kentucky: Waives all tuition and fees at state-supported insti-
             tutions of higher learning to any resident age sixty-
             five or older on a space-available basis.

Louisiana: Waives tuition and registration fees at public col-
             leges and universities to any person age sixty or
             older. Also reduces textbook costs for these stu-
             dents by 50 percent.

Maryland: Waives tuition to the University of Maryland sys-
             tem for up to three courses per term for any
             retired person age sixty or older on a space-avail-
             able basis. Also waives tuition to community col-
             leges for residents age sixty or older.

Mississippi: Waives tuition for residents age fifty-five or older
             for one credit class per semester, with unlimited
             auditing, on a space-available basis.

Nevada: Waives registration fees for credit or audit for per-
             sons age sixty-two or older.

New   Institutions may reduce tuition fees to $5.00 per
Mexico: hour for up to six hours per semester for residents
             age sixty-five or older on a space-available basis.

North   Waives tuition at colleges and universities
Carolina: for residents age sixty-five or older on a space-
             available basis.

South   Waives tuition at any public college for residents
Carolina: age sixty or older on a space-available basis.

Tennessee: Waives tuition and registration fees at public col-
             leges and universities for residents age sixty-five or
             older on a space-available basis.

Texas: State-supported schools may waive tuition for per-
             sons age sixty-five or older to audit any course on
             a space-available basis.

Utah: Waives tuition at institutions of higher learning
             for residents age sixty-two or older on a space-
             available basis.

Virginia: Waives tuition for auditing courses at any state
             institution of higher education for residents age

sixty or older with annual incomes less than $10,000 on a space-available basis.

Washington: State universities and community colleges may waive tuition to residents age sixty or older enrolled for credit on a space-available basis.

Chapter Ten

RVs and Retirement

O
f all the lifestyles open to low-income retirees, few accommodate a shoestring budget as well as recreational vehicle retirement can. This presumes, of course, that your motor home, trailer, or camper is paid for or at least that you aren't facing stiff monthly payments.

If you've ever owned an RV, chances are you've fantasized about how it might be to actually *live* in your rig instead of merely vacationing. You imagine yourself taking off and never landing, following the seasons, catering to your whims, happy as a seagull soaring in the breeze. It's an exciting, awesome idea. You can totally change your lifestyle, rent out the house, put things in storage, and set out with no particular destination in mind! Many people do just this. The best part is, for those searching for low-cost retirement, RV living can fill the bill. It depends on how you go about it, of course.

This enthusiasm for RV living is growing rapidly. Years ago, before the phenomenal growth of the recreational vehicle industry, RVs were primarily used for weekends and summer vacations. Travel trailers were rarely self-contained (although some models had flush toilets that needed to be hooked to sewer connections before they could be used). Pickup trucks with cab-over campers were the forerunners of today's luxury motor homes. Those few folks who traveled full-time in cramped little trailers were considered to be gypsies, eccentrics, or adventurers. Living in the back of a pickup was, well, the sign of a loser.

Times have changed, and RVs have changed with them.

Today, uncounted thousands of retired folks spend months at a time in fifth-wheels, motor homes, and deluxe cab-overs. If you still believe RVs are for gypsies, a visit to your local RV sales lot will leave you slack-jawed in astonishment. Instead of the old Porta Potti facilities of yesteryear, you'll find complete baths, including sunken tubs, showers, and designer vinyls. Microwaves and freezers are all but standard, as are three-way refrigerators that can operate on propane, the rig's 12-volt battery system, or 110-volt park current. Furnishings are plush and tastefully matched to the rest of the decor, and an ingenious use of space provides incredible storage room. It isn't surprising that many folks spend a lot of time in their RVs during retirement, when they finally have time to enjoy them to the fullest.

RV Parks Galore

RV destinations offer accommodations that vary in quality from super deluxe to extra grungy. Prices vary from costly to free. Later in this chapter you'll find out how you can even get *paid* to park! In addition to higher prices, higher quality parks have certain features in common: swimming pools, Jacuzzis, shuffleboard courts, restaurants, and sometimes even golf courses.

An all-important part of the better RV parks is a clubhouse. It's more than just a place to go for a cup of coffee and to meet other RV enthusiasts. The park clubhouse serves as the headquarters for the park's social activities. Dancing, bingo, arts and crafts, jazzercise, card parties, potlucks, and group tours are just a few of the organized pastimes available in the typical clubhouse. There's no excuse for ever being bored.

There are two kinds of RV parks. There are parks that cater to tourists in transit, places where people typically stay for a few days and then move on. These facilities can cost $20 to $40 a day, depending on what is offered. Full-time RV folks cannot afford these luxury places. They look for parks that cater to long-term residents, where space rents vary from as low as $50 a month to more than $300. For example, one of the better RV parks in Tucson, Arizona, charges $355 a month (plus electricity) for the winter months, but only $1,545 for year-round rent (that figures out to less than $130 a month). About half of the spaces are rented out for the year; the owners leave their rigs parked during the summer and return to their cooler hometowns. From October through May, the park hires a full-time social director, who arranges a complete calendar with tennis tournaments, swimming, hobbies, and just about anything else one might wish to do. "Our people don't just sit around twiddling their thumbs," says the park manager. "We don't give them the chance to be bored."

Rents for RV parks vary depending on quality and location. Many perfectly adequate RV parks charge as little as $150 a month. One lady in Florida remarked, "Our park rent here costs us less than our fuel-oil bill if we stayed home all winter, so I figure we're living here rent-free. We just weatherproof our house and forget it until the snow melts!"

Not long ago I read an ad in *Trailer Life* for an RV park in Mesa, Arizona. It advertised affordable rates and an astonishing range of attractions. I'll list them here so you can see what you get for your money: clubhouse, ballroom, lounge, library, pool/billiards, card parlor, Olympic-sized pool/Jacuzzi, kitchen/snack bar, four tennis courts, putting green, golf driving cage, shuffleboard, horseshoes, exercise gym, lapidary shop, silversmith studio, woodworking shop, ceramics studio, arts and crafts facilities, table tennis, laundry/ironing rooms, and a sewing room. Apparently, the only hobbies missing are bungee jumping, goldfish swallowing, and underwater basket weaving!

Those addicted to slot machines will find many of Nevada's casinos very accommodating for RV travelers. For example, the last time we looked, Sam's Town RV park in Las Vegas charged about $10 per night, which included (besides hookups) a fifty-six-lane bowling alley, 2,000 slot machines, two floors of casino with keno, and a race-and-sports book. And if that wasn't enough, they offered free dance lessons. Most casinos don't bother charging for parking; they simply request that RVs park in a designated area, but they provide no hookups. Naturally, they're eager for you to stay so you can spend your money in the casino. By the way, some of Nevada's gambling casinos, starting with Harold's Club in Reno, have made it a policy to hire senior citizens as part-time or full-time workers. How would you feel about dealing a few hands of blackjack next winter?

The variety of RV parks almost defies description. Those with their own golf courses present a country-club atmosphere, complete with nineteenth-hole cocktail lounges and gourmet dining rooms. Others sit right on the beach for easy access to surf-casting and splashing around in your bathing suits. There are even parks for nudists, where people splash around in their *birthday* suits! Ordinarily, you must be a member of the American Sunbathing Association to enter, but most parks allow trial visits by respectable-looking couples. And because park residents do laundry less frequently, they also save on laundry detergent.

What Will the Kids Think?

A big problem for many retirees who want to start "full-timing" in their RVs is the shock, disbelief, and disapproval of their children. They cannot believe their parents could do such a thing! The whole idea seems irresponsible to them. "Why do they want to worry us like this? Why do they have to do weird things? Why can't they stay home and be like everyone else?" They forget how we were appalled at the weird clothes and hairdos our kids used to wear or by their CDs of so-called music with lyrics we didn't want to hear!

As one lady put it, "My only real problem getting started into full-timing was convincing my children, relatives, and friends that I had not lost my senses. To them, 'Grandmother' means dressing in a long skirt, apron, bonnet, and high-top shoes. She's a person who sits by the fire, knitting sweaters while cookies bake in the oven. 'Grandmother' certainly doesn't mean flitting around the country alone in an old motor home, dressed in a sweatshirt, jeans, and sneakers!"

If you want to humor the kids a bit, you can put a CB radio and cellular phone into your rig and get vehicle insurance with a good emergency road service provision. But in the final analysis, it's your retirement, and now it's your turn to worry *them* a little.

One caution that all experienced full-timers will give to newcomers: Don't burn your bridges. You may want to re-cross them should you decide that full-timing is not as romantic as you thought. If you own a home, you might consider leasing it out for a while, "just to make sure." Some make arrangements with their tenants to reserve the garage, a room, or part of the basement for storing their things. Renters can also forward mail and telephone messages.

RV Clubs and Retirement

Many RV travelers feel that part of the fun of owning a rig comes from belonging to a club. Rallies, camp-outs, and tours are just a few of the organized activities available through RV clubs. Newsletters keep members well informed about upcoming events. Depending upon the season and weather, club members meet at designated campgrounds, set up an enclave, and start socializing. There are clubs for rockhounds and prospectors, for jewelry making, quilting, handicapped travelers, computer buffs, and just about any other kind of hobby you can imagine for which you aren't likely to be arrested. Anything you want to know about RV lifestyles you will learn by belonging to one or more clubs.

For the full-time RV traveler, however, club membership is more than just an entertaining pastime; membership is essential. Folks who scrape by on very limited budgets and who must squeeze the maximum value from every dollar do not hesitate spending money for club dues. They consider club membership every bit as important as gasoline when living full-time in their rigs.

Club publications present news of rallies and new campgrounds, and they keep you posted on other members' whereabouts. Some list free parking places provided by members for the overnight use of fellow members. The sticker on your RV announcing that you are a member acts like an invitation for other club members to introduce themselves. You are able to enjoy the inexpensive benefits of RV ownership without feelings of uneasiness about being a stranger among strangers.

Good Sam

The largest RV club of all, Good Sam, started years ago when a Utah trailerist sent a letter to *Trail-R-News* magazine (now *Trailer Life*). The letter suggested that the magazine offer subscribers a decal for their rigs, something that would indicate their willingness to stop and help fellow RVers in distress. The idea caught on and mushroomed into the Good Sam Club.

Because few insurance companies were interested in covering RVs, it seemed only natural that the club should provide policies tailored to members' needs. Before long it became the major insurer of travel trailers and motor homes.

Today the Good Sam Club boasts more than 750,000 members, with 2,200 chapters around the country. In addition to insurance with emergency road service, policyholders receive discounts at hundreds of campgrounds in the Good Sam Park program, a campground directory, a subscription to *Trailer Life* magazine, trip routing, and even RV financing. (The insurance isn't mandatory for club membership.) Free services include mail forwarding, credit card loss protection, lost key service, lost pet service, commission-free traveler's checks, and a monthly news magazine, the *Hi-Way Herald*.

Trailer Life, by the way, is a valuable publication for RV travelers, whether full-timers or weekenders. It is full of important news, features on how to repair your rig and interesting places to visit, and analysis of general trends in the RV industry. Information on Good Sam Club can be obtained from P.O. Box 11097, Des Moines, IA 50381; (800) 234–3450.

Escapees

Several clubs specialize in serving the needs of those who live full-time in their RVs. The best known and largest is the Escapees (SKP), with 12,000 members. Founded by Joe and Kay Peterson several years ago, the club has grown by leaps and bounds as more and more people discover the joys of full-timing. They maintain several RV parks scattered around the country, where members can stay at reduced rates, even boondock for just a few dollars a day.

The Escapees' national headquarters is at 100 Rainbow Drive, Livingston, TX 77351; (888) 757–2582. The club publishes a monthly news magazine covering important news about rallies and get-togethers, new places to park, tips on equipment maintenance, and hints for making life easier on the road. Members report where they are and what they've been doing so friends can keep in touch. SKP members often remark, "We feel like we're part of a large, close-knit family."

Another important facility of the club is a mail forwarding and message service. An 800 number both accepts phone messages and allows you to retrieve them. Mail is forwarded automatically. This system solves the problem of keeping in touch with the world while gypsying.

Free Lodging in State and National Parks

Perhaps the main reason you wanted an RV in the first place was to visit scenic national parks, recreational wonderlands, and picturesque parts of the country. Making camp alongside a lake or beside a sparkling trout stream—that's what it's all about, right? Most folks, restricted to a two-week vacation, have to squeeze into any campsite where they can make reservations. When park campsites are full, it's off to a $26-a-night commercial park with coveys of screaming children underfoot.

Every vacation season, however, county, state, and national parks are in need of volunteer workers. If you're retired and have your own transportable housing, you may make application as a campground volunteer host. If you're accepted, the park will reserve a prime campsite for you at no cost whatsoever! You can stay the season for free. Even better, a few parks will even pay you to park for the entire season! While the pay may be minimal, the work is also minimal, yet interesting and rewarding.

The host's duties consist of registering visitors, helping campers locate their campsites, and answering questions. For serious emergencies, a two-way radio or cell phone keeps volunteer hosts in touch with park rangers. Usually, the requirement is four hours of work a day in exchange for a free site hookup and perhaps a few benefits. One volunteer said, "We never keep to the minimum. It's too much fun."

Private resorts, campgrounds, and tourist attractions also need seasonal help, but they are expected to pay a salary or hourly wages. Sometimes regular housing units, such as cabins or rooms, are provided for workers without RVs. But living accommodations can be spared for only a few people—the rest of the rooms or cabins must be rented to make a profit. When you bring your own housing with you, however, it's a different story. These places love their RV staff members! And they know that when the season is over, you're out of their hair until next year.

Because many volunteer and paid jobs are in rustic locations, managers and employers are delighted to find seasonal workers who need nothing more than water and electricity hookups. When the season is over, the workers pack up and move on to better weather, leaving behind nothing but good memories. Often, before they leave, arrangements are made for the coming season.

Job opportunities are available as campground managers, bookkeepers, off-season caretakers, maintenance workers, and gatekeepers. The most common volunteer jobs offer free parking and hookups (but no salary) to campground "hosts," whose duties consist of answering the questions of new campers and making them feel at home. Other jobs require more responsibility and offer a salary.

We interviewed a couple who spent the summer at a county park on a scenic white-water river, a favorite place for river rafting and trout fishing. This was their first time doing this. "We sent out ten applications," Brenda said, "and within the week we received two positive replies. We took this one because it paid a monthly stipend as well as the free hookups." Her husband said, "They even installed a telephone in our trailer so we could be in contact with park headquarters."

When asked how much their summer on the river cost them, they did some mental calculations, and Joe said, "We were spending about $65 a week at the market. We know, because we only drove into town twice a week. Our only other expenses were laundry, telephone calls to our kids, and dinner out once a week." Brenda added, "Videocassettes, too. We rented four or five a week. No television here." After doing some work with a hand calculator, they came up with an average figure of $293 a month. They didn't mention their pay, but it surely covered a portion of their expenses.

Seasonal Retirement

Every winter, trailers, campers, and motor homes by the hundreds of thousands flock toward retirement destinations in Texas, Florida, California, and Arizona. This is an ideal compromise for those who refuse to give up their paid-for homes or who cannot stand the thought of leaving their grandchildren permanently. For winter's duration, they golf, bicycle, stroll the beaches—whatever suits their fancy—instead of huddling inside next to the fireplace. If they feel like fishing, they needn't chop a hole in the ice first. Money saved on heating bills back home pays for a large part of the trip.

By nature, RV travelers are friendly folks. They *have* to enjoy parking shoulder-to-shoulder with their neighbors. You'll find few strangers in RV parks. Winter travelers generally have two sets of friends: those who live in their hometown and those who live in the RV winter neighborhood. As winter parks begin receiving visitors, old friends meet and celebrate a joyous renewal of last year's companionship. "We've been coming here for the last six years," one lady told us, "and we have more friends in this park than we've ever made back home!"

Not all part-timers travel seasonally; some use their rigs to visit friends and relatives scattered around the country. Because weather isn't the most important consideration, they travel during the uncrowded and inexpensive times of the year. One couple we interviewed has two sons living on the West Coast, a son in New Jersey, and a daughter in Miami. "We make it a point to spend a month a year visiting each one," explained June, a petite brunette who helps drive the 30-foot motor home. "We never wear out our welcome, and we have our own home. We don't have to interfere with our children's privacy by staying in their homes."

Working and RV Travel

In Chapter 3 we talked about working and retirement. As mentioned, many RV travelers follow the seasons, visiting the nicest parts of the country in the best seasons and working at temporary jobs. They often earn enough to cover their expenses and don't have to touch their Social Security or other "mail-box income." The good news is that plenty of temporary jobs are available at most popular seasonal resorts. Employers love to have workers who bring their own housing with them—and who don't mind leaving when business drops off at the end of the tourist season.

RV owners often receive preferred consideration over those who need conventional housing.

This is a great way to follow the weather and stay within a shoestring budget. Like a loose-knit club, thousands of RV full-timers travel the country, working their way from one vacation hot spot to another. They have their own "bible," a publication called *Workamper News* (also mentioned in Chapter 3), which is chock full of information on temporary job opportunities. Subscribers write enthusiastic letters to the editor telling of jobs like guiding visitors at the Wild Bill Hickok Museum in Deadwood, South Dakota; working in casinos in Lake Tahoe; selling Christmas trees in Wisconsin; doing office work in an RV campground in Florida; and managing a gift shop in Bar Harbor, Maine.

Chapter 3 provides details on how to find temporary jobs and how to subscribe to *Workamper News*.

Desert Boondocking

The deserts of the Southwest draw hundreds of thousands of RVs, the vast majority driven by retired people as they visit the cities and desert outback for winter stays. Snowbirds have become a major economic boon for host communities. Yuma, Arizona, for example, doubles its population of 50,000 every winter. Phoenix hosts around 200,000 seasonal residents, bringing almost $200 million to the economy. An enormous number of these winter visitors bring RVs with them.

The Southwest offers plenty of conventional RV resorts with the usual recreation facilities. But for many, the desert Southwest presents unique opportunities for "boondocking," an ingenious technique of camping without paying overnight fees. "Freebies" is another term for the same thing.

Most RV owners boondock occasionally; that's one of a rig's advantages. Roadside rest areas are perfect for getting sleepy RV drivers off the interstates. A supermarket parking lot can be a lifesaver when it's too late to find an RV park. A friend or relative's driveway is much better for a weekend visit than a motel or trailer park a dozen miles away.

But southwestern desert boondockers have raised the concept of boondocking to a fine art. A boondocker's badge of pride is the ability to spend the entire winter boondocking—enjoying sunshine, companionship, and recreation—without spending a nickel for rent. Needless to say, free housing and no utilities help enormously toward the notion of shoestring retirement, with elimination of the two most expensive items in basic budgets: rent and utilities.

Desert boondocking started informally many years ago, when a few campers began pulling off the road onto government land to spend a few days or weeks just loafing. They'd simply set up camp wherever they pleased and make themselves at home in the sagebrush and cactus. The vast majority of southwestern desert lands in states like Arizona and California are public property—so nobody complained. Before long, the word got out that free camping in the desert was the perfect way to spend an economical and pleasant winter. Every fall, small cities of campers began blossoming all over the desert, staying until the following spring.

Rather than attempt to evict thousands of RVs, the U.S. Bureau of Land Management (BLM) began selling camping permits for the entire season and encouraging the boondockers to congregate in certain locations. The fee is a mere $25 a year, which goes toward providing drinking water, dumping stations, and cleanup. (This fee is due for an increase and may be higher by the time of publication.) Recently, the BLM started offering free campsites (presumably with utilities) for volunteers who will do a small amount of work, monitoring the permit-holding campers and checking sanitary conditions.

Don't get the wrong impression and equate boondocking with poverty. You'll see some rigs boondocked in the desert that cost more than many fancy homes. Their owners can afford to spend the winter anywhere they care to, yet here they are, happy campers in the cactus. They come from all walks of life, all trades, professions, and occupations. It's a lifestyle that isn't necessarily connected with a need for economical living.

Almost all desert boondockers are retired and have one thing in common: a love for outdoor winter retirement. To be sure, some really can't afford a winter vacation any other way. In fact, some have to live this way because their incomes are so low. So you will find shabby old trailers and campers on rusted pickups parked next to shiny new motor homes valued at $150,000. RV camping is truly a social leveler. This is democracy at the grassroots level (or is it cactus-roots level?).

In addition to the low rent of just $25 for the season, boondockers enjoy the lowest utility bills possible—they pay *nothing*. There are no 110-current plugs in the desert, no water hookups, no natural gas, and no garbage/sewer charges. Bottled gas cooks meals and sometimes provides light. Radios, televisions, and indoor lights are powered by 12-volt batteries, which are charged by solar panels. Conserving drinking water and battery power becomes second nature after a while. This is living at its simplest—and at its cheapest!

Those who prefer solitude simply wheel off the road wherever they choose—within the permit area, of course—and drive until all traces of civilization are out of sight. They set up camp and sometimes stay for weeks before having to make a run into the nearest town for supplies. They are disturbed by no sounds other than the distant yapping of coyotes or feisty little birds chattering away in the sagebrush. The BLM maintains several campgrounds in Arizona and eastern California near the Colorado River. Some have improvements, such as water and dumping stations, and one, near Holtsville, California, is even said to have a hot tub!

Arizona Choices

Now you might imagine that desert RV camping would be the very epitome of isolation. Oddly enough, desert camping can be perfect for the gregarious, the talkative, and those who love to make friends, as well as for hermits. Those who enjoy company park their rigs near each other, with a campfire as the central focus. Those who like to be alone simply move farther into the sagebrush and tend their own campfires.

Every winter, the biggest RV boondocking area of all—Quartzite, Arizona—changes from empty desert into a virtual city. Although rigs don't park cheek by jowl, as they must in commercial RV parks, the campers have to get close together to make room for the others. Because so many friendly neighbors are camped nearby, folks who normally wouldn't dream of boondocking feel absolutely secure here.

Throughout late spring, summer, and early fall, Quartzite lives the life of a typical desert crossroads community, almost deserted. But when winter rolls around, things change quickly. During the winter, as many as 150,000 RVs converge upon Quartzite. When you drive toward Quartzite's center, RVs fill the desert as far as the eye can see. No one knows for sure how many people are there at any one time, since rigs are continually arriving and departing, or moving from one boondocking site to another.

Entrepreneurs of all descriptions set up shop, selling wares and services to the flood of RV owners who begin arriving in mid-fall. Hobbies become businesses, and pre-retirement skills once again become valuable. Signs on motor homes, campers, and trailers announce, "Alterations and Tailoring," "Air Conditioners Serviced," "Ceramics," "Auto Repair," and "Rental Library." One motor home advertised a copy machine and word processing (presumably the rig had its own generator). People set up stands in front of their rigs to sell knickknacks, clothing, arts and crafts, trinkets, and essentials. Automobile mechanics carry tools in their pickups and essentially bring the garage to your vehicle while they make repairs. One man who deals in flea-market kinds of merchandise said, "Whenever my wife and I spend the winter here, we always take home more money than we left with."

During the winter Quartzite puts on a carnival mood. Making friends and going to potlucks, dances, and club meetings keep the social types busy; trading paperbacks, campfire conversations, and card games are for the quieter types. An outdoor ballroom called the Stardusty hosts twice-a-week dances. Then, when the late spring sun begins beating down on aluminum roofs, when air conditioning begins to sound nice, the rigs abandon their makeshift city to the baking heat of the desert summer.

Many snowbirds boondock or stay in RV parks in the Yuma area. Near Yuma, just off Interstate 8, is Sidewinder RV Park. Sleepy Hollow is a few miles farther, just across the border from the Mexican town of Los Algodones. Last I heard, monthly rates were reasonable, in the neighborhood of $100. Sleepy Hollow features a band that plays for dances every weekend. The musicians are regulars who come here every winter.

Los Algodones is Mexico's answer to high-cost U.S. medical bills. Thousands of U.S. and Canadian citizens journey here every year to take advantage of bargain eye care, dentistry, low-cost prescription drugs, and general medical care. See Chapter 5 for details.

Another encampment is located north of Yuma near Imperial Lake and Dam. Campgrounds bear names like Hurricane Ridge and Beehive. Government-constructed rest rooms, holding-tank dumps, and freshwater make winter-long camping comfortable and inexpensive.

California's Unique Slab City

During World War II, General Patton searched for a desert training ground to prepare his armored division for war. He wanted terrain that simulated North Africa's desert, a place to get his tank crews in shape for the planned invasion. He found it near the small town of Niland, not far from southern California's Salton Sea. A large camp went up, and the troops readied for battle. After the war, the camp was dismantled and its buildings razed to the ground, but the cement slabs upon which the buildings rested are still there—thus the name The Slabs, or Slab City.

These cement platforms made wonderful RV pads, so it wasn't long before a few campers began spending winters in the sunshine of the southern California desert. The elevation is low, nearly sea level, making for winters that are as balmy and pleasant as the summers are hot and insufferable. The news quickly made the rounds of RV boondockers. Slab City became a rival to Quartzite. And instead of the nominal $25 a year, Slab City is free!

Between 5,000 and 10,000 people congregate here every winter; by June, all but a handful are gone. RVs of all descriptions and prices pull off the paved road, head into the desert, and park haphazardly, sometimes next to friends, other times seeking solitude. Compatible RVers cluster together, forming regular neighborhoods, each with a central campfire area surrounded by lawn chairs and chaise lounges.

Some campers started a church complete with regular services. The church, in a large mobile home, doubles as an information center when services aren't underway. This must be how it was back in the covered wagon days, for amid all of this chaos there is an admirable sense of community and order. There is a heartwarming, natural sense of respect for neighbors' rights.

With no formal rules or regulations, the residents seem to know instinctively just what to do as individuals to make things work. Even though there are no law enforcement officers, there are few or no lawbreakers. When an occasional troublemaker drifts into Slab City, he or she receives a silent treatment that is followed by determined group action should the offender not catch the hint.

An unspoken notion of the Golden Rule inspires folks to care for their neighbors. Should a camper not appear outside by 10:00 in the morning, neighbors check to see if everything is okay.

Most RV units have CB radios that serve as a telephone system. Some CBs are always monitoring channel nine, ready to call Niland, about 2 miles away, in the event of a medical or other emergency. At any given time, a retired nurse or two will be staying here, so medical assistance is always close by.

Although the vast majority of the Slabs' residents are retired, a few younger families join the community every year. A county school bus makes a daily stop to pick up the handful of children who live there.

Once a month, a government agency out of San Diego arrives with surplus commodities, and the Salvation Army drops in two or three times a month to distribute vegetables, canned goods, and other foods. Some campers need this help; most don't, even though they welcome the freebies. As one lady said, "When you're living on Social Security, you feel that anything the government hands out is something your taxes have already paid for!"

With no rent or utilities, there is little to spend money on at the Slabs. Several retirees tell us that they not only get by on their Social Security checks—they save some of it every month! The Niland post office receives many retirement checks for Slab City residents. The extra money spent in the town doesn't go unnoticed by the town residents, who deeply appreciate their winter neighbors. The campers annually pump $4 million into the economy of Imperial County.

Not everyone will be happy at Slab City, though. My wife and I agree that it's fun for a while and that we thoroughly enjoy the extremely interesting mixture of campers. Yet a long-term visit here would grow tiresome for us. It's a long journey to the nearest library, bookstore, or shopping center. Before long, we catch up on our reading, get tired of playing cards with neighbors, and weary of our own cooking. We begin dreaming of Chinese food and pizza with sausage and anchovies. For a while, we enjoy not worrying about deadlines or telephones, but the truth is, after a while, we miss them.

Texas's Rio Grande Valley

Another important destination for RV retirees is in the great state of Texas. RV parks throughout Texas draw travelers from all over the United States and Canada. Although Texas undoubtedly has boondocking locations, the emphasis here is on traditional RV parks. The main attraction is that part of Texas bordering Mexico: the Rio Grande Valley, a country famous for truck farms, grapefruit groves, and nowadays groves of RV parks.

Each winter, trailers, campers, and motor homes of all descriptions converge on the Rio Grande Valley and become seasonal abodes for several hundred thousand temporary retirees. "Winter Texans," they're called. They are welcomed by the local businessmen and residents, who acknowledge the tremendous boost retirees give the economy. Orange groves, palm trees, and 80-degree afternoons make for pleasant living while winter winds paralyze the countryside back home.

Winter retirement in southern Texas isn't an especially new idea. It started back in the 1930s, when midwestern farmers, their work shut down by cold weather, would make their way to the warmth and sunshine of the Rio Grande Valley. Pulling old-style house trailers or driving homemade campers, these cold-weather refugees began arriving in such numbers that the Rio Grande Valley area gained the nickname "the poor man's Florida." When RVs came into their own and shed the connotation of poverty, the Rio Grande Valley came into its own as a winter retirement Eden.

The number of winter visitors keeps growing. Ten years ago, about 50,000 snowbirds wintered in the Brownsville-Harlingen-McAllen area; today they number more than 200,000! There has been a boom in RV park construction to accommodate the crush. There are well over 500 parks around here, some with several hundred spaces each. One popular RV retirement destination is the town of Mission, near McAllen. More than 10,000 RVs arrive here every winter, with more than one hundred RV parks making room for them. RVers almost double the year-round population of Mission, which bills itself as "the Mecca for Winter Texans."

An interesting contrast exists between the lifestyles of the desert boondockers and winter Texans. While the desert folks pride themselves on living frugally, organizing unique social groups and creating their own entertainment, the Texas crowd prefers having things done for them. RV parks are big business here, and they compete for winter residents by offering complete programs of entertainment and activities. Social directors plan pancake breakfasts, ice cream socials, square dances, and other events to get people mingling and having a good time. Swimming pools, hobby rooms, classes, indoor shuffleboard, tennis, dance halls, libraries, pool rooms, sewing rooms, and special halls for recreation and socializing are other common features. Even bare-bones parks usually have a lively recreation hall to go with the laundry facilities. Park rents here are more than $300 a month for the truly ritzy places to about $200 for the more ordinary ones—certainly within the range of a shoestring budget.

With such a tremendous influx of people every season, pressure is put on stores, restaurants, and service enterprises to keep up with the additional demand for goods and services. This naturally creates a demand for seasonal workers. Many retirees state that they have no problem finding work if they so desire. Many RV parks hire their extra help exclusively from their seasonal residents. Some RVers have "steady" jobs—they work for the same employer every year.

McAllen is the largest town in this network of retirement cities; Mission, Harlingen, and Brownsville fill out the list. Near the mouth of the Rio Grande is South Padre Island, a long, narrow spit of land that also draws RVs. The southernmost tip is covered by the town of South Padre, but just a few miles north civilization gives way to sand dunes, good fishing, and RV boondocking.

We've discussed only a small portion of RV seasonal retirement here. Excellent winter RV parking can be found throughout the southern United States from Florida to the West Coast. For summer travel the selection is even wider in the northern states and into Canada.

Wintering in Mexico

Because Texas and the desert Southwest wintering places are so close to the Mexican border, it would be surprising if adventuresome RV owners didn't venture farther south for sun and tourism. Of course they do, and they've discovered some delightful and economical places to spend the winter. RV caravans are very popular, with ten to thirty rigs traveling together as their owners have fun exploring Mexico. Hundreds of RV parks accommodate visitors. Some visitors prefer to boondock for free in Baja California.

My wife and I had become enamored with RV travel south of the border while in the process of writing *RV Travel in Mexico*. Unfortunately, the book is out of print, but you'll often find it in your library.

When we began work on *RV Travel in Mexico*, we loaded our 24-foot motor home with fresh water, fishing gear, a couple of lawn chairs suitable for sunning, and plenty of reading material. The next few months were spent on a delightful odyssey through various parts of Mexico. In all, we did more than 3,000 miles of traveling, boondocking on lovely beaches, visiting colonial towns, sometimes overnighting by hooking up to electricity behind large gas stations, occasionally staying at luxury resorts where coats and ties were preferred in the restaurants, and making some enduring friendships. It's easy to understand how this carefree lifestyle can become addictive.

On Mexico's western side, the most popular RV winter retirement areas are found in the Baja California peninsula and in the mainland state of Sonora. Baja is particularly well liked, partly because the peninsula is so dry that much of it is uninhabitable unless you bring your own lodging and water supply. Many wonderful beaches have no hotels or tourist accommodations; they spread empty and desolate along the beautiful Sea of Cortez or the rolling Pacific. Without an RV, no matter how rich you might be, you can only glimpse these sights as you drive past. With your own rolling home, you can enjoy beaches and scenery that those poor millionaires must forgo. Boondocking is *in*.

Not unexpectedly, as more and more "winter Mexicans" crowd the Baja beaches, local residents see commercial possibilities. Along the Baja California coasts, many beaches belong to *ejidos* (Indian communal lands) under tribal control. Although all Mexican beaches are open to the public, ejidos can charge for overnight parking. That's why some of the more popular beaches are no longer free—although they might as well be because camping charges are so low. Typically, a caretaker makes the rounds every evening and asks for a couple of dollars or so for overnight parking—depending on the beach. In return, the caretakers make sure things are tidy and keep an eye out for suspicious characters.

The beach where we've spent the most time is Santispac, just south of Mulegé, about halfway down the peninsula. Several hundred RVs arrive here every winter, beginning in October and staying until the weather begins heating up in April. With their rigs lined up along the beach, campfire pits in front, and sometimes a palm-thatch *palapa* built for shade, these temporary expatriates enjoy a bountiful season of companionship, fishing, swimming, and just plain loafing. Beach caretakers also keep their eyes on trailers and palapas left through the summer when Baja sunshine makes Death Valley seem cool. From the reports we get, theft is rarely a problem.

"The same folks tend to come to our special beach every season," explains one lady. "It's like a big homecoming every time another rig pulls in. With campfires every evening, it's like a winter-long beach party." Her husband adds, "With rent almost free, it costs us less than $300 a month to spend the winter in Mexico.

It could be less, but we like to eat breakfast at the beach restaurant, and we often eat dinner in town."

For those who hesitate to boondock (although with a hundred rigs in a row, it hardly seems like boondocking), more than a hundred RV parks are scattered around Baja. You'll find one just about anywhere you'd care to visit, as well as a few in places you wouldn't visit on a bet. Facilities range from super-luxurious star resorts complete with gourmet restaurants to rustic fishing camps with no amenities other than hospitality, cold beer, and friendly faces.

By the way, 99 percent of your RV neighbors will be from the United States or Canada; few Mexicans own RVs. Those who can afford them prefer to stay in first-class hotels when traveling. They don't quite understand why we think traveling in a small tin box is fun. (I don't understand it either, but it *is* fun.)

Space rents for RV parks range from a couple dollars a day to as much as $35 a day at one luxury place. One of our favorite commercial parks is at Bahía de Los Angeles. There, a cement patio and an electrical hookup cost about $10.00 a day. A water truck passes through with drinking water and will fill your tanks for a small fee. The sea provides a bountiful harvest of clams and scallops, not to mention fish for those willing to toss a line in the water. Kids knock on the door every evening to see if you want to buy their freshly caught fish or live pin scallops still in the shell. A nearby restaurant serves excellent meals of fish, lobster, and tough but tasty Mexican steaks.

Two little markets in the village supply basic foods, such as chickens, coffee, and sterilized milk. Folks on tight budgets depend on the sea for much of their food, with clam chowder, sautéed scallops, or rockfish fillets "Veracruzano" providing wonderful gourmet dinners. "We load up our cabinets with canned goods and such before we leave San Diego," said one lady in Bahía de Los Angeles. "We seldom have to buy groceries here other than eggs, tortillas, and fresh veggies. We feel as if we are eating for free." "We made a deal for two month's space rent at $190, so I don't see how we could possibly spend more than $500 out of pocket for two months," said her husband, "and that's including the gas to get here and back!"

When driving in Baja during our last trip, I counted the number of vehicles on the road and noted that about half of them were RVs with U.S. or Canadian license plates. Sometimes it looked as if we *norteamericanos* had taken over the peninsula for our own campgrounds. My personal experience has been very positive in Mexico. The questionnaires we hand out to RV travelers in Mexico include a question about safety. Unanimously, people tell us they feel very secure driving in Mexico. Well, that shouldn't be too surprising: If they didn't feel safe they wouldn't be there.

North for a Cool Summer

Seasonal travel is not the snowbirds' exclusive kingdom. Summer heat and humidity send thousands on the reverse trek. Retirees who select Phoenix or Tucson for retirement because of the lovely winter weather can be bored silly by the searing heat of July and August. That's why you'll see Arizona license plates in Montana, Michigan, and Maine during the summer. Spring and fall are beautiful in Missouri and Indiana, but summers are suffocating and might better be spent elsewhere.

We interviewed one Phoenix couple who visit the Oregon coast every summer. Their favorite town, Brookings, seldom sees summer highs above 70°F, and the couple always sleep under an electric blanket. "We've never used the motor home's air conditioner in Brookings," the husband said, adding, "We've never seen the temperature reach 80!" Other RVs visit here in the winter, as well, because the fishing is good all year and it never freezes. Be prepared for winter rain, however.

Folks who choose to retire on the Gulf Coast of Florida because of mild winters dearly love to escape the hot summers there. The hills of West Virginia, North Carolina, Kentucky, and Tennessee offer welcome deliverance from Florida's steamy summers. The Atlantic Coast, particularly up around Maine, offers some delightfully cool places to park and relax. This might be the time to visit those Canadian RV friends you see every year in your winter neighborhood.

RV Budgets

The question of how much it costs to live full-time in an RV is a complicated one. All of us have different incomes and budgets. Those with huge mortgages on a deluxe motor home will naturally spend much of their income on payments. Some spend a lot of time driving from place to place, consuming gasoline or diesel fuel and staying in fancy resorts every night. Getting from one place to another isn't cheap—RV fuel consumption is much higher than that of a typical sedan. But the average RV full-timer moves only to change locations for the season, and ideally the rig will be paid for. Renting park space by the month rather than by the night reduces costs drastically. The truly economical lifestyles include a considerable amount of boondocking and freebies.

One lady, who makes her home in a 24-foot RV, told us, "Last winter, when I left my Michigan home base to go to the California desert, I found I could easily get by on $350 a month." She went on to add that during the winter, before she started full-timing, her heating, gas, and electric bills at home totaled close to $300 a month, so getting by on $350 was easy.

Not everybody can manage full-timing on $350 a month, of course. We all know folks who spend more than that on cigarettes and booze. So how did our friend do it? She stayed at California's Slab City for zero rent. The gentle desert climate all but eliminated the need for heat or air conditioning (Slab City has no utility hookups anyway). She used three 5-gallon tanks of propane for cooking and an occasional touch of warmth when the temperature dropped below 60°F outdoors. A solar panel supplemented her 12-volt system for lights, radio, and cassette player (TV reception is lousy in Slab City). Her total utility costs came to less than $25 for the full three-month sojourn—an average of $8.00 per month.

"Since I'm single, my food costs are low," she said. "Neighbors at Slab City always share rides for shopping in Niland, so I drove the 2 miles to town just every other week or so. I needed to dump my holding tanks anyway. My gasoline bill was almost nothing."

In addition, she shared expenses with three other single ladies for a day trip to Mexico (about an hour's drive), plus one overnight expedition to challenge the slot machines and black-jack tables in Nevada (about four and a half hours away). "We shared a large room—at the senior-citizen rate of $33 with two double beds—and we took advantage of the 99-cent breakfast specials and the enormous buffets in the casino restaurants. That was the only month that I spent $350, and then only because I couldn't make the slot machines pay off!"

Chapter Eleven
Singles and Retirement

Perhaps you've noticed how ads in retirement publications picture retired couples? Always strikingly handsome, tenderly holding hands as they gaze lovingly upon their new retirement home (or Cadillac, or yacht, or whatever the advertisement is pushing). The husband is attired in an expensive Irish-tweed sport coat, and his distinguished, platinum-toned hair sweeps back from an aristocratic forehead. (He's never bald, is he?) His wife's hairdo discreetly reveals a few silver highlights. (If we didn't know she was retired, we'd assume she was about thirty-seven years old.) This typical retired couple is successful, affluent, and looking forward to a future of golf games, gourmet dinners, and bridge parties as they entertain brilliantly in their fabulous new home.

You don't need someone to tell you that this picture is far from accurate. Besides the fact that few of us men can brag about our aristocratic foreheads, most of us actually look our ages and many really are bald. More importantly, many retirees don't have that loving other person to hold hands with. Many people approach retirement alone. They also find themselves far from affluent, with their minds on matters other than bridge and golf games.

What happens when your spouse dies unexpectedly just before your planned retirement date? All those wonderful plans you've made get knocked into that famous cocked hat. What about the homemaker who spends her productive years raising a family, only to find herself divorced once the children

213

are on their own? Where do you go from there? I think I can speak from experience in this matter; my first wife died unexpectedly after thirty years of marriage, just as we were planning our retirement.

Single retirees face different challenges than married couples do. Their economic and lifestyle strategies must be different, too. If being single is not something new, most people without relationships do fine, at least while they are working. But once they leave the workplace, where most of their friends are, some find themselves faced with unexpected changes of lifestyle. The problem is most severe in the case of single women.

Women and Single Retirement

For every 100 older men in the United States there are 146 older women. This ratio increases with age to a high of 260 women for each 100 men for those eighty-five and older. Only 41 percent of these women are married, compared with 78 percent of the men eighty-five and older. Furthermore, more than half of America's women are on their own by the time they are fifty-five years old—before they reach retirement age. Women who retire at age sixty can expect to live another twenty-five years or so and can expect to have to make do with less, so it's doubly important they plan well for retirement.

Divorced or widowed women who manage to find careers in the workplace often find their social lives revolving around work. But once single women leave the workplace, they find a void that needs to be filled by friends and family. Should a retired woman be short of either, she faces a lonely future.

Women also have fewer options or activities that society considers "acceptable" and with which they feel comfortable. A man can be perfectly happy tent camping and fishing in the woods, wearing the same socks a week at a time. Most retired single women not only feel uncomfortable camping in a flimsy tent but also hate fishing—and dirty socks. A man may think nothing of living just about anywhere, but many women feel apprehensive in all but the most secure situations.

Chances are that she will also be short on retirement funds. It's well known that women earn significantly less than men for equal work, so they end up with lower Social Security payments, company pensions, and savings accounts. Furthermore, because of age discrimination, women are frequently pressured to quit work and draw their pensions or Social Security at the earliest possible age, rather than waiting until maximum benefits are due. Finding part-time work is also more difficult for older women. The result of women's low lifetime earnings is that the typical woman's Social Security checks are often half that of a man who earned good wages all his working life. Single people, both men and women, need different retirement strategies than married couples do to survive on a shoestring. But single women need miracles.

Single Transitions

One might assume that the transition into retirement is easier for folks who never married, or for those who have lived most of their adult lives as single persons. Why should retirement be a traumatic experience? After all, aren't they accustomed to a single life? It might seem that the only thing to do now is to adjust to a lifestyle that doesn't include working every day. Often it is an easy adjustment. Yet some find retirement especially lonely, particularly if their entire social lives have centered on their jobs. At work they had fellow employees to socialize with, friends to talk with, and companions at lunch. When they stop working, all of that is suddenly gone. Also gone are regular paychecks, medical benefits, and Christmas bonuses. It's a different world out there when you quit work.

For those fortunate enough to have built up a network of friends and acquaintances, leaving this umbrella probably doesn't make much sense. Although you may be living in an expensive area, you might well be better off staying where you are and keeping your friends. This can often be done by cutting back on your most expensive budget item—housing.

But if your friends do come mostly from your business or workplace world, and if you have few nearby family connections, you could find that you have little to lose by going someplace more economical, perhaps a place with a nicer climate. You can then start building a new life, acquiring new friends, and exploring new interests. If you're already living in a high-cost area, moving somewhere more economical might be the ticket to a better life. This is true for both singles and couples.

In many economical retirement locations, particularly in smaller towns, small furnished apartments can be found for much less than $500 a month, including utilities. These apartments are perfectly adequate for a single person trying to get by on a shoestring. We recall looking at a studio apartment in a small town on Oregon's Rogue River—a delightfully peaceful and pretty place for economical living. The rent was about $375. Shopping was a four-minute walk from the door. A single woman would feel perfectly safe here.

Once settled, you can see how you like the area, making friends and exploring a new lifestyle. As a new kid on the block, you may find that the best way to begin making new friends and acquaintances is through volunteer work. Go to the local senior-citizen office and apply for work with RSVP or another volunteer program. Within days, you'll start building a new network of friends, and before long you will have more friends than you ever made by working every day. One of our correspondents, a retired man, told us that he makes friends through square dancing. He says, "Just check with the clubs, like the Elks, the Eagles, and the American Legion, as well as with the local chamber of commerce."

Shared Housing

Earlier we discussed the concept of shared housing as an effective way for couples to cut their living expenses. But as a single person, shared housing can dramatically lower your cash flow, at the same time elevating your standard of living. Later on, in the "Traveling Singles" section, we'll talk about the "single supplement" penalty, in which single persons are charged just as much for some things as a couple pays. Hotel rooms, cruise cabins, and house rentals, for example, are doubled for the single person. Monthly rents or house payments are the same, whether one person or a family of ten occupies the domicile.

The possibilities are intriguing. Instead of paying $400 a month for rent and utilities in an ordinary, cheap (perhaps risky) neighborhood, you can join with partners to pool your resources, permitting you to reside in a upscale neighborhood, with tranquil and eye-pleasing surroundings. Your lifestyle also benefits from the low crime rates and better police protection typically found in more affluent residential districts.

Instead of a cramped, two-room apartment in the inner city, you could live in a lovely suburban home with three or four bedrooms, a gourmet kitchen, a large living room, and a separate TV room, complete with a landscaped patio for barbecues and lounging. You might prefer to share a spacious apartment or condo in an elegant section of town with a private deck and a view of the ocean (or the river or the mountains).

Sharing is definitely not the same as renting a room in a private home. Being a lodger involves little commitment, and you are rarely considered part of the household. You are a stranger, a paying guest in someone else's home. The key to a successful living arrangement is the word *shared*. The ideal situation is one where you and your housemates agree on formal rules and arrangements and form a surrogate family. Sometimes it is wise to get everything in writing, so there can be no misunderstandings. If it happens to be your home you are sharing, rather than a rental, you need to be sure you are protected (and because it's your place, you may end up being a little more autocratic).

House sharing is a particularly successful strategy for single or widowed women, when two, three, or four pool their resources to enjoy dignified, comfortable living arrangements without giving up individuality. Having friends living together also provides the security of a support group in emergencies. Should someone in the household become ill or have an accident, having caring friends around could be a lifesaver. Women usually prefer to have other women for house partners, but mixed-gender sharing is also common. This doesn't necessarily have to involve romance or intimacy (assuming that's not what you want), if that is made crystal clear from the beginning. Having a gentleman around the place to fix the roof and change the storm windows can come in handy, while a man might appreciate women's cooking skills from time to time or a sympathetic ear when he feels low.

Let's look at the financial side of home sharing. Assume that the standard of living and lifestyle to which you would like to become accustomed requires at least $1,200 a month for rent and utilities. This amounts to $14,400 a year. That's quite a chunk of your budget, right? By sharing with two companions, your expenses drop to $400 a month, a savings of $9,600 a year— over a ten-year period, a savings of nearly $100,000. This is money you could spend on travel, a new automobile every once in a while, or any frivolous expense you might care to indulge in. If you manage to share an automobile between house-sharing companions, the savings are even more.

If you're a single home owner, you might find that a compatible companion or two sharing house payments and everyday expenditures makes perfectly good sense. While your expenses are cut drastically, you still accumulate equity in your house. Sharing household chores makes living easier and gives you more time to get out of the house and enjoy your retirement. With friends watching over the house and paying the expenses, you can travel without worrying. On the other hand, it could make equally good sense to sell the house, put the money into investments, and move in with someone else. (Of course, please consult your financial adviser and family members before making an important decision of that nature.)

How do you go about finding partners? A glance at any newspaper classified section often turns up individuals seeking home sharing. You might place your own ad (with a box number so that you don't receive unwelcome visitors). Screen the candidates carefully to make sure you like and trust them. It goes without saying that compatibility is the highest-ranking consideration in house sharing. An alternate way of choosing companions is through the *Travel Companion Exchange Newsletter* (described in the "Traveling Singles" section). Although this service is basically for putting singles in touch with travel companions, it's also a possibility for locating home-share companions. Jens Jurgen, the founder of the group, says, "It takes time and flexibility to find housemates who are compatible with your lifestyle and nature. Making a decision to live with someone requires far more 'checking out' than merely traveling together." References and credit checks are a must, he advises.

However, making a trip together isn't a bad idea. If you can survive a cruise, a tour, or a motor-home trip together, you'll get a preview of what living together might be like. The best part is that two can travel almost as cheaply as one. The worst thing that could happen is that you will ruin a two-week vacation, but you will also avoid a semi-permanent disaster.

Retirement Communities

Not everyone can be comfortable pulling up stakes and relocating as a stranger in a strange neighborhood or living in someone else's home. A convenient, worry-free alternative for singles is the concept of a non-prepay retirement community, the kind where you simply rent by the month. In a living situation like this, you will find a large number of people of your age group from which to select your friends. Aside from medical insurance, clothing, and phone use, most of your basic expenses are covered.

The retirement communities we investigated in Oregon are typical of most sections of the country, offering high-quality living in secure apartments with fees starting at $1,200 a month.

This charge includes two or three meals daily (served in a pleasant dining room), weekly housekeeping and linen service, twenty-four-hour staffing, cable TV, social and recreational programs, scheduled transportation, off-street parking, and all utilities except telephone. These are generally large complexes, often with a social director who arranges bridge games, arts and crafts, evening entertainment, and other activities. A van will take you for shopping and doctor appointments. We've also looked at places that charge as much as $3,900 a month, but these places are so luxurious that it's like being on a permanent cruise. However, it isn't difficult to find similar accommodations for much less per month, but these will be smaller complexes, sometimes with only a dozen or so efficiency apartments. The amenities aren't as nice, and sometimes only dinner is served. With fewer residents, you could be stuck with people you don't care for, and you won't get much in the way of entertainment. But the homes are much more affordable; we saw one small apartment that rented for $900 a month, the same as a Social Security benefit for some folks.

There are several advantages to this type of living arrangement. Besides the fact that your monthly expenses are predictable, without having to make a serious commitment, you can explore the community to see whether it is desirable for your long-term retirement. One manager of a retirement facility pointed out that she encourages people to do a three-month trial before pulling up stakes in their hometowns or doing anything drastic.

"This is particularly important upon the death of a spouse," she said. "Too often the surviving spouse isn't capable of making rational decisions in the short run. She may feel utterly isolated, lonely, and trapped in an empty home. In a retirement community, she'll be surrounded by friendly people. Because she has no long-term obligation, this is a relatively painless way to try out a new lifestyle and to try on a new community for size."

One caution: Most residents of retirement homes naturally

will be older—there are no multigenerational retirement homes. Look around and see if you'll find compatible companions, retirees of your own age and enthusiasm with whom you can relate. Just because you're retired doesn't mean you're old!

You'll find retirement establishments all over the country. To locate them, simply open up the yellow pages to "Retirement." To choose a retirement community in another city, visit your local library and ask for the out-of-town phone books. Then choose the city or town where you might want to retire, check the listings for something that sounds nice, and do some shopping for price and quality. Charges vary widely, depending upon the community, the area's cost of living, and the quality of the facility.

Be careful about places where you must "buy in" to the facility or sign a long-term lease. There is nothing wrong with these concepts; it's just that if you are looking around for low-cost retirement alternatives, you probably aren't interested in putting up $50,000 in nonrefundable front money just to see whether you like your new retirement location. If you find you aren't happy, you would be far better off if all you were responsible for was a thirty-day notice before shoving off. Also, don't expect to find reasonable rents in a large city or in an expensive area. Like everything else in an expensive location, the cost of a retirement home is likely to be extravagant, too.

When you find something you can afford, check it out. The best time to visit is for lunch or dinner, when you can sample the quality and variety of the food. How is the place decorated? How does the staff interact with residents? Are they professional and caring? Is the place quiet or noisy? Do people seem friendly? Do they socialize well? Don't hesitate to speak with residents to see how they like living there. Many retirement communities have furnished guest apartments set up for trial visits. At the least, arrange to stay a weekend to get the feel of the place.

Traveling Singles

Many people view retirement as a time for foreign travel. After all those years of two-week vacations, mostly spent fixing things around the house, some travel seems to be in order. Unless your budget is so restricted that trips farther than the grocery store are out of the question, this is your chance.

Of course, it will have to be done on a shoestring. As a person who has specialized in budget travel, I can assure you that it can be done—and that it can be fun! In fact, a lot of the fun is just in seeing how inexpensively you can travel, particularly in foreign countries. Budget travelers often pass time comparing expenses. The person who found a great room for $20 is one up on the poor dunce who paid $25 and didn't get breakfast.

If your budget won't even allow for a $20 room, you can often travel to the great vacation hot spots and receive your room free as part of a work package. Chapter 3 tells about how to find part-time jobs in resorts during the height of the season and earn some money, as well.

Travel for singles can, however, be unfairly made expensive because of something called the single supplement. That is, most hotels charge a single person the same price as two people in the same room. Some cruise ships are reluctant to book a single in the first place. It turns out that the real profit is what the cruise ship takes in on drinks, gambling, and side excursions. They make twice as much when there are two people in a cabin. When taking a taxi, it costs just as much for one passenger as for two or more. And on and on.

The solution is to find a travel companion to share costs. Compatible friends enjoy their trips much more than singles, not just because of companionship, conversation, and sharing of experiences, but also because they have more confidence to go more places and do more adventurous things than they would by themselves. And by sharing costs the travel budget goes much further.

If you have no adventurous acquaintances, how do you find a compatible partner? Sometimes it's difficult finding someone with the time, money, and desire to take a trip with a stranger. Senior-citizen newspapers often have classified ads from those looking for travel companions.

One way to find a traveling partner is through a singles travel club that helps singles in search of companions get in touch with each other. The recognized national leader in this partner-matching field is Travel Companion Exchange (TCE) of Amityville, New York. For twenty years TCE has been bringing together travelers of similar interests through a newsletter and computer match-up service. Members list their interests and places they'd like to travel and describe the kind of travel companion they would like to find.

"This isn't a lonely hearts club or a dating service," says Jens Jurgen, the company president, "although it works well in that respect. We've had a lot of marriages. I remember one elderly lady who met and married a gentleman through the service. Then, a few years later I saw her name on the list again. Her husband died on a trip on the Orient Express, so she signed up to find another one!"

Jurgen says, "I realize that opposite-sex matches are not always platonic, but that doesn't trouble me. I'm catering to the needs of single people needing traveling companions." Romance isn't necessarily the objective. Jens points out that men often don't like to share with another male. "After the army, never again," seems to be the attitude. And women, although open to sharing with another female, often prefer a man. Some of the reasons given: "I like to have someone to dance with," and "I feel more secure with a male travel partner, and I like help with the luggage."

For inexperienced, elderly, or handicapped travelers, having a partner makes sense. Women traveling alone miss a lot by their reluctance to visit some very interesting places. It goes without saying that you must be very careful when using this kind of service. You need to make it quite clear what the traveling relationship will be and what it will not be. TCE suggests that you and your prospective companion meet and get to know one another before setting out on adventures. One woman complained that her lady traveling companion "smoked like a chimney and wouldn't drive under 80 miles an hour." A few meetings beforehand might have helped them avoid subsequent bad feelings. Though TCE is multigenerational in nature, there are plenty of retired members, with the majority of listings by people over fifty—and some up to eighty-five years old. Contact the Travel Companion Exchange, Box 833, Amityville, NY 11701; (631) 454–0880; or on the Web at www.travelcompanions.com. There's a yearly membership fee.

RVs for Singles' Retirement

Single RV travelers have their own clubs. In Chapter 10, we discussed the Escapees RV club; it has a group called SOLOs, which is for singles only. The singles RV club we know best is Loners on Wheels (LoW). The members we've interviewed are enthusiastic about the club and continually talk about what it has done for them. This is a singles-only club, although married couples are not discouraged from joining in the evening campfire get-togethers or dances. Members stress that this is not a lonely hearts club, although that's not to say romances do not bloom. Should a couple begin traveling together in the same rig, or if they get married, they are expelled from the club on the grounds that they have "committed matrimony". However, there's no ill feeling toward those errant members who have fallen by the wayside. In fact, there's a general celebration and a genuine invitation to keep in touch.

The club has its own home park in Deming, New Mexico. Members can stay there for $2.00 a day for boondocking (without water or electricity hookups) or $150 a month with utilities. There are LoW chapters in almost all states in the United States and all the Canadian provinces, with temporary regional headquarters in popular seasonal campgrounds where members congregate. Club rallies are held year-round, following the weather, in places like Florida, Texas, Mexico, California, Canada, and just about anywhere else RVers might want to visit. For full information, write to Loners on Wheels, P.O. Box 1060, Poplar Bluff, MO 63702.

As part of the research for this book, my wife and I decided to visit a LoW gathering to see firsthand what it was all about. So one balmy January evening, we drove our motor home off the pavement to make camp amid thousands of trailers, campers, and motor homes in the California desert setting of Slab City.

It was a pleasant, moonlit night, with a slight breeze blowing in from the nearby Salton Sea. We breathed sagebrush-perfumed air deeply as we walked across the sandy desert to where the Loners have their semipermanent headquarters. Several official trailers were set up around a large cement slab, which served as a dance floor at night and a shuffleboard court by day. A blazing campfire had drawn a dozen Loners, who were drinking coffee, cocktails, or hot cider. They were chatting and making plans for a square dance the next afternoon.

We explained that we were doing research for a book and were interested in talking to single retirees. We'd come to the right place; the campers were eager to talk to us. "Man or woman — life is a difficult experience to handle alone," remarked one single man who had just moved into retirement. "I've found the solution to my loneliness through RV travel and belonging to Loners on Wheels."

As is the case at most LoW camp-outs, about 60 percent of the campers here were women. I asked one lady, "How do you feel about safety out here in the desert?" She explained that before retirement, she had been a bank teller in a big city, adding, "During the two years before I retired, I was held up at gunpoint five times! Now ask me again how safe I feel here!"

Another woman, a widow, said, "If it weren't for this club and all of the wonderfully supportive friends in it, tonight I would be sitting alone watching television in a little two-room apartment in downtown Seattle." She smiled at her friends and said, "I've never felt safer in my life."

An eighty-five-year-old lady known as Duchess Grubb added, "This is a lifesaving group that has literally gotten people out of wheelchairs. We have camp-outs and rallies going on every month somewhere and caravans going in all directions." Duchess lives in her RV half of each year, commuting from her Pacific Northwest home—where she spends summers—to Death Valley and the Salton Sea for the winter.

"Traveling with friends makes all the difference in the world," explained another LoW member. "I'd never have the courage to do it alone." With other club members in a caravan—always ready and willing to assist—RV traveling becomes relatively anxiety-free. Socializing over breakfast, cooking dinner together, or singing around the evening campfire there is no time to be bored or to feel alone. Because most RV clubs have a philosophy of "Never let a stranger into camp without a hug," RV retirement becomes a heartwarming experience. For singles, it is the most economical retirement lifestyle we've seen. This gives "retirement on a shoestring" a special meaning.

Over the past years, we've interviewed several LoW members, asking about their budgets. The replies vary widely, from one lady who claimed to live on $360 a month, to others to spend up to $1,200 for basics. When we asked one single RVer if he could estimate his budget, he replied, "I don't have to estimate. I can tell you to the nickel. I spend $833 a month. That's what I get from Social Security, and I spend it all!"

Josi Roth, president of Loners on Wheels, says, "I know one man who brags about living on $550 a month, and I believe him. Of course dinners out and local shows are not included, but he does travel and he enjoys a nice standard of living. Many people do it easily on about $1,200 a month. They keep moving to a minimum as fuel has become pricey today. During one winter at the Slabs, I spent approximately $100 a month for propane (for heating), gasoline (for electric generator), and more gasoline for grocery shopping and twice monthly drives to the rest stop in Brawley to fill up with water and dump my holding tanks. Add groceries, and it was a cheap winter. However, being a shopping junkie took care of the rest of my income."

*C*hapter Twelve
Foreign Retirement

I t's not as easy as it once was, but it's still entirely possible to retire in a foreign country on a shoestring budget. But not in just any foreign country. At one time, American travelers with a few dollars in their jeans felt like a millionaires, sipping fine wine in Paris cafes, savoring beef Wellington in London restaurants, or playing roulette in Monaco. A seventeenth-century stone cottage with a view of the Mediterranean rented for $200 a month, and a sumptuous meal—including wine—cost $10. Many retired North Americans routinely traveled abroad to spend several months a year in Provence or on the Costa del Sol because it was cheaper than staying home. No longer. Today you'll feel indigent in most of Europe. That Mediterranean cottage will now cost $3,000 a month, and that sumptuous meal has a sumptuous price. Even European economy prices would be expensive here at home. Furthermore, it costs a small fortune to get there; you still can't catch a bus to France. The days of living in Europe on a shoestring are sweet memories.

But if you have a dream of an exotic retirement, don't despair. There are still a few foreign countries where a shoestring budget can sustain a dignified, comfortable, and stimulating lifestyle. Instead of retirement in Europe, look closer to home—to Mexico and Central America. The countries I'll discuss in this chapter do not require that you spend a lot on transportation to visit. Airfares are expensive, but you can drive your car or travel by bus. Long stays or permanent retirement are practical on a budget backed only by Social Security. Most importantly, these countries welcome retirees.

Before we go any further, I'll make an important point: I do not recommend foreign retirement for folks who have little or no cash reserved for emergencies. Yes, you can easily live on a shoe-string budget in some countries, but if you *have* to live on a shoe-string budget, my recommendation is that you shouldn't try it! Unexpected expenses can and will arise; without a safety net, you may well find yourself in a pickle.

Why? Back home, there are city, county, and state agencies to make sure you are somehow taken care of in emergency situa-tions. But Mexico and Central American countries do not pro-vide welfare assistance even for their own citizens—and they certainly won't for you. Welfare in the third world is the respon-sibility of family and friends—not the government. If you run out of money, you'll either be on your own or else dependent upon the charity of fellow North Americans. Furthermore, if you are truly indigent, the host government can take a very dim view of your being there. You are rarely permitted to work in foreign countries unless you are a legal resident, and you can get into trouble if you try.

Becoming a legal resident of a foreign country poses a prob-lem for some low-income retirees. You need a minimum monthly retirement income to receive resident status. If you fall below this minimum, you won't qualify for year-round residency. The good news is that, except for in Mexico, an average Social Security check should be enough to qualify you for residency. However, the process of obtaining legal residency can be expen-sive unless you have the perseverance to arrange it all yourself.

Don't let a lack of steady income discourage you. Many expa-triates simply stay the limit of their visas and then make a bus or automobile trip to the nearest border to renew them. After a day or two at the beach, they return to their adopted country. They look forward to these inexpensive sojourns, which are necessary every three or six months, depending upon the country. If your budget doesn't allow for this travel, these mandatory trips across the border could strain your resources. Be aware that there's always the possibility that both Mexico and Costa Rica might at some time in the future begin enforcing rules that limit you to six months each year without applying for residency. But again, your Social Security check will usually cover your minimum income requirements.

A final consideration is that neither Medicare nor Medicaid is recognized outside the United States. You will be on your own as far as medical and hospital bills go. The bright side of this picture is that doctors and hospitals charge a fraction of what they do back home, and medical plans for a year can cost less than a month's medical insurance in the States. But unless you join the country's health insurance program, you will need cash to pay your medical bills, however small they may be.

If you do have backup funds for emergencies, you might enjoy the excitement of living in another culture. There's no question that you can do it in style and on very little money. In Mexico, Costa Rica, and Guatemala, your generic Social Security check of $850 to $1,350 a month can cover all expenses. This amount allows a couple a quality lifestyle that would be totally unthinkable in the United States or Canada. Many retirees cover all basic expenses, dine out frequently, do some traveling, and even hire part-time servants.

While it's true that living costs are dramatically lower in some countries, you must remember that there are limits to your lifestyle; nothing is free. If your liquor bills are $800 a month, you'll be hard-pressed to survive on $850 a month. If you decide to rent a villa with a swimming pool for $800 a month, you'll have to make some drastic adjustments to your food budget!

The big plus of foreign living is that you'll find it extremely easy to make friends with your new neighbors—the native people as well as North Americans. A special camaraderie arises among expatriates in a foreign setting. They come together as if by magnetism. You'll find close friends among people you may never have spoken with back home. There are no strangers in an expatriate community.

You'll also have adventures exploring scenic coasts, spectacular mountains and forests, and picturesque villages. Making new friends among the native people and learning to speak the language are other benefits. My wife and I enjoy living in a foreign country so much that we spend half of each year in Costa Rica. We've previously lived in Mexico, and briefly in Spain and have traveled extensively in South America. But we choose Central America as our present part-time retirement destination.

By the way, in the following sections on retirement in Mexico and Central America, I often use the word *gringo*. Understand that this is not a pejorative term in Latin America. It generally means any person who is light-skinned and who speaks English as a first language. Latin Americans sometimes call Germans and Swiss *gringos* simply because they are often blond and light-skinned. The practice is similar to our using *Aussie* for an Australian or *Brit* for anyone from the British Isles.

Let's start our discussion of foreign retirement with Mexico. It's the most accessible foreign country suitable for shoestring retirement.

Retirement in Mexico

Nineteen years ago, Don Merwin and I coauthored a book called *Choose Mexico for Retirement*, describing how to retire in that country on a monthly expenditure of $400. This fantastically low budget even allowed for servants and travel about the country! In those days Mexico was a true paradise for North Americans retiring on a shoestring.

Our book sold 50,000 copies the first year. Thousands of retirees from the United States and Canada discovered the joys and benefits of retirement in a friendly country that welcomes foreign neighbors. The newcomers found fascinating lifestyles in colonial cities, picturesque villages, and tropical beach settings. Living graciously on a shoestring budget was only part of the equation. The vast majority didn't make the move to Mexico because of finances; that was a secondary consideration. The $400 figure was a minimum budget, and most spent several times that figure for elevated lifestyles. The attraction was the opportunity for gracious living among other expatriates, a choice of perfect climates, and immersion in a different culture. The fact that the equivalent of a Social Security income provided a standard of living far better than they could hope for at home for the same money was merely icing on the cake.

As you might expect, the cost of living has risen steadily over the years. Although today it would take at least twice as many dollars to maintain the $400-a-month lifestyle of nineteen years ago, we must realize that costs have risen in North America over those intervening years as well. Social Security benefits have also risen. A minimum budget today would be in the neighborhood of $800 to $1,000 a month. It's difficult to state an exact amount because the dollar-to-peso exchange rate can fluctuate over time. At the time of writing, the value of the dollar is steadily dropping against the peso, which means that prices for those using dollars are rising, even though prices in pesos remain constant. There's every chance that soon the reverse will happen, and dollars will be worth more pesos in exchange, in which case prices will drop for those of us on the dollar standard.

What can you do with $800 today? That's about $200 a week, about four times what most skilled laborers earn. On $200 a week, it's possible to rent a modest home or apartment, eat well (including dining out at least once a week at a nice restaurant), and take care of all your basic needs. On incomes of about $1,000 to $1,200 a month, a couple can do some traveling and afford to hire a maid to take care of the house and do the laundry. This budget even covers medical insurance. One thing that makes this lifestyle possible is that you don't need to spend money on heating and air conditioning.

Don Merwin and I take turns occasionally spending a month or so in Mexico in order to update *Choose Mexico*. During one visit before devaluation, my wife and I traveled to a popular retirement area, rented an apartment for a month, and kept scrupulous records of our expenditures. We found that a basic monthly budget would come under $800, so rest assured that it is still possible.

A semiretired couple who live in Mazatlán had this to say: "Labor, food, and locally manufactured goods are much less expensive than their counterparts in the United States. We go to the movies here every week—a ticket costs $2.00, and popcorn is 80 cents. Our maid, who comes in six days a week, eight hours each day, is paid approximately $50 per week, and she is very well paid by Mexican standards. On the other hand, if you want to buy imported electronics or appliances, be prepared to pay double for it."

In one respect, year-round retirement here isn't as easy as it used to be. The Mexican government raised the minimum income requirement for a resident permit and becoming a full-time resident. At one time a couple needed just $550 a month in retirement income; today it's around $1,000 for a single person and $1,500 for married couples. However, this income require-ment is cut in half if you own your own home in Mexico, which brings the amount to only $750, well within the range of most Social Security checks.

However, if you can't qualify financially, it isn't an insur-mountable problem. Tourist visas are good for six months at a time. You simply make a bus trip to the border every half year, do some shopping, obtain another tourist visa, and return for another six months. A large number of retirees don't care to live in Mexico full-time anyway. They prefer to spend November through March enjoying the sunny weather here, and they then return to enjoy the best part of the year at home.

Where North Americans Live Mexico is a large country with an amaz-ing variety of climates, landscapes, and panoramas. From tropi-cal Pacific beaches to high, snow-clad mountains, you can find almost any kind of environment imaginable. The climate on the central plateau can be described as "perpetual spring," and the Pacific and Gulf coasts enjoy "perpetual summer."

Many locations in Mexico make wonderful places to retire, too many to be described here in a few paragraphs. From Baja California to the Yucatán Peninsula, retirement locations are described in the book *Choose Mexico*. Many bookstores and libraries have copies, so before you make any decisions, check it out.

In Chapter 10, we discussed RV retirement in Mexico during the winter months. This can certainly be done on a shoestring. But spending a summer in Baja California would be only slightly less uncomfortable than spending a summer in a pizza oven. The Mexican mainland is where most North Americans choose conventional retirement living.

Some folks dream of finding an out-of-the-way place where the residents are all natives, a place where retirees can live an idyllic existence. However, unless you are fluent in Spanish, you'll probably want to try your retirement in a place where other North Americans can keep you company. That isn't because Mexicans aren't friendly; it's simply because you'd soon become bored silly with no one to communicate with.

One area with lots of expatriates and a perfect spring climate is Guadalajara and environs. More than 30,000 North Americans call this region home. Between the city and the many small communities around Lake Chapala, you'll find many clusters of English-speakers among whom you will immediately be accepted as friends. Helping newcomers get their start in Mexico is part of the tradition here. Rents can be expensive in some Guadalajara neighborhoods and lakeside communities, but you'll have no problem finding accommodations to match your budget just a short distance from the high-priced places. We have a friend who recently found a small house near the lake for less than $200 a month.

Others prefer the tropics, settling in romantic places like Acapulco, Puerto Vallarta, or Mazatlán. Although these places have a deserved reputation as expensive, jet-set resorts, you'll discover that there are always low-cost homes for rent, although they may be away from the beaches. The more popular the resort, the more low-cost housing is needed for the many Mexican employees who work for tourist businesses. This is where you'll find housing bargains in working-class neighborhoods.

Choose Mexico details a large number of retirement possibilities in Mexico. With research and shrewd planning, retiring there on your Social Security check is entirely possible.

Driving in Mexico Most Mexican highways are adequately paved, but they are not designed for high-speed driving. Mexican drivers tend to drive slowly on the highway; many feel that the slower they drive, the longer their vehicles will last. It's best to adopt this local practice; it's a lot safer that way. The worst thing about most Mexican highways is that they often lack shoulders and have neither centerlines nor markings on the side of the pavement. This is all right when driving during the daytime, but it's *not* safe at night. A slight miscalculation or oversteering when oncoming headlights blind you can send you over an embankment. An encounter with a Brahma bull sleeping on the pavement can be deadly for the animal *and* for you. Repeat after me, "I will *never* drive at night in Mexico!"

An even more important piece of driving advice: Never drive in Mexico without *Mexican* automobile insurance. Non-Mexican insurance is not valid. Fortunately, insurance is inexpensive if you buy from the right source. Don't believe guidebooks that tell you that all Mexican insurance costs the same. Details on insurance and other essentials can be found in *Choose Mexico* or a good travel guide for Mexico.

Is Mexico Safe? This frequently asked question is frustrating for anyone who has traveled in Mexico. The misinformation and distorted views of Mexico held by many North Americans are difficult to dispel—until they actually travel there. The truth is that the Mexican people are gentle, polite, and law-abiding. The law is very strict and tough on habitual criminals. Upon the third conviction, a convict automatically receives a twenty-year sentence. As you can imagine, this policy discourages criminals. People who have retired in Mexico will often tell you that they have no fear of walking the streets of an average Mexican town at any time, day or night. That's not to say Mexico doesn't have its share of crime, particularly in the bigger cities; in Mexico, as anywhere in the world, the larger the city, the more crime.

I've heard many horror stories over the years about someone's brother-in-law's friend who had difficulties with the police after being involved in a minor accident. Well, I suspect that the rest of the story is that the brother-in-law's friend didn't have insurance. In my years of driving in Mexico—nearly 100,000 miles to date—I've never been unfairly hassled by the police. I've been stopped many times for speeding, but each time I knew full well that I was breaking the law. I just hadn't expected to get caught. I've interviewed many Americans who have been involved in accidents in Mexico; they've had nothing but praise for their insurance companies and the local authorities.

In an issue of *Loners on Wheels Newsletter*, a retired single lady, driving her motor home toward Cancun, Mexico, described an accident this way: "Two days into Mexico, like a turkey I stopped for a feathered turkey sitting in the road. A big green truck loaded with oranges didn't stop. The trucker's insurance paid for my damages. It's strictly against the law in Mexico to hit anyone stopped on the road! The police and my insurance adjuster couldn't have been nicer. Two days later, the garage had miraculously patched up my RV, so my trip continued."

I'm sure bad things happen in Mexico just as they can occur anywhere. I'm convinced, however, that the incidents are fewer and farther between than they are here in the United States.

Retirement in Central America

To a person who hates winter and who loves foreign living, the Central American countries of Guatemala, Honduras, and Costa Rica are extremely attractive. From the age of eighteen, when my parents retired in Mexico, I spent every winter I could enjoying that country's sunny warmth and charming tropical beaches. Then, in 1973, I discovered Central America during a three-month vacation through Guatemala, Honduras, El Salvador, Nicaragua, and finally Costa Rica. That trip began my ongoing love affair with Central America.

Until recently, the name Central America carried images of civil war and dangerous traveling. Travel there was only for the most adventurous. Civil wars in El Salvador, Nicaragua, and Guatemala made newspaper headlines and received continual attention on the evening news. Finally, after years of strife, peace has returned to Central America. And with the return of peace and safe traveling has come a flood of tourists and retirees.

It's difficult to know for certain how many U.S. and Canadian citizens have retired in Central America; my guess is that the number is close to 30,000 in all. The majority live in Costa Rica, although a growing number are choosing Guatemala, and a few are moving to Honduras. My wife and I have joined this wave of expatriates; we spend part of the year at our home on Costa Rica's Pacific coast.

Two places often touted as great spots to retire in Central America are Belize and Honduras. I've never traveled in Belize, so I can't recommend it one way or another. I can only say that I've heard mixed reviews. And most of my friends who've traveled in Belize have been robbed at one time or another.

El Salvador and Nicaragua occasionally receive strong praise from guidebook writers. I am familiar with both countries and frankly wouldn't recommend either as a great place for retirement. There are a number of reasons, not the least of which are widespread poverty, social unrest, and the lack of other expatriates to whom you can turn for friendship and support. Furthermore, the towns and countryside in El Salvador and Nicaragua can't compare with the prettier regions of Central America.

Honduras, on the other hand, has some charming places that attract occasional expatriates. It sometimes receives lavish praise as a place to retire, but outside of a few tourist locations, you'll seldom find enough expatriates to constitute a retirement community. Such a community is critical for successful living in a foreign country. You could be very lonely with no other English-speakers to socialize with other than visiting tourists. In addition,

Honduras is a very poor country with a long history of military intervention in the government.

This leaves us with Costa Rica and perhaps Guatemala for Central American retirement on a shoestring. I know both countries well.

Costa Rica

Costa Rica has avoided the civil and military strife that has mired its sister republics in a quicksand of turmoil and tragedy. It has been a bastion of peaceful tranquillity and a haven for American retirees. Costa Rica's devotion to democracy and peaceful cooperation with its neighbors have helped it to retain its enviable position as a showcase for prosperity, respect for law, and personal freedom.

Costa Rica's tradition of peace and democracy, as well as its dramatic mountain ranges, has caused it to be called "the Switzerland of the Americas." Of all foreign countries, Costa Rica attracts the highest percentage of foreign retirees. Among a population of some three million people, nearly 20,000 are North Americans who live in Costa Rica as retirees or businesspeople.

As in Mexico and Guatemala, you'll find a wide range of climates in Costa Rica. You can choose between a year-round spring climate in the central plateau or a lush, tropical beach climate along the Pacific and Caribbean coasts. About half of the population lives in the temperate highlands in the center of the country. From there, it's a two-hour drive to the Pacific Ocean or two hours east to the Caribbean. Take your pick. In the highlands, it's permanent springtime, with daily high temperatures in the 70s. In the tropics, it's permanent summer, with highs in the 80s.

Nature lovers journey here from all over the world to enjoy rain forests, cloud forests, and abundant wildlife, as well as gorgeous beaches and world-class ocean fishing. Costa Rica isn't the only place with these attractions, but it's just about the only place where you can see them and feel safe. You needn't worry about being caught in a cross fire between rebels and soldiers.

In fact, Costa Rica doesn't even *have* soldiers! It abolished its army more than fifty years ago and thereby avoided the sickness that plagues most Latin American countries: military dictatorships. Money that in other Central American countries is squandered on corruption and funneled into the Swiss bank accounts of high-ranking officers is instead spent on schools, hospitals, and roads. The lack of an army and the existence of a large middle class are key factors in Costa Rica's exceptionally high standard of living.

Inflation has climbed slowly here over the past few years, with the ratio of the dollar to Costa Rican currency following suit. At this time, the country's monetary unit, the colón, trades at about 400 to the dollar. The colón floats according to a free market and is not government controlled as currency is in some countries. Therefore, as prices rise, the number of colóns we receive for the dollar goes up as well. This system keeps prices steady for foreigners with dollar bank accounts. For example, over the past five years, prices in colóns have doubled as the currency's value dropped. But a dollar is now worth twice as many colóns, so relative costs have remained constant. The result is a low cost of living, not as low as in Mexico or Guatemala, but much lower than in the United States or Canada.

The average U.S. Social Security check is much more than the average middle-class Costa Rican earns. The income requirement for becoming a *pensionado* in Costa Rica is $600 a month in pension. And it's entirely possible to get by on this amount. A $600 paycheck is considered a good income for most Costa Rican families. That's about what a college professor earns, or about double what a skilled construction worker earns. However, again I caution against living in a foreign country without adequate funds. It would be unwise to try living here if you had no backup resources and if $600 was all you could count on.

To give you an idea of prices in Costa Rica, our basic phone bill is less than $5.00 a month, with local calls almost free. Where we live, our electric bill rarely tops $20 a month because our home has neither a furnace nor air conditioning—we don't need them. It never gets so warm that our ceiling fans don't do the job. Groceries generally cost less than they do back home; local produce is downright cheap, although imported goods are expensive. Medical expenses are affordable. The most expensive hospital room in San José—in a modern, well-equipped facility—will set you back not much more than $100 a day. That's for a private room with bath, telephone, TV, and an extra bed for family members if they wish to stay overnight. For about $50 a month, retired residents can buy into the Costa Rican medical system; that's *everything* fully covered.

Most North Americans will say that one of the best parts about living in Costa Rica is its friendly citizens. This is an egalitarian country without strong class distinctions. The people are outgoing, happy, and full of humor. They sincerely like North Americans, perhaps because we are so much like them. The educational system here is one of the best in Latin America, with literacy levels said to be higher than in the United States.

Tourists are restricted to ninety days, with an additional ninety-day extention, in Costa Rica, but that's long enough to get the flavor of living here and to decide if it's an appropriate place for retirement. In San José, where most retirees live, or at least start out living, you might rent one of the many apartments that are available by the week or month to experience the essence of living within the culture. I recommend that you then travel by bus around the country to look for your ideal location.

North Americans in Costa Rica, unlike those in other foreign countries, don't feel the need to cluster together in expensive compounds. We tend to feel comfortable in just about any neighborhood. Therefore, suitable rentals usually can be found in working-class neighborhoods for $150 to $300 a month, or even less if you look around.

Becoming a retiree in Costa Rica requires a lot of navigating through red tape and various government ministries, filling out forms in triplicate while the bureaucrats use their rubber stamps to mark everything in sight. It's best to hire a specialist to take care of things for you. You'll need proof that your income is at least $600 a month, a police report from your hometown, and other items. For details, consult my book, *Choose Costa Rica.*

However, it really isn't necessary to go for pensionado status unless you plan on living in Costa Rica full-time. Many foreigners prefer not to apply for residency, so they renew their three-month tourist cards for another three months for a six-month stay. (Any travel agent can take care of this for you; it isn't necessary to approach the immigration office.) They then travel to a beach resort across the border in Nicaragua or Panama for a seventy-two hour visit in an inexpensive hotel, after which they are eligible for another six-month stay in Costa Rica. Presently, the government is very lenient with this situation, but there's always the chance that they might become strict and insist on residency for full-time residents.

My friends claim that I tend to be uncritical about places I like, stressing the upbeat and minimizing the downbeat. So be aware that Costa Rica, like the other foreign countries mentioned in this chapter, is a third-world nation. Roads are not up to our standards, bureaucracy is maddening, and servants tend to have a *mañana* attitude. And there is crime. Central America has some of the most highly skilled pickpockets this side of Italy and Spain. Burglaries, while not as prevalent as in some parts of the United States, are more often focused on affluent foreigners. (Even on a shoestring budget, we gringos seem affluent.)

But the quality of crime is different from that back home. Outright robberies and muggings are so rare that they make front-page headlines in Costa Rica. In the United States, unless you live in a very small town, you're not likely to see a mugging or a liquor store holdup reported in your local newspaper at all, much less on the front page. Most retirees in Costa Rica will tell you that personal safety is as high or higher than in their hometowns. in USA

The best approach in Costa Rica is the same as in any foreign country: Be careful of your wallet in city crowds. Have neighbors watch your house when you're gone. Burglars almost never enter a home when it's occupied or watched.

Getting to Costa Rica can be quick and expensive by airplane, or slow and inexpensive by bus or automobile. My wife and I have traveled all three ways. When we have the time, we enjoy the drive, and the bus trip is fun, too. Our last drive took a month as we visited friends in Mexico and Guatemala along the way. We did lots of sightseeing, taking in Mayan ruins and wonderful beach resorts; it was a monthlong vacation. Buses are exceptionally inexpensive, with deluxe buses zipping through Mexico, complete with movies and "flight attendants" serving drinks and meals.

Guatemala

With peace finally settling over the region, Guatemala is once more becoming a practical place for retirement. Of all the economical retirement styles described in this book, Guatemala has to offer the ultimate in shoestring economics. The government requires a monthly income of only $300 in order for you to obtain a pensionado, or retiree resident visa. The astounding thing is, if need be, you can actually live on $300 a month! As best as I can tell, at least 1,500 U.S. citizens and an undetermined number of Canadians have chosen retirement in Guatemala. The big drawback here is a high crime rate, particularly crimes against wealthy Guatemalans. More about this later on.

To get an idea of what it costs to live here, I interviewed a retired couple who live in the mountains on the edge of Guatemala City. The husband took an early retirement from his job in the United States and came to Guatemala to look things over. He fell in love with a lovely Guatemalan lady, bought a home, and settled into retirement.

He said, "My company pension is less than $1,100. That covers all our household expenses, including two full-time maids.

We also send two poor children to school, pay for their clothes, books, and tuition, plus a few dollars to their families so they won't take the kids out of school and make them work. And I put $300 in our savings account every month."

If this budget is too expensive for your taste, a single person can really cut costs by renting a room with meals from a family that specializes in board and room for foreign students at local Spanish schools. The city of Antigua is a very popular place for this arrangement. For as little as $175 a month, you can receive three meals a day, a clean room, and laundry service. You don't have to be in school—the family is happy to have you under any circumstances. Of course, your meals will be basic and plain. A friend who was staying in one of these places said, "For this price, what do I care? I usually have dinner in a restaurant with friends anyway."

Where to Retire Gringos tend to congregate in just a few locations in Guatemala. Two favorite retirement sites are the old colonial city of Antigua and the Indian town of Panajachel on the shore of beautiful Lake Atitlán. Two other places around the perimeter of Guatemala City are also suitable for gracious retirement living: the suburbs of San Cristóbal and Vista Hermosa. These can be somewhat more expensive, and out of the shoestring-budget class, but still a great value for your money. Guatemala City itself is a place to avoid. The streets are filled with litter and pickpockets and are very unsafe.

Were it not for the crime rate, I can't imagine any place better than Guatemala for low-cost living, and I would recommend it enthusiastically. But foreigners who choose to live or retire in Guatemala consider crime as just another inconvenience of living in a third-world country. Duncan Aitken, who lives in Panajachel, says, "Things seem to be improving, but compared to what? Actually, the police are a large part of the problem. The old national police force is slowly being disbanded and replaced with a better trained and much better paid force. So corruption is definitely down."

Kidnapping has been the most serious problem in Guatemala, but not for foreigners unless they are high-profile and very wealthy. Victims are selected with a clear idea of how much money they have. They're usually fingered by someone employed by the victim's family or by an employee at the victim's bank who has access to financial records.

Duncan Aitken adds, "The Guatemalans themselves are most often the victims of crime, and they are in an uproar over the situation. The politicians are under intense pressure to control crime and are doing what they can—and their efforts have tangible results—but they have a lot of work to do yet."

Guatemala isn't like Costa Rica, where you can live just about anywhere you please in relative safety. Foreigners in Guatemala congregate in safer areas, live where friends live, and avoid high-crime areas. During my last trip, a government official and a police captain assured me that personal safety was improving. However, unless they get a better handle on crime, some caution is in order. Should you decide to try Guatemala, it's best to stick to tourist places like Antigua or Panajachel, where special police patrol the streets to make then safer for North Americans. Talk with other foreigners to get their opinions of just how safe a neighborhood might be.

Learn to Speak Spanish One way of visiting Guatemala and trying it out is to attend one of the language schools there. Not only is this a fascinating way to learn more about the country, but it is incredibly inexpensive. In Antigua, the location of many Spanish schools, room and board with a Guatemalan family can be arranged for as little as $50 to $60 a week! Schools provide one-on-one teaching for as little as $4.00 an hour.

One couple described their experiences this way: "Our school consisted of four buildings scattered throughout the town, most of which were formerly homes of wealthy families. Students work one-on-one with a teacher, and one student-teacher pair occupies each room. The room contains one small table, two wooden chairs, and a 40-watt lightbulb. The windows, in general, do not have glass, but rather shutters and the requisite iron bars to prevent intruders.

"School occupied most of our waking hours. We attended seven hours a day, five days a week, with a two-hour break for lunch. We were so saturated with Spanish that studying at the break was impossible. At night we did a few chores, rushed home to dinner, and then studied.

"At first, the teachers spoke slowly and distinctly to us. By the time we left, they were speaking at nearly normal speed, and we were really grasping their words. It was truly amazing how much clearer all of the native people were speaking compared to how they used to speak when we arrived just two months before!

"We don't regret it for a minute. We learned an incredible amount of Spanish; however, it is only a beginning, and we surely need to study further so, yes, we will go back."

Peace Corps

For foreign retirement on a shoestring, here's the best option of all: Join the Peace Corps! It isn't as crazy as it might seem at first glance. The Peace Corps actively seeks out older, retired citizens who have much to contribute. No other group in this country embodies the years of leadership, skills, experience, and proven ability of our senior citizens. You're never too old to serve in the Peace Corps. Volunteers must be at least eighteen years old, but there is no upper age limit. The oldest Peace Corps volunteer ever was eighty-six when he completed his service.

For the first time in their lives, many senior citizens find themselves without commitments to a career or family, so they find fulfillment and excitement in helping others. In addition, they're getting *paid* for it! They're having the time of their lives and at the same time are participating in programs that affect literacy, health, and hunger and help promote world peace and friendship. Retired singles and couples have put their expertise to work in Africa, Asia, South America, Central America, and the Pacific Islands.

The Peace Corps is involved in fields that are being redefined continuously: the health, well-being, and development of other peoples and nations. Every day on the job means learning something new from the people around you, the culture you are immersed in, and the problems that you face.

Most Peace Corps assignments require a four-year college degree; however, if you don't have a college education, you can still qualify by having three to five years of work experience in a needed specialty such as a skilled trade or business management. When evaluating your application, the Peace Corps considers the "whole person," looking at your life experiences, community involvement, volunteer work, motivations, and even your hobbies. It's possible for married couples to qualify as volunteers, both working and living in the same community. In fact, about 10 percent of Peace Corps volunteers are married. Peace Corps recruiters can help you evaluate the skills and experiences needed to qualify for a foreign assignment.

Do you need to speak another language to get into the Peace Corps? Not at all. During your training period, you'll receive intensive language instruction to prepare you for living and working in your foreign community. Some countries prefer volunteers who have mastered the native language, such as French or Spanish, but it is not often a requirement. The Peace Corps is prepared to teach more than 180 languages and dialects.

Peace Corps volunteers receive living expenses and a monthly stipend to cover incidental needs, so there is no need for them to spend savings or other income. At the conclusion of your volunteer service, you will receive a "readjustment allowance" of $225 for each month of service. Therefore, if you complete your full term of service, you will receive $6,075 tax free. This severance pay comes in handy for making a transition back into life at home. The compensation you receive from the Peace Corps doesn't affect your Social Security earnings. Because all expenses are paid, many older Peace Corps volunteers bank their entire Social Security, pension, and interest income during their two-year tour of duty.

The Peace Corps provides two vacation days for every month of service. That's twenty-four days a year that you can use to travel home for a visit or entertain family and friends who come to see you. Most volunteers use their vacation time to visit other countries in the region and learn about other countries' people, cultures, and traditions. The cost of your vacation travel is your responsibility, but once you are there, you can travel inexpensively, traveling like a native rather than a tourist.

At the end of your tour of duty, you qualify for career, education, and other advice and assistance through the Peace Corps' Office of Returned Volunteer Services (RVS) and its Career Center in Washington, D.C. RVS publishes a bimonthly job bulletin and career manuals, provides self-assessment tools to help returned volunteers explore career options, and facilitates career-planning activities.

Here is a terrific opportunity to make a contribution to peace, utilize your life's experience helping others, and have the time of your life. Be aware that there are always more applications than openings, so getting a position in the Peace Corps isn't a slam dunk. But you just might have the skills and experience that are needed.

Your regional recruiting office is the best place to get more information about your suitability for Peace Corps volunteer positions. Also, many recruiters were volunteers themselves, so they can explain firsthand what it's like to be in the Peace Corps. For information or an application, write to Peace Corps, Room P-301, Washington, DC 20526; or call (800) 424–8580. To access job listings for the Peace Corps, call the twenty-four-hour Job Line at (800) 818–9579.

Chapter Thirteen
Some of Our Favorite Retirement Places

I f you've analyzed your situation and have determined that moving to another location is your best option for economical retirement, you'll find some suggestions in this chapter. Because you'll be leaving your hometown, your friends, and maybe some family members behind, you may as well consider moving to another state. If you live in a cold climate, moving to a place with warmer winters will go a long way toward helping your budget.

Housing prices in some parts of the country have risen to the point where it doesn't make sense to talk about "retirement on a shoestring." After all, expensive housing is one of the major causes of expensive living. In the California community where my wife and I live—on the central California coast—home prices have risen steeply. Our local government is busy building new "affordable housing units" to accommodate low-income families. The price of an ordinary, "affordable" home will begin at $350,000. (No, that isn't $350,000 per block. That's per house!) Well, compared with a median sales price of about $600,000 in an ordinary neighborhood, I suppose it is affordable. But prices haven't shot up everywhere. Many parts of the country, even in California, have seen little change in the economy other than a gradual inflation connected with the price of gasoline and utilities.

To see how much the cost of living has gone up since our last edition of this book two years ago, in mid-2003 we conducted a survey of low-cost communities in various locations around the nation. We queried real estate professionals living in twenty small towns with populations between 10,000 and 20,000. Among the questions, we asked the average price of a three-bedroom home in a comfortable, middle-class neighborhood, and whether the prices had risen significantly. We stipulated that the home be in a neighborhood where a retired couple would feel safe and that it be located within easy walking distance of shopping.

The replies confirmed our belief that in the more economical retirement locations, real estate has not gone wild at all. In fact, many real estate contacts reported very little price movement over the past two years. Homes can still be found for average selling prices in the $80,000 range. In most of these economical locations, a three-bedroom home can be rented for around $500 a month and a two-bedroom home for $400 a month. Similar neighborhoods in expensive areas would feature rents at least twice as high.

We've confined our research on economical towns to smaller places, 50,000 population or below. As a general rule, smaller towns have more constant economies that don't see fluctuation in the local workforce or inflationary pressures on wages. That means local residents don't keep chasing real estate prices up. With affordable housing, the other major expense that can't be controlled is utilities. This can vary with each community, so you'll have to keep an eye on that when deciding where to move. Items such as gasoline and car maintenance can vary widely, depending on the state and region where you live. For example: A gallon of gasoline can cost 50 cents more in one part of the country that another. An auto mechanic may earn $10 an hour in some regions and $28 an hour elsewhere. See the cost-of-living chart for some economical retirement places.

Some of Our Favorites

When my editor suggested that we list our favorite economical retirement locations, it sounded like an easy task. After all, my wife and I have visited and inspected many, many parts of the country in the course of our research travels. However, when we sat down to compile our list, we discovered that we had to choose from a list of almost 300 nice places we had visited over the past fifteen years of retirement explorations.

We found it next to impossible to choose just a few favorites. We would miss too many desirable retirement havens by restricting our list to specific towns or cities. Furthermore, space in this book doesn't allow detailed analysis of each community. That job is best left to one of my other books, like *Where to Retire;* or one of the "Choose" books, such as *Choose the South for Retirement, Choose the Northwest, Choose the Southwest, Choose California,* or *Choose Florida.* These guides highlight the specifics of living in each community and discuss the many places necessarily excluded from this chapter.

You will notice that the states listed here generally enjoy milder winters, and that we emphasize locations in the South or Southwest. Some of the southern communities mentioned are among the most economical in the nation for real estate, rentals, heating costs, and general cost of living.

My wife and I feel that the communities presented here would satisfy our retirement needs, but that doesn't necessarily mean they would be suitable for everyone. I can't stress too much the need to investigate for yourself not only the cost of living in your new hometown but the lifestyle and the friendliness of your new neighbors. Just because a place has a low cost of living doesn't mean you'll be happy living there.

It's Nice To Feel Wanted

An interesting development in retirement is taking place in many communities around the nation. A growing awareness of the economic and social value of retirees from outside the region has transformed the way many towns and small cities think about retirees. This is particularly true in the South.

Many towns are creating "retirement recruitment committees" to reach out across the nation to welcome newcomers and
to invite retirees to relocate there. Money is being spent at both
the community and state levels to lure out-of-state retirees.
You're on their wanted list.

This all came about a few years ago when town and city
administrators began looking for ways to modernize and upgrade
their economies. At first they tried giving subsidies and tax breaks
to lure industries to relocate to their communities. Then they discovered that a factory employing low-wage workers (who often
have no medical benefits, who have children to burden the
schools, and who have little extra money to spend) can be a drag,
not a boost, to economic development.

On the other hand, retired couples moving into the area do
wonders for the economy. Retirees typically *create* jobs instead of
taking jobs. They have Medicare and don't depend on local
charity for health care. They have no children, yet they pay taxes
to support the schools just the same. They have money to spend
on extras, and they don't contribute to the local crime rate.
Retirement experts estimate that one retired couple moving into
a community is the economic equivalent of almost three new
jobs being created.

As a result, many small towns are giving up on factories and
instead are concentrating on attracting out-of-state retirees. They
eagerly recruit new neighbors who contribute economically and
socially. They do this through active welcoming committees.
The idea is spreading, especially through the South, with
involvement on the state as well as local levels. At least one state,
Arizona, has decided to follow suit with its own recruitment program. Many communities in other states are forming retirement
committees on their own.

Typically, the program works like this: When the committee
learns that someone has made inquiries at the chamber of commerce about retirement, a volunteer gets on the telephone and
invites the prospective retirees for a visit. Committee members
show newcomers around the area, introduce them to other

TOWNS WITH BELOW-AVERAGE LIVING COSTS

Below are some of the more inexpensive places in the country. As you can see, the below-average price of housing has a lot to do with low living costs. Utilities and health care are also important. Note the below-average cost of medical care in these towns.

These towns are listed as examples only. The author cannot vouch for their livability, although we've visited many of them. Some are okay places for retirement, others are best politely described as "provincial."

PERCENTAGES *BELOW* NATIONAL AVERAGE OF COST OF LIVING, REAL ESTATE, AND HEALTH CARE

TOWN AND STATE	COST OF LIVING	REAL ESTATE	HEALTH CARE
Cookeville, TN	-16.4	-22.4	-23.1
Conway, AR	-14.2	-24.3	-16.9
Kingsport, TN	-13.5	-15.5	-16.4
Joplin, MO	-12.8	-20.5	-2.3
Nevada, MO	-12.7	-14.2	-17.9
Murray, KY	-12.4	-23.4	-15.4
Johnson City, TN	-12.2	-13.9	-17.4
Douglas, GA	-12.2	-22.9	-9.5
Lubbock, TX	-11.8	-19.0	+2.5
Dyersburg, TN	-11.7	-22.6	-20.8
San Antonio, TX	-11.6	-16.8	+1.1
Salina, KS	-11.6	-18.8	-14.4
Lancaster, SC	-11.5	-19.0	-2.0

TOWN AND STATE	COST OF LIVING	REAL ESTATE	HEALTH CARE
Ardmore, OK	-11.1	-20.4	-22.6
Paducah, KY	-11.1	-22.3	-16.9
Fort Smith, AR	-11.1	-26.1	-11.2
Memphis, TN	-11.0	-17.9	-9.2
Texarkana, TX-AR	-10.8	-21.6	-5.9
Jackson, MS	-10.6	-11.3	-25.3
Anderson, IN	-10.5	-19.2	-8.5
Dothan, AL	-10.2	-22.6	-15.3

TOWNS WITH ABOVE-AVERAGE LIVING COSTS

Listed here are some expensive places. With high-priced real estate and medical care, it would appear that these towns would be out of the question for most people thinking of retirement. But folks who live there, who already have housing they bought years ago, before the market went crazy, find a comfortable living situation. Many food and miscellaneous items such as clothing and gasoline aren't priced too much above other places. Notice the cost of health care in some of these places, however! Do not get sick there.

These towns are listed as examples only. The author doesn't recommend them for anyone planning on retiring on a shoestring and points out that he would live there only at gunpoint or as a participant in a protected-witness program.

PERCENTAGES *ABOVE* NATIONAL AVERAGE OF COST OF LIVING, REAL ESTATE, AND HEALTH CARE

TOWN AND STATE	COST OF LIVING	REAL ESTATE	HEALTH CARE
Chapel Hill, NC	+13.7	+25.1	+5.9

TOWN AND STATE	COST OF LIVING	REAL ESTATE	HEALTH CARE
Sacramento, CA	+19.3	+23.2	+46.6
New London, CT	+19.6	+39.6	+14.8
Philadelphia, PA	+20.3	+36.9	+4.9
New Haven, CT	+20.3	+42.6	+43.2
Fairbanks, AK	+22.3	+13.7	+60.8
Oakland, CA	+28.0	+69.1	+33.5
San Diego, CA	+29.6	+67.1	+32.5
Washington, DC	+31.1	+65.3	+23.4
Juneau, AK	+31.7	+44.8	+68.7
Trenton, NJ	+35.3	+87.2	+56.3
Framingham, MA	+37.4	+84.4	+32.5
Los Angeles, CA	+37.9	+109.1	+13.0
Boston, MA	+42.5	+97.2	+35.5
Honolulu, HI	+44.9	+88.7	+17.2
Chicago, IL	+48.2	+134.3	+35.0
Newark-Elizabeth, NJ	+50.4	+123.8	+55.9
Bergen-Passaic, NJ	+53.1	+136.6	+64.6
Stamford, CT	+53.9	+152.6	+31.8
Jersey City, NJ	+65.9	+186.5	+72.1
San Francisco, CA	+79.6	+237.6	+52.0
New York (Manhattan), NY	+126.4	+342.2	+74.2

retirees, and invite them to social affairs specially designed to make newcomers feel welcome.

What does this mean to retirees? Instead of moving into an unfamiliar town, as a stranger among strangers, retirees immediately enjoy a circle of welcoming friends and acquaintances. Often the committee volunteers have themselves moved in from other states; you'll have interests in common. You'll quickly learn what the term *hospitality* really means.

When you request information from a chamber of commerce, no matter in what part of the country, be sure to ask if there is an active retirement committee. If there is one, you can be confident that you will be welcomed to the community as a valued friend.

CLIMATE OF SELECTED CITIES

CITY, STATE	AVERAGE HUMIDITY	DAYS OVER 90°F	DAYS UNDER 32°F	JULY AVG. HIGH (°F)	JULY AVG. LOW (°F)
Atlanta, GA	70	19	59	86	69
Birmingham, AL	72	39	60	88	70
Clarksville, TN	71	37	75	90	69
Memphis, TN	69	64	59	88	72
Raleigh-Durham, NC	71	25	82	88	67
Kansas City, MO	69	40	106	83	69
Wichita, KS	66	62	114	87	70
St. Louis, MO	70	37	107	85	69
Chicago, IL	67	21	119	79	63
Philadelphia, PA	67	19	101	86	67

Compare the number of days over 90°F with the number of days below freezing in this table. You'll see that southern cities are warmer than northern cities in the winter.

Retirement in the South

For many people, the thought of retirement in the South evokes images of backward, prejudiced, and unfriendly neighbors who are united against outsiders. Nothing could be further from the truth. While you may have found some of these attitudes a generation ago, today you will find an open, welcoming climate throughout most of the South. A mixture of the modern and the traditional, most southern neighborhoods are among the safest and friendliest in the nation and offer amenities such as golf courses and community colleges.

Earlier we talked about the importance of senior-citizen centers in retirement strategies. You need to be aware that in many southern communities, these facilities often provide only minimal services. Local people sometimes look upon them as an adjunct to welfare, simply as a place to hand out free meals and a place for indigents to hang out and watch TV. Where this is true, the social and helpful functions of senior centers are usually fulfilled by other local organizations. Volunteer projects are often coordinated by a garden club or similar social group. This isn't always the case; sometimes there are wonderful senior centers—you'll have to check them out during your visit.

Most people also expect the South to be terribly hot in the summer. Well, it is, at least for folks like my wife and me, who spend summers on the California coast where it's always cool. But the main difference between southern summers and northern summers is the length of the warm weather, not its intensity. On the other hand, northern winters are famous for being long and severe.

Alabama One of the states most active in retiree recruitment, Alabama has dozens of small cities and towns with active Retirement Advantage committees to recruit retirees. For detailed information about these communities, call (800) 235-4757. You'll receive the state's retirement magazine as well as information about the towns that are awaiting your visit. One of the advantages to relocating here is extremely low property tax rates. In the towns we researched, taxes on a home worth $90,000 were typically less than $500 a year.

The countryside varies from the Appalachian Mountains in the northeast to rolling farmlands in the center and wire grass flatlands in the southern part of the state. The weather is typically southern, with mild winters and hot summers. Ozark and Enterprise, located in the southeastern part of the state, are exceptionally friendly and welcoming to retirees. Quality real estate is affordable, with plenty of rentals available in Enterprise, and high-quality homes in Ozark listed at almost give-away prices. Florida's beaches are only a ninety-minute drive away. There's a cosmopolitan makeup to the local citizenry; folks come from all over the country, not just the Deep South. A large percentage of new retirees are ex-military.

For rural communities eager to bring in retirees from out of state, try Greenville and Camden. Situated in the south-central part of the state, these towns are about 40 miles from the Florida state line and not far from Florida beaches. Right on the beach, the communities of Gulf Shores and Orange Beach offer great saltwater recreation, although housing costs have risen sharply lately.

Among the dozens of places in Alabama trying hard to convince you to join the community are Jasper, Mentone, Anniston, Gadsen, and Scottsboro.

ALABAMA (MONTGOMERY) WEATHER

	TEMPERATURE (°F)				ANNUAL PRECIPITATION (IN.)	
	JAN	APR	JUL	OCT	RAIN	SNOW
Daily Highs	57	77	92	78	49	0
Daily Lows	36	53	72	53		

Florida Florida has always been the darling of East Coast retirees. Although it is losing some of its magic, the state still draws more retirees than any other state in the Union. Those who think Florida is expensive may have a surprise coming. This state offers some of the best retirement bargains, dollar for dollar and feature for feature, in the country. Of course, you can find housing costs lower in places like Oklahoma or Idaho, but winter heating bills cancel out the advantage.

The state's climate ranges from exceptionally mild to semi-tropical. While midday temperatures in the summer, heavy with humidity, can be oppressive, outdoor activity in early mornings and evenings is the preferred mode of exercise. Some of the interior regions of Florida are very reminiscent of the Midwest.

Daytona Beach and St. Augustine are on the peninsula's Atlantic side, and although not particularly inexpensive, they have less-costly communities just a short drive away. Daytona's 23-mile-long white sand beach is perhaps its most famous feature, and it's one of the few places in Florida where autos are permitted to drive along the shore. Besides good beaches and pleasant winters, excellent senior-citizen services add to the value of retirement here.

On the northern Gulf beaches, you'll find affordable communities like Panama City and Fort Walton Beach, but tourism runs up the cost of living. Around Pensacola you'll find a selection of towns ranging from ordinary to almost luxurious. The state's western beaches have a string of towns that are rather expensive, yet with pockets of affordable housing tucked away here and there.

Inland Florida becomes quite rural once you get away from the metropolitan districts. Places like Ocala, Destin, Leesville, and other small cities have homes, farms, and acreage priced less than you might expect. Also, just east of the Tampa–St. Petersburg area is a semirural area where very affordable real estate and inexpensive mobile-home living make for true shoestring retirement. Mobile-home living here is the least expensive

mode of Florida retirement. We've looked at livable places selling for $8,000 and park rents of $150 a month.

FLORIDA GULF COAST WEATHER (TAMPA)						
	TEMPERATURE (°F)				ANNUAL PRECIPITATION (IN.)	
	JAN	APR	JUL	OCT	RAIN	SNOW
Daily Highs	70	82	90	84	47	0
Daily Lows	50	61	74	65		

FLORIDA INLAND WEATHER (GAINESVILLE)						
	TEMPERATURE (°F)				ANNUAL PRECIPITATION (IN.)	
	JAN	APR	JUL	OCT	RAIN	SNOW
Daily Highs	67	81	91	81	52	0
Daily Lows	42	55	71	59		

Georgia Georgia can be divided into three regions for retirement.
The Atlantic Coast, often called the Colonial Coast; the north-
eastern part of the state, in the foothills of the Appalachians; and
the lower part of the state, known as the Plantation Trace. The
state is full of small towns suitable for retirement, but whether
many out-of-state retirees move there is another question. So far,
the state of Georgia hasn't become deeply involved in retirement
recruitment, although there is some recruitment at the local
level.

Long a favorite with retirees looking for inexpensive places to
live, Georgia's northeast corner has suffered from too much popularity; the cost of housing has increased quite a bit in the last
five years. Rabun County has been the perennial favorite, a collection of tiny villages, Clayton being the largest. Nearby
Habersham County is the second most popular place for retire-

ment, with Clarkesville and Dahlonga the largest communities.

The Plantation Trace, along the southern edge of the state, has long been a place for northerners to vacation and play golf in the winter. It's just now gaining popularity with retirees. A low cost of living is part of the attraction. You might look at Thomasville as an example of a progressive small city where retirement may be a good idea.

The Colonial Coast is a collection of exceptionally expensive places and some rather moderately priced communities. Jekel Island, Skidmore Island, and parts of Savannah are far out of reach for a shoestring budget. The mainland city of Brunswick, just a short drive from the spiffy island places, abounds in affordable places for rent or sale.

GEORGIA WEATHER (MACON)

	TEMPERATURE (°F)				ANNUAL PRECIPITATION (IN.)	
	JAN	APR	JUL	OCT	RAIN	SNOW
Daily Highs	58	78	92	78	45	1
Daily Lows	36	52	71	52		

Kentucky Most of Kentucky has any number of low-cost places to retire. Finding the most appropriate small towns may take some investigating, however. As in many small southern towns, you could feel a bit out of place if you are the only "outsiders" in the community. Exceptions will be found wherever there are retirement committees, but there are few such programs in the state.

For retirement anywhere, it's hard to beat a college town. Bowling Green, Murray, and Danville are three Kentucky university locations we've investigated. You're always sure to find kindred spirits who've moved from elsewhere because of the school and attendant benefits. Of the three towns, only Bowling Green is "wet," where you can order wine with a meal.

Somerset, toward the lower section of Kentucky, is also becoming popular with retirees.

KENTUCKY WEATHER (DANVILLE)						
	TEMPERATURE (°F)				ANNUAL PRECIPITATION (IN.)	
	JAN	APR	JUL	OCT	RAIN	SNOW
Daily Highs	40	66	86	68	46	16
Daily Lows	23	44	66	46		

Louisiana A fascinating mélange of historical and cultural ingredients, Louisiana is becoming interested in attracting retirees. Call (318) 367–6447 for information on towns with retirement committees.

One of the oldest towns west of the Mississippi, Natchitoches is famous for its stately homes, which date from as early as the 1700s. A university town with an intellectual atmosphere and retirees from all parts of the country, Natchitoches has a low cost of living and friendly residents. The movie *Steel Magnolias* was made here using local residents, scenery, and homes. Nearby is the Toledo Bend Lake area and towns such as Leesville and DeRidder, which have very active retirement committees.

West and south of Baton Rouge is "Cajun Country," the most famous part of Louisiana. At one time, Cajuns were noted for their closed society. They jealously maintained their French language and their private ways of living. Times have changed, however, thanks to television, modern transportation, and open communication. Retirees are welcome, and living is easy in this charming region. This area is for folks who like "country," who fit into a down-home atmosphere, and who relish crawfish gumbo. Popular towns are Houma, New Iberia, and Lafayette.

LOUISIANA WEATHER (SHREVEPORT)					
TEMPERATURE (°F)				ANNUAL PRECIPITATION (IN.)	
JAN	APR	JUL	OCT	RAIN	SNOW
Daily Highs 61	79	91	80	56	0
Daily Lows 41	58	73	56		

Mississippi Mississippi's "Hometown" retirement program is the most vigorous and enthusiastic of all the retiree-attraction programs in the country. With twenty cities "certified" as excellent places to retire, you can be pretty sure you'll find a place for you. As an added incentive for retirees, Mississippi recently passed legislation exempting all pensions from state income taxes.

One of our favorite towns in the state, Oxford was described in the chapter on education and retirement. Other towns worth investigating are Columbus, an old-style southern city, and Hattiesburg, a city of 49,000 people just ninety minutes from the gulf. The gulf area's Biloxi and Gulfport have long been traditional low-cost retirement areas, although new big-time gambling casinos have recently upped the ante. Holly Springs, near Memphis, is also a possibility. Starkville and Meridian, in the eastern part of the state, are also very active in retiree recruitment.

For a list of Mississippi's twenty certified retirement cities write to P.O. Box 849, Jackson, MS 39205, or call (601) 359–5978.

MISSISSIPPI WEATHER (HATTIESBURG)					
TEMPERATURE (°F)				ANNUAL PRECIPITATION (IN.)	
JAN	APR	JUL	OCT	RAIN	SNOW
Daily Highs 57	77	93	79	53	1
Daily Lows 35	53	71	51		

North Carolina We're convinced that some of the most beautiful and scenic places in the world are found in the Blue Ridge and the Great Smoky Mountains. October, when leaves are turning, is a marvelous time for a visit. Hardwood trees display a full explosion of color, with brilliant reds, yellows, purples, lavenders, and all colors in between, while evergreens provide a conservative background of green. We've also made the rounds in the spring, when the dogwoods, azaleas, and mountain laurel trees are in full bloom.

This mountain region has been prime retirement country for more than a century. Places like Blowing Rock, Boone, Newland, and other gorgeous settings in the Great Smoky Mountains draw many retirees in search of milder summers and picturesque winters. Living costs here range from very low to very high, so shopping around is strongly recommended. Asheville was once on the list of affordable places to live, but popularity has taken its toll—with higher real estate prices.

The Piedmont and coastal regions of North Carolina also have some reasonable places for retirement, but you'll have to look around. Because so many people are moving in from the North and Northeast, prices have skyrocketed in many towns.

NORTH CAROLINA WEATHER (ASHEVILLE)						
	TEMPERATURE (°F)				ANNUAL PRECIPITATION (IN.)	
	JAN	APR	JUL	OCT	RAIN	SNOW
Daily Highs	48	69	84	69	48	17
Daily Lows	26	43	62	43		

South Carolina Like North Carolina, South Carolina has a mountain region, a piedmont, and a coastal region. Charleston is South Carolina's jewel, but there are few inexpensive neighborhoods. But just west is Summerland, an old-fashioned hometown not far from glamorous Charleston. Farther north is the waterfront city of Georgetown, where antebellum homes are as common as bungalows. While not exactly priced for the shoe-string budget, they are relatively affordable.

In the piedmont region, Aiken is a lovely Deep South city where a mixture of northern and southern newcomers take full advantage of retirement opportunities. Aiken's robust business district makes it look larger than it actually is. It's the shopping and employment center for a large area.

SOUTH CAROLINA COAST WEATHER (CHARLESTON)

	TEMPERATURE (°F)				ANNUAL PRECIPITATION (IN.)	
	JAN	APR	JUL	OCT	RAIN	SNOW
Daily Highs	57	73	88	75	47	1
Daily Lows	41	58	75	60		

Tennessee Tennessee is a popular state for retirement for those who don't want to go too far from their hometowns in the North or Northeast. Retirees can easily return for a visit whenever they please, and the grandkids can visit often. Resort developers are taking advantage of this market by building golf-course housing complexes.

Because of the large military base nearby, Clarksville has become a popular retirement place for servicemen from all parts of the country. An exceptionally friendly population and reason-able costs are the pluses. Clarksville sits conveniently on an inter-state highway that whisks you to the big city of Nashville in less than forty-five minutes. The nearby town of Dover is typical of a small Tennessee town, with very low living costs. Dover is becoming popular because of its proximity to the Land between the Lakes and its outdoor recreational opportunities.

Crossville sits in a rolling, wooded and agricultural country-side, typical of many midsized towns in Tennessee and

Kentucky. Nearby Fairfield Glen attracts retirees from Michigan, Ohio, and Indiana, but the prices are higher than in Crossville itself. Two golf-course communities nearby offer properties at relatively moderate prices. Two towns in Tennessee that have been drawing many retirees are Dayton and Loudon, both on lakes, with water recreation galore.

TYPICAL TENNESSEE WEATHER (CLARKSVILLE)						
	TEMPERATURE (°F)				ANNUAL PRECIPITATION (IN.)	
	JAN	APR	JUL	OCT	RAIN	SNOW
Daily Highs	46	71	90	72	48	11
Daily Lows	28	48	69	48		

Virginia–West Virginia Earlier in the book we discussed special conditions whereby retirees find that an economic slowdown, such as a factory closing, an industry change, or a military base closing, pulls the floor from under the real estate market and causes the cost of living to drop dramatically. All too often, this occurs in places where you wouldn't care to visit much less live. Empty factory buildings, rotting fishing piers, mining dumps, or denuded forestlands don't exactly create an ideal retirement atmosphere, even though living is cheap. There has to be more.

As described in Chapter 6, the Appalachian region of Virginia and West Virginia doesn't suffer from any of the above ailments, since it started out with a prosperous infrastructure in the first place. Yet because of an economic downturn, it is one of the most affordable regions you can find. This area, self-styled as "Four Seasons Country," has a number of delightful small towns that are great for retirement. The bonus is that an active retirement welcoming committee is eager for you to take up residence there.

Our favorite places here are the towns of Tazewell and Richlands in Virginia and the small city of Bluefield, which straddles the state line. Incidentally, Bluefield State College reaches out to the community with its Creative Retirement Center. On the West Virginia side are Princeton and Beckley, two lovely towns with plenty of low-cost housing. Two remarkably charming towns in West Virginia are Fayetteville, in a wooded valley to the north, and Lewisburg, a colonial town toward the eastern portion of the state. Homes built in the 1700s are common here, and quality homes on large parcels of land are absolutely affordable. For information about this region, contact the Creative Retirement Center, P.O. Box 4088, Bluefield, WV 24701. The e-mail address is info@mccvb.com. The toll-free phone number is (800) 221–3206.

FOUR SEASONS COUNTRY (VIRGINIA–WEST VIRGINIA)					
TEMPERATURE (°F)				**ANNUAL PRECIPITATION (IN.)**	
JAN	APR	JUL	OCT	RAIN	SNOW
Daily Highs 40	67	86	68	42	34
Daily Lows 26	44	65	45		

Midwestern States

The states of Arkansas, Oklahoma, and Texas have some interesting and economical places for retirement. The Ozark Mountains are the centerpiece of recreational and scenic values in western Arkansas and eastern Oklahoma. Texas has few mountains except in the western part, but it has lots of Gulf of Mexico beaches for recreation.

Wages and prices in general are low, especially in smaller towns, so the cost of living is favorable. Most locations enjoy a true four-season climate, with occasional light snows in the winter and delightful fall and spring seasons. Summers, of course, are similar to those in the southern states. Texas has a more varied climate, with milder winters near the Gulf, and a drier climate the farther west you travel.

Arkansas Because it's not far from large population centers such as St. Louis, Kansas City, and Chicago, Arkansas has been drawing many retirees from those locations. The four-season climate features fairly mild winters, combined with Ozark Mountain scenery in the northwestern third of the state. Most Arkansas towns are "dry," except in some of the more populous areas.

We recently discovered the town of Mena in the Ouachita Mountains, an offshoot of the Ozarks. The local retirement committee has several enthusiastic volunteers who've moved here from far northern locales. Housing is very reasonable, and personal safety is exceptionally high. Not far away is Fayetteville, which is discussed in Chapter 9.

Bull Shoals, Mountain Home, and Lakeview are lakeside communities offering real estate bargains and reasonable living costs. Added attractions are friendly neighbors, good fishing, and lovely scenery. Traditional retirement areas like California and Florida are losing retirees, who move here to take advantage of an exceptionally low crime rate and gorgeous scenery. About 60 miles north of Little Rock, Heber Springs and Greers Ferry draw many retirees who love fishing. The towns overlook a 40,000-acre lake with 300 miles of wooded shoreline and waters overrun with bass, stripers, walleye, catfish, and lunker-sized trout. The Hot Springs area is another popular retirement locale.

ARKANSAS WEATHER (FAYETTEVILLE)						
	TEMPERATURE (°F)				ANNUAL PRECIPITATION (IN.)	
	JAN	APR	JUL	OCT	RAIN	SNOW
Daily Highs	48	74	94	76	40	7
Daily Lows	27	49	71	49		

Oklahoma Some very pleasant and scenic retirement locations bring people from all over the country to enjoy economical retirement. However, Oklahoma also has some rather dreary-looking places. You'll do well to stick with the prettier places because that's where the out-of-state retirees congregate.

Grand Lake o' the Cherokees/Tenkiller is part of a large network of lakes on the fringes of the Ozark Mountains. Some of the nation's best real estate values are found here, tucked away among picturesque forests, Ozark hills, and unsophisticated small towns. The Grand Lake is large enough for good-sized sailboats and permits private boat docks. Some areas, however, are only for those of you with hermit tendencies. Not far away is Bartlesville, a city that has preserved Oklahoma hospitality and affordable living.

OKLAHOMA WEATHER (TULSA)

	TEMPERATURE (°F)				ANNUAL PRECIPITATION (IN.)	
	JAN	APR	JUL	OCT	RAIN	SNOW
Daily Highs	46	72	94	75	39	9
Daily Lows	25	50	72	50		

Texas The third most populous state in the Union, Texas offers a large menu of economical retirement locations. Austin and San Antonio are two of Texas's bargain spots for big-city real estate and apartment rentals—if you like big cities. Overbuilding has caused prices to remain stable or to drop in a market of ever-increasing costs.

Texas has a long coastline on the Gulf of Mexico, and two of the more popular towns there, Corpus Christi and Galveston, suffer from split personalities. On the one hand, there are lots of seasonal tourists. On the other hand, there are the cities' full-time residents. The trick to retiring on a shoestring in Corpus or Galveston is finding a home away from the tourist crush. The payoff is a mild climate with great gulf fishing and endless beaches. Padre Island has several small communities that attract retirees, especially the half-year types.

Border towns with easy access to Mexico for shopping and recreation, such as Laredo and El Paso, rank very low in cost of living. Modern American conveniences and old Mexican charm blend to give these places a distinctive character.

Along the Rio Grande Valley, small cities like Harlingen, McAllen, and Brownsville are the choice of countless part-time retirees, as mentioned in Chapter 10. However, more and more retirees are making this region their permanent home. Those who can stand summer heat will find rock-bottom housing prices here. In addition to the sweet aroma of citrus blossoms in December, residents enjoy a particularly colorful Christmas because of the abundance of poinsettias throughout the area. The Mexican city of Reynosa sits across the river from McAllen and is a popular shopping destination.

TEXAS GULF COAST WEATHER (GALVESTON)

| | TEMPERATURE (°F) | | | | ANNUAL PRECIPITATION (IN.) | |
	JAN	APR	JUL	OCT	RAIN	SNOW
Daily Highs	59	73	87	78	40	0
Daily Lows	48	65	79	68		

WEST TEXAS WEATHER (EL PASO)

| | TEMPERATURE (°F) | | | | ANNUAL PRECIPITATION (IN.) | |
	JAN	APR	JUL	OCT	RAIN	SNOW
Daily Highs	58	79	95	79	8	6
Daily Lows	30	49	70	49		

Southwestern States

The Southwest has much less rainfall and humidity than the rest of the country. While some regions are very dry and hot, especially in the summer, the very low humidity makes the air feel comfortable. In Las Vegas, a temperature of 95°F is downright comfortable, whereas 95°F in Florida would make you a prisoner in your air-conditioned home.

Winters in most southwestern locations are very mild, often with typical daytime high temperatures over 70°F. While it can get chilly in the evening, things warm quickly as soon as the sun comes out. Except in the mountains, you rarely see snow in most southwestern communities, and even in the high elevations the snowfall is sparse. In fact, precipitation of any kind is scanty, ranging from as little as 3 inches of rain yearly in Yuma to as much as 21 inches in Flagstaff. Compare this with 52 inches of rain annually in Gainesville, Florida.

The truly hot summers in many Southwest locations aren't something you can conveniently ignore; you'll need some kind of air conditioning. The good news is that inexpensive "swamp coolers" do wonders because of the low humidity. Trying to use these contraptions back east would indeed turn your living room into a swamp before long.

Arizona Arizona is a state with varied climates and landscapes. It includes some of the most expensive places to live in the entire region, such as Scottsdale and Carefree, as well as some of the most inexpensive, places like Bullhead City and Payson. The low-desert locations are exceptionally hot in the summer, yet pleasant in the winter. The higher mountain towns see snow in the winter but have delightful summers. Just about anywhere you choose to retire in Arizona will place you with neighbors who've moved here after retirement.

Ajo and Bisbee are two mining towns that drew bargain-hunting retirees when large mining corporations suddenly closed down operations, sending the towns into economic tailspins. Property values dropped to almost giveaway prices. The real estate markets in both towns have recovered to some extent, but prices are still attractive. A large number of the residents today are retirees who hail from all parts of the country.

Lake Havasu City, Parker, and Bullhead City are three low-desert retirement towns on the banks of the Colorado River. They all offer great real estate bargains. Very hot in the summer but pleasantly warm and dry in the winter, the area loses population when the snowbirds fly away in late April. Bullhead City is just across the river from Laughlin, Nevada, one of the fastest-growing casino complexes in southern Nevada. According to the local chamber of commerce, about 80 percent of Bullhead City residents are retirees! Yuma, near the Mexican border, is another low-cost retirement area, with subdivisions of inexpensive homes. Hot summers are the drawback, but more and more people are staying year-round as time goes on. Senior-citizen services appear to be excellent.

Another of our discoveries is the town of Payson, about an hour north of Phoenix. Tucked away in the shade of enormous pine trees, Payson is a great place for shoestring living. The community features mobile homes and inexpensive homes on forested lots. Because of its higher elevation and cooler summers, it has traditionally been a weekend getaway from Phoenix.

ARIZONA HIGH-DESERT WEATHER (TUCSON)					
TEMPERATURE (°F)				ANNUAL PRECIPITATION (IN.)	
JAN	APR	JUL	OCT	RAIN	SNOW
Daily Highs 64	80	99	84	11	1
Daily Lows 38	50	74	57		

ARIZONA LOW-DESERT WEATHER (YUMA)

	TEMPERATURE (°F)				ANNUAL PRECIPITATION (IN.)	
	JAN	APR	JUL	OCT	RAIN	SNOW
Daily Highs	69	86	107	91	3	0
Daily Lows	43	56	80	62		

ARIZONA MOUNTAIN WEATHER (FLAGSTAFF)

	TEMPERATURE (°F)				ANNUAL PRECIPITATION (IN.)	
	JAN	APR	JUL	OCT	RAIN	SNOW
Daily Highs	42	57	82	64	21	97
Daily Lows	15	26	50	31		

Nevada Nevada is a large state and very underpopulated, but only a few places might be considered for retirement. Although we like places like Las Vegas and Reno for retirement, they've become rather expensive lately. Although the cost of living is not low, employment opportunities and gambling excitement make life here worthwhile for some. Competition between casinos forces them to offer tremendous values in restaurant food and entertainment, which makes going out easy on a shoestring budget. The good part about retirement for many is the opportunity for part-time work. Local casinos often make it a point to hire senior citizens as part-time workers. The bad part is that too many people have a weakness for gambling. About 80 miles outside of Las Vegas, in the middle of the desert, the town of Pahrump draws many retirees to its warm climate and low cost of living, although it's a bit too isolated for some. And without any public transportation, an automobile is a must.

NEVADA WEATHER (RENO)						
	TEMPERATURE (°F)				ANNUAL PRECIPITATION (IN.)	
	JAN	APR	JUL	OCT	RAIN	SNOW
Daily Highs	45	63	91	70	7	24
Daily Lows	20	29	48	31		

New Mexico New Mexico has traditionally been a popular place for retirement, with places like Santa Fe, Taos, and Albuquerque the favorites. However, these places have become quite expensive. Nevertheless, we've found a few inexpensive places we can recommend.

Roswell has been receiving many favorable reviews in magazines and books as a retirement destination. It's a nice-looking town, and local boosters are eager for newcomers to move in. Historic Silver City has a picturesque, turn-of-the-century downtown and some excellent housing opportunities. Its higher-altitude location moderates the summer climate. Another mountain location, Ruidoso, has an incredibly lovely ambience, with tall pines and a rushing river flowing through town. Carlsbad is a small city that actively encourages retirees to relocate. The local chamber of commerce is very helpful. Carlsbad's main drawback is its location so far from the closest metropolitan area, El Paso. An exceptionally economical if not scenic location, Truth or Consequences is in the desert not far from a large lake for water recreation. Housing is particularly inexpensive here.

NEW MEXICO WEATHER (ALBUQUERQUE)						
	TEMPERATURE (°F)				ANNUAL PRECIPITATION (IN.)	
	JAN	APR	JUL	OCT	RAIN	SNOW
Daily Highs	47	71	93	72	8	12
Daily Lows	22	40	65	43		

Pacific Coast States

Here you'll find the most varied climates in the country—perhaps on the entire continent. From desert terrain that makes the Sahara look like an oasis, to rain forest, to sunny beaches fringed by palm trees, to glaciers and year-round snowpack, the Pacific Coast states have it all. In a matter of hours you can leave the mountain ski slopes and be swimming in the Pacific. You can live in a coastal town where temperatures seldom reach the mid-seventies, even in July and August, yet it never snows or freezes. Nearby places have hot summers and snow-free winters, yet they are forty-five minutes from snow country, where a 3-foot snowfall overnight is a common occurrence.

The Pacific Coast is also a study in economic and social contrasts. Here you'll find some of the most expensive real estate in the nation, yet not far away is housing that compares favorably with places in the Deep South. Some of the most densely packed metropolitan areas are just a few miles from small, rural towns that offer real country living. And, as in the Southwest, much of the land in the Pacific Coast region is in the public domain. Virtually all of the national forests and state lands are open to the public. These open lands can be within an hour's drive of the center of enormous cities like Los Angeles and Seattle.

One other condition is very different from the rest of the country: Beaches are all public. By law, all beachfronts must be open to anyone who cares to go there. Public passage must be provided. This is in stark contrast with the Atlantic Coast and, to a great extent, the Gulf Coast. There, valuable waterfront properties include the beach, and trespassers are unwelcome. Even some rivers in the Pacific Coast region have guaranteed public access. That is, the first 10 feet of riverbank are available for recreational use. All of this public access to shore and rivers means a great deal to fishermen, beachcombers, and picnickers.

California California has some of the most expensive places to live in the country, ranking just behind New York City. But you can find inexpensive areas where high prices haven't caught up. There are so many places to consider here that it's difficult even to make suggestions. The book *Choose California for Retirement* will give you a more complete look at retirement here.

For year-round mild climate, the northern coast is the place to go. Eureka and Arcata are examples. Air conditioning is unknown, winter brings almost no snow, and some very inexpensive housing can be found there. Many small towns, such as Fort Bragg and Mendocino, dot the coastline south toward San Francisco. At the opposite extreme, desert living is inexpensive in towns like Indio, Desert Hot Springs, and Brawley. Expect hot weather here.

To the east, away from the Pacific Ocean and tucked away in California's northern mountains, are several little-known retirement gems. Outdoor recreation is available year-round, and property is inexpensive. Redding is a small city with a low cost of living. The highway east from Redding winds through several likely locations, with the town of Burney being a good candidate for retirement. The region is lush with evergreen forests and close to deep lakes and mountain streams for bass and trout.

Some folks prefer the four-season climates of the Sacramento and San Joaquin Valleys, with mild winters but hot summers approximating those back east. Not all communities are affordable here, but you'll encounter a few localities with inexpensive homes. Clinging to the banks of the Sacramento and Feather Rivers as they wend their way toward San Francisco Bay are several towns worth investigating. Dunsmuir and Mount Shasta are at the upper reaches, and Paradise, Oroville, and Marysville are very popular for inexpensive retirement. These towns are near Gold Country and the foothills of the Sierra Nevada. Interesting retirement towns in the Gold Country include Tuolumne, Angels Camp, Fiddletown, and Calaveras.

CALIFORNIA COASTAL WEATHER (EUREKA)

	TEMPERATURE (°F)				ANNUAL PRECIPITATION (IN.)	
	JAN	APR	JUL	OCT	RAIN	SNOW
Daily Highs	53	55	60	60	39	0
Daily Lows	41	44	52	48		

CALIFORNIA INLAND VALLEY WEATHER (FRESNO)

	TEMPERATURE (°F)				ANNUAL PRECIPITATION (IN.)	
	JAN	APR	JUL	OCT	RAIN	SNOW
Daily Highs	54	74	98	80	11	0
Daily Lows	37	47	64	50		

CALIFORNIA MOUNTAIN WEATHER (MOUNT SHASTA)

	TEMPERATURE (°F)				ANNUAL PRECIPITATION (IN.)	
	JAN	APR	JUL	OCT	RAIN	SNOW
Daily Highs	42	58	85	65	37	105
Daily Lows	26	33	51	37		

Oregon Oregon has always been popular with Californians looking for affordable retirement locations. It's become so popular that prices have risen to match demand. However, wages and prices are low compared with where retirees are coming from—high-priced California cities like San Francisco and Los Angeles. Oregon has no sales tax but manages to make it up with high property taxes.

Inland Oregon valley cities, with quality living, access to outdoor sports, and low housing, are popular with California retirees. The winters are mild with very little snow, and the surroundings are green year-round. Despite Oregon's reputation for rain, this area receives about half the precipitation of most eastern and midwestern cities, but without the oppressive winter weather.

Especially inexpensive is a group of small communities scattered along the scenic highway that winds its way across the mountains toward the ocean at Crescent City. This area is known as the Illinois Valley, named after the Illinois River that runs through here. You'll find several "wide spot in the road" communities such as O'Brien, Kirby, and Selma. Cave Junction is one example of small-town living with rock-bottom real estate prices and pleasant surrounding countryside. Good fishing and hunting are bonuses.

All along the Oregon coast, interspersed between beaches and cliffs, are places such as Brookings, Coos Bay, Florence, Gold Beach, and Port Orford. The weather here is some of the mildest in the nation, with almost no frost and temperatures over 75°F rare. Residents refer to the area as Oregon's "banana belt." There's some justification: Flowers bloom all year locally, and about 90 percent of the country's Easter lilies are grown here. Retirees comprise an estimated 30 percent of the population. Along the Columbia River, you'll find some interesting retirement towns such as Hood River, The Dalles, and, farther upstream, Hermiston. Inland, in the high-desert country, Klamath Falls and Pendleton are also worth a look.

OREGON COAST WEATHER (ASTORIA)						
	TEMPERATURE (°F)				ANNUAL PRECIPITATION (IN.)	
	JAN	APR	JUL	OCT	RAIN	SNOW
Daily Highs	47	56	68	61	70	5
Daily Lows	35	40	52	44		

OREGON INLAND VALLEY WEATHER (MEDFORD)					
TEMPERATURE (°F)				**ANNUAL PRECIPITATION (IN.)**	
JAN	APR	JUL	OCT	RAIN	SNOW
Daily Highs 45	64	91	69	20	8
Daily Lows 30	37	54	40		

Washington Although it's the most northernmost state on the West Coast, Washington's western region has mild winters, much of them almost snow- and ice-free, and cool summers. The coastal region is famous for rain, just as the central and eastern portions of the state are famous for being dry. About 25 percent less rain falls on Seattle than on parts of Florida, but rain typically falls gently for hours at a time in Seattle, in contrast to Florida's typically brief but intense thunderstorms.

Aberdeen is a town deep in the economic doldrums, and real estate prices and rentals are about the lowest we've seen anywhere. At one time, many homes were selling below $30,000. The U.S. Department of Housing and Urban Development has converted repossessions into subsidized housing. If you can qualify, you might find very inexpensive rents. Like all Northwest locations near the ocean, Aberdeen's weather is perfect for those who hate freezing weather and hot summers. You'll never need air conditioning here. But it's unpleasant for those who love hot sunshine and don't like winter rain.

Just across the Columbia River from Portland, Oregon, the city of Vancouver offers low housing costs and mild weather. It also has an ideal tax situation. Why? The state of Washington does not collect state income taxes, yet it provides substantial property tax relief to low-income senior citizens. However, the state does have a sales tax. Vancouver residents handle this quite well; they simply cross the Columbia River into Oregon when making major purchases, because Oregon has no sales tax! As for winter weather, you'll never need a snow shovel in Vancouver.

COASTAL WASHINGTON WEATHER (SEATTLE)

	TEMPERATURE (°F)				ANNUAL PRECIPITATION (IN.)	
	JAN	APR	JUL	OCT	RAIN	SNOW
Daily Highs	44	57	75	60	39	7
Daily Lows	34	41	54	45		

INTERIOR WASHINGTON WEATHER (YAKIMA)

	TEMPERATURE (°F)				ANNUAL PRECIPITATION (IN.)	
	JAN	APR	JUL	OCT	RAIN	SNOW
Daily Highs	37	64	88	65	16	25
Daily Lows	20	35	53	35		

Appendix

SALES TAX BY STATE

STATE	FOOD ITEMS TAXABLE?	STATE RATE	LOCAL RATE	MAX. RATE
Alabama	Yes	4.00	6.00	11.0
Alaska	Yes	—	7.00	7.00
Arizona	No	5.60	3.00	8.60
Arkansas	Yes	5.12	4.75	9.87
California	No	6.00	2.50	8.50
Colorado	No	2.90	5.00	7.90
Connecticut	No	6.00	—	6.00
Florida	No	6.00	1.50	7.50
Georgia	No	4.00	3.00	7.00
Hawaii	Yes	4.00	—	4.00
Idaho	Yes	5.00	3.00	8.00
Illinois	Yes	6.25	3.00	9.25
Indiana	No	6.00	—	6.00
Iowa	No	5.00	2.00	7.00
Kansas	Yes	5.30	3.00	8.30
Kentucky	No	6.00	—	6.00
Louisiana	Yes	4.00	5.50	9.50
Maine	No	5.00	—	5.00
Maryland	No	5.00	—	5.00
Massachusetts	No	5.00	—	5.00
Michigan	No	6.00	—	6.00
Minnesota	No	6.50	1.00	7.50
Mississippi	Yes	7.00	0.25	7.25
Missouri	Yes	4.22	4.12	8.35
Nebraska	No	5.50	1.50	7.00
Nevada	No	6.50	0.75	7.25

STATE	FOOD ITEMS TAXABLE?	STATE RATE	LOCAL RATE	MAX. RATE
New Jersey	No	6.00	—	6.00
New Mexico	Yes	5.00	2.25	7.25
New York	No	4.00	4.50	8.50
North Carolina	No	4.50	3.00	7.50
North Dakota	No	5.00	2.50	7.50
Ohio	No	5.00	2.00	7.00
Oklahoma	Yes	4.50	5.35	9.85
Pennsylvania	No	6.00	1.00	7.00
Rhode Island	No	7.00	—	7.00
South Carolina	Yes	5.00	2.00	7.00
South Dakota	Yes	4.00	2.00	6.00
Tennessee	Yes	7.00	2.75	9.75
Texas	No	6.25	2.00	8.25
Utah	Yes	4.75	2.25	7.00
Vermont	No	5.00	1.00	6.00
Virginia	Yes	3.50	1.00	4.50
Washington	No	6.50	2.40	8.90
West Virginia	Yes	6.00	—	6.00
Wisconsin	No	5.00	0.60	5.60
Wyoming	Yes	4.00	2.00	6.00

Index

About the Author

John Howells and his wife, Sherry, spent many months of travel by automobile, motor home, and airplane gathering information to produce this book. They interviewed retired folks in all sections of the country, collecting experiences, advice, and valuable insights into successful retirement lifestyles.

John has written and coauthored several other books about retirement locations. Among them are *Choose Mexico for Retirement*, *Choose the Southwest for Retirement*, and *Choose Costa Rica for Retirement*. He also writes about retirement and travel for mature Americans in magazines such as *Successful Retirement* and *International Living*. He is a member of the board of directors of the American Association of Retirement Communities. John and his wife live in California and Costa Rica.